Militant Islam

Militant Islam provides an innovative sociological framework for understanding the rise and character of recent Islamic militancy. It takes a systematic approach to the phenomenon, incorporating examples from around the world.

A number of sociological concepts and theories are applied to militants including those associated with social closure, social movements, nationalism, risk, fear and 'decivilising'. These are examined within three main themes; characteristics of militant Islam, multi-layered causes and the consequences of militancy, in particular Western reactions within the 'war on terror'. Interrelationships between religious and secular behaviour, 'terrorism' and 'counter-terrorism', popular support and opposition are explored. Throughout the book, examples from across Muslim societies and communities are drawn upon, enabling the popular tendency to concentrate upon 'al-Qa'ida' and the Middle East to be challenged.

This book will be of interest to students of Sociology, Political Science and International Relations, in particular those taking courses on Islam, religion, terrorism, political violence and related regional studies.

Stephen Vertigans is Reader in Sociology at Robert Gordon University, Aberdeen. He has written and co-written a series of books, articles and conference papers on Muslim communities, terrorism and religion, especially resurgent and militant Islam, and is currently researching a range of terror groups across the world.

Militant Islam

A sociology of characteristics, causes
and consequences

Stephen Vertigans

**With contributions from
Donncha Marron and
Philip W. Sutton**

Routledge
Taylor & Francis Group

LONDON AND NEW YORK

First published 2009
by Routledge
2 Park Square, Milton Park, Abingdon, Oxon OX14 4RN

Simultaneously published in the USA and Canada
by Routledge
270 Madison Ave, New York, NY 10016

Routledge is an imprint of the Taylor & Francis Group, an informa business

Typeset in Times by
Book Now Ltd, London
Printed and bound in Great Britain by
CPI Antony Rowe, Chippenham, Wiltshire

British Library Cataloguing in Publication Data
A catalogue record for this book is available from the British Library

Library of Congress Cataloging in Publication Data
Vertigans, Stephen.
Militant Islam: a sociology of characteristics, causes and consequences/
Stephen Vertigans with contributions from Donncha Marron and
Philip W. Sutton.
    p. cm.
Includes bibliographical references and index.
1. Terrorism—Social aspects. 2. Islamic fundamentalism—Social aspects.
3. War on Terrorism, 2001—Social aspects. I. Marron, Donncha. II.
Sutton, Philip W. III. Title.
HV6431.V464 2008
303.6′25—dc22   2008011385

ISBN10: 0–415–41245–5 (hbk)
ISBN10: 0–415–41246–3 (pbk)
ISBN10: 0–203–89107–4 (ebk)

ISBN13: 978–0–415–41245–2 (hbk)
ISBN13: 978–0–415–41246–9 (pbk)
ISBN13: 978–0–203–89107–0 (ebk)

Contents

Acknowledgements

A number of people have been involved in the production of this book whose contributions I would like to acknowledge.

The original proposal for *Militant Islam* was developed with Phil Sutton. Due to other commitments, his contribution to the final manuscript has been limited to Chapter 2. It has been a pleasure to work with Phil on the early stages of this and other projects but I hope this book is at least close to our original aims. I am also extremely grateful to Donncha Marron who wrote Chapter 5 and provided insightful comments as the book evolved. I am also appreciative of detailed analyses provided by Chris Thorpe and Val Vertigans.

Much of the material has been discussed with a range of audiences at other universities, conferences and student forums, and their observations played an important part in the development of the central ideas. Finally, the book would not have been possible without the sympathetic support of Joe Whiting and assistance of Natalja Mortensen and Suzanne Chilestone at Routledge.

Earlier versions of Chapters 2 and 4 appeared, respectively, as Sutton, P. W. and Vertigans, S. (2006) 'Islamic "New Social Movements"? al-Qa'ida, Radical Islam and Social Movement Theory', *Mobilization: An International Journal of Social Movement Research,* 11(1): 101–116, and Vertigans, S. (2007) 'Militant Islam and Weber's Social Closure: Interrelated Secular and Religious Codes of Exclusion', *Contemporary Islam* 1(4): 303–321. Some of the material included in the Introduction and Chapter 1 appeared in Vertigans, S. (2007) 'Routes into "Islamic" Terrorism: Dead Ends and Spaghetti Junctions', *Policing: A Journal of Policy and Practice*, 1(2): 447–59.

Introduction

Beyond 'al-Qa'ida' and politics: a sociological contribution?

Since 2001, studies of militancy associated with Islam have shifted attention from a generic 'Islamic fundamentalism' to domination by the spectre of al-Qa'ida. This form of militancy seems ubiquitous, yet without a distinct, substantive or quantifiable core, the same entity can appear nowhere. Populist coverage of the phenomena has tended to replicate these misapprehensions, understandably concentrating upon terror attacks and their physical impact. Gruesome images of dead Jews, Christians, Hindus, Muslims, agnostics, men, women, children, government officials, police officers, military personnel, bank employees, pop singers, journalists, authors, medical doctors, university students, school pupils, wedding guests and tourists have all been transmitted across the world. These pictures and the tendency to connect all acts of political violence committed by Muslims to a generic 'al-Qa'ida',[1] have contributed to an inflation of a specific 'Islamic threat'. To some extent, this is a consequence of political discourse in the West and media reporting. However, as the plethora of publications during these early years of the twenty-first century indicates, academics have also been heavily instrumental in these processes of inflation. Consequently, the obvious question to commence this book with is: Why is yet another text about militant Islam required?

First, the overwhelming majority of publications about militant Islam are written from the realms of politics, international relations and area studies. From this analysis, it is possible to gain an understanding about the role of power and nation-states, the political decisions, opportunities, constraints and threats that have been instrumental within militancy today. By comparison, sociological contributions have been minimal.[2] Consequently, the impact of social processes and activities behind people becoming militants and such groups forming has been underexplored. Through applying sociological ways of thinking, it is argued that changes in religious and secular processes and cross-cutting allegiances within societies and global relations can be highlighted and levels of understanding enhanced. In so doing, a sociological approach can expand upon other studies that tend to overrely upon the causal analysis of economic, political and psychological factors. It is argued that changes, and in particular the perceptions of them, have led to a re-evaluation of both Islam and Western forms of discourse.

Second, sociological theories and concepts can help to address the normative tendency to condemn[3] and personalize accounts by illuminating processes and experiences that have hitherto remained neglected. Such inattention may be partly explained by the traditional reluctance for sociologists to examine political violence.[4] The neglect is compounded when violence is associated with religion which has 'been banished to the sidelines in the contemporary field of theoretical struggle' (Calhoun 1999: 237). And, the secularist tradition within sociology can be considered to have contributed to many Western academics being 'confused and bewildered by religious crusaders' (Oberschall 2004: 34) with religion considered, Beckford (2003) suggests, as marginal or deviant phenomena. Beckford (2003: 151) notes that 'exponents of social theory have shown little interest in religious movements ... studies of religious movements have failed to exercise significant influence on social theory.'

As part of this intra-disciplinary shift towards inner 'specialisms', Islam within sociology has become epistemologically isolated as a 'religion' to the neglect of interrelated social, cultural, political and economic activities and relations. This is not, however, to suggest that this text will provide a comprehensive review of sociological contributions to the study of Islam because such a task is beyond the intended scope. Instead, insights and ideas from a range of empirical and theoretical sociological sources and other disciplines have been chosen based purely on their relevance to explaining the processes under investigation.

Third, building upon the above point, there has been a tendency across academic disciplines to examine militant Islam generally, and related terrorism in particular, in isolation. Thus, at present, we are considered to be encountering a 'new terrorism' (Jenkins 2001), a 'new wave' (Rapoport 2003) undertaken by 'new types of post-cold war terrorists' (Hudson 1999) or a 'new generation' (Hoffman 1998). If concentrating on the methods of attack, then there are grounds for claiming that this is indeed a distinctive age of terrorism and militancy. In so doing, however, there is a danger that commonalities across militant groups, religious and secular, are lost. For example, despite the tendency to concentrate on violence with Islam, there have been militant Jewish groups like the Gush Emunim, Hindu Shiv Sena, the Sikh Bhindranwale group, elements within the American Christian far right and Japanese cult Aum Supreme Truth that have all propounded violence to various degrees.[5] Similarly, Bergesen and Han (2005) and Duyvesteyn (2004) have argued that there are numerous examples of secular groups from earlier periods with characteristics associated with the 'new' groups. By drawing upon concepts, beliefs and behaviour associated with 'New Social Movements', social closure and nationalism, it is argued that militant groups share experiences, sentiments and practices with other forms of non-violent discourses. In other words, some of the characteristics and causes associated with militant Islam may be less distinctive than is widely thought.

Fourth, beyond the concentration upon the physical impact of attacks, for example, the destruction of the 'Twin Towers', the devastation to mass transportation networks in London and Madrid, the grim outcome of attacks in public arenas in Algeria, Bali, Darfur, Iraq and Israel, studies of consequences of militancy upon the West are limited.[6] Yet political, cultural, social, economic and legal reactions are fundamentally important both to the likelihood of defeating the 'enemy' and for the ways of life people in the West may experience. Increasingly, militant Islam and Western policies and behaviour are interwoven. A sociological application can help both to uncover these neglected relationships and to explain why strategies of counter-terrorism being implemented in defence of Western values like freedom are restricting the values they are designed to defend and, in particular, why this is arousing so little popular protest.

The sociological approach that has been adopted in this work is not rigidly tied to a dominant methodology or theoretical stance. In so doing it is hoped that a detached and reality-congruent exploration of militant Islam and Western reactions has been written within a framework that incorporates individual behaviour, social networks, nation-state institutions and global relations. Irrespective of academic allegiance, the book is therefore primarily designed to enhance levels of knowledge and understanding about militant Islam and Western counter-terrorism.

Introducing militancy

This section briefly introduces the subject matter, namely militant Islam, and some of the central components that will be developed throughout the following chapters. However it is not intended to provide detailed analysis of the exegesis of religious texts; instead, theological aspects of Islam are drawn upon only where they are explicitly relevant in understanding the interaction between ideas, activities, experiences and cultural, economic, legal, political and social conditions and processes. Pointers will be provided for readers requiring more theological knowledge.

When studying militant Islam, it is quickly noticeable that the field is dominated by the Middle East. This is understandable. Islam originated from the Arabian peninsula which is also the birthplace of the most prominent of contemporary militants, Osama bin Laden, and fifteen of the militants who committed the 2001 attacks on the United States. Subsequent events in Iraq, Lebanon and the Palestinian territories have also raised the spectre of militancy in the region. And of course, the strategic significance of the oil-producing countries contributes to growing anxieties about potential threats to supplies. Post 2001, attention has extended to the 'enemy within', resulting in considerable focus being placed upon Muslim communities in the West. Events in parts of Africa and Central, South and Southeast

Asia are relatively neglected. Thus, as Devji (2005) points out, the association of *jihadism* with the Middle East, and it could be added the West, needs to be addressed because much of the *jihadi* activities occur in places like Afghanistan, Chechnya, Pakistan, the Philippines and Sudan. And overgeneralizations within the Middle East and across Muslim societies are also prominent. Experiences and practices within Muslim societies are different: daily lives can be incomparable across and within social settings; interpretations of colonialism and the West are heavily influenced by a region's proximity to such relations, both spatially and across time; political perspectives are prompted by a combination of historical and contemporary events and exposure to forms of communication and transportation. Yet such vicissitudes are often overlooked in discussions of the 'Muslim world', Islam in the Middle East or South Asia, etc. and the 'British Muslim community'. To understand militancy, it is suggested that a more sensitive global perspective is required, particularly in areas in which militants are becoming more influential. In this text, examples are drawn from across Muslim societies and communities in a manner that reflects the diversity of beliefs, practices and experiences, and the commonality of some social processes and loyalties.

Comparative analysis of militant groups can be confusing because of the different terms that are used and the different meanings applied. There are a range of concepts used to describe what is referred to as militancy in this text. 'Radical', 'fundamentalist' and 'Islamist' are all epithets that describe a range of demands and behaviours. Islam in this context can be a religious force, political movement, spiritual response to a crisis of modernization or reactionary challenge to secularization and Westernization (al Zayyat 2004; Milton-Edwards 2005). However, all these words are also associated with other usages,[7] so to try to minimize confusion, 'militancy' has been adopted to establish the distinctive behaviour under investigation. Nor is the adaptation of one term to describe all forms of associated behaviour without problems. To suggest that people who kill civilians on behalf of Islam are Muslims is controversial. For many religious leaders and believers, people who belong to groups associated with al-Qa'ida and act in the name of Islam are not Muslims. Conversely, militants will denounce Muslims not engaged in the 'armed struggle'. This creates a problem for social scientists in deciding whose application, if any, is correct. In this text, W. I. Thomas' (1928) famous adage is adopted: if people define situations as real then they are real in their consequences. As Marranci (2006: 31) points out with regard to those involved in the attacks on America, 'they felt they were Muslim' and this was an integral part of their identities. In other words, if people think they are Muslims, then their classification will suffice: to prove otherwise is a task for theologians and not social scientists. A multitude of groups, theological interpretations and practices exist which reflect the broad range of characteristics associated with militancy, integrating religion and politics across different social relations, activities and experiences. From this perspective it is important to identify some commonalities and crucial differences into the social processes behind these interpretations forming the behaviours that ensue and the consequences of these actions and reactions.

In this text, militancy is associated with political violence[8] undertaken in the name of Islam and the utilization of the concept of *jihad*. Islamic doctrine is utilized to justify violence and killing by ideologues who often lack formal religious credentials. This is distinct from the broader resurgent Islam that is about religious belief and is more closely integrated with the *ulema* and personal faith that incorporates communal acts of prayer and fasting. Militancy also encompasses politics and a desire not only to change individual behaviour and levels of spirituality but also to extend the influence of religion across political, economic and legal spheres based upon interpretations located within the *Qur'an* and *hadiths*. Therefore, militancy generally is, as Devji (2005) observes, about much more than acts of violence. It is in part about feelings of empowerment[9] designed to reposition Islam within individual identities and social activities. In the process, the split between religion and other aspects of life is eradicated and Islam becomes dominant within psychologies and across social relations. This differs from most Muslims whose faith tends to be more clearly divided on sacred and profane grounds. For these Muslims, Islam is an individual matter or is embedded within social relations outside politics, for example, religious places of worship, charities, welfare and other forms of communal activities, and where political engagement is noticeable it is through peaceful means. In other words, as Esposito (1999), Halliday (2002) and Marranci (2006) have argued, in opposition to writers like Kramer (2001), Lewis (1990, 2002) and Pipes (1989), Islam alone cannot explain violence. Religion maybe an integral part of many Muslims' identities, influencing family life, employment, communal loyalties and social activities, but is not politicized and, for these people, is not connected to violence.

Consequently, it is important to stress that this book examines the behaviour of a very small minority of the 1.3 billion Muslims on the planet. Islam is, for the majority, one form of identification that does not inevitably result in psychological separation from non-Muslims. Religious allegiances are one of many that are integrated with other loyalties and physical and social characteristics, for example, age, gender, nationality, ethnicity, region, class, race, sports and art. In other words, the global bloc of Muslims facilely demarcated on the grounds of faith can also be divided according to a multitude of competing fidelities. Contrary to some perspectives of globalization, Islam may be a global religion but is not universally interpreted. Important theological and practical differences can be discerned across the world, like, for example, when comparing the more austere Islam found within the Middle East and the rich diversity to be found within Africa and Southeast Asia.[10] Yet to return to an earlier point, it is the minority who hold some beliefs that conflict with those of the majority in Muslim societies and across the West that attract immense interest. The latter sections of this book are designed, in part, to understand this disproportionate interest.

Finally in this section, it is important to challenge the tendency to categorize violent political acts by Muslims within a generic category of 'al-Qa'ida'. Thus, terror attacks directed against Western institutions or citizens are categorized with conflicts in diverse places like the Philippines, Chechnya, Kashmir and the Palestinian territories, and intra-state struggles in Pakistan, Iraq, Egypt, Sudan, Algeria, Central Asia and Indonesia. Not only is this incorrect but facilely classifying all groups together and attributing all actions to 'al-Qa'ida' inflate the threat, providing legitimacy to the possibility of a militant core and raising levels of fear. At a local level, Burke (2006) and Valiyev (2006) note, governments are frequently utilizing international concerns about the 'group' to enable them to suppress an opposition that has a number of valid concerns. This further strengthens the extent of fear over the 'group' providing legitimacy for heightened security and aggressive posturing that, as later chapters detail, challenge the values that are considered to be the basis for defence. Conversely, governments' reactions to terrorism inflate the threat and provide the opposing discourse with a strengthened sense of credibility in its potentialities. In some respects, al-Qa'ida is a pernicious permutation that does not exist in the manner in which it has been identified within the West. As Burke (2003) highlighted, and which Chapter 1 explores, al-Qa'ida is not a distinct organization with clearly defined lines of demarcation, particularly since the destruction of the established training facilities and networks following the American invasion of Afghanistan. Increasingly, al-Qa'ida is an idea, a form of discourse interwoven with behaviour. By focussing upon behaviour, namely acts of terrorism, commentators are able to draw similarities in methods and outcomes. Yet this approach is essentially and understandably emotive, influenced by atrocities and their horrific aftermaths. The multitude of reasons behind the actions are lost or neglected. By focussing instead upon the social processes and activities which result in a range of militant Muslims becoming engaged in violence on behalf of al-Qa'ida–related and non-associated groups, we aim to provide more representative accounts for this form of behaviour.

Review of the book

The book is loosely divided into three interlinked themes, namely sociological characteristics, causes and characteristics. In so doing, it is designed to identify the distinctions and commonalities within militancy, to explore the underlying factors that are contributing to the phenomena, to unravel interrelationships between militant and Western actions and to investigate public reactions in the West to acts of terror and counter-terror.

Chapter 1 aims to establish the evolution of the militant discourse, the transmutations that have occurred and the centrality of historical and

contemporary events and processes. The primary focus is upon characteristics and causes of militancy which are then developed in later chapters.
Important philosophical or theological sources are drawn upon and, where
appropriate, further reading recommendations provided.

A number of these issues are explored in Chapter 2 which challenges the
tendency to examine religious movements generally, and militant Islam in
particular, in isolation. By applying concepts from the field of social movement studies, it is argued that if attention is shifted beyond the use of
violence, important similarities can be noted between secular 'New Social
Movements' like environmentalism, student movements and feminism and
al-Qa'ida–related groups. Commonalities include interconnections with contemporary fears and uncertainties, reaction to, and utilization of, globalization, loosely organized 'networks of networks', use of symbolic actions
and similar constituencies. These factors lead to the following question: If
militancy shares processes and experiences with other forms of protest
movements, does this suggest that they are part of a broader challenge to
Western-inspired globalization and associated values?

The application of non-religious sociological ideas and theories is further
explored in Chapter 3, which examines the modernist/primordialist debate
within the sociology of nationalism with respect to Islamic national and
transnational loyalties. It is argued that although studies of nationalism tend
to neglect the continuing significance of religion, Islam retains fundamental
significance in forms of collective identity based around an 'imagined community' and interplays between the past and present, local and global. And
by applying related concepts to nationalist groups like Hamas and Kashmiri
Jaish-e-Mohammed and transnational groups associated with al-Qa'ida, our
levels of understanding about these groups' appeal are enhanced while
enabling important distinctions within militant Islam to be drawn.

In Chapter 4, Max Weber's concept of social closure is adapted to enable
social processes behind allegiances forming within militant and secularist
groups to be explored. Fractures between the groups are also illuminated.
The roots of the interrelated methods of exclusion and usurpation, that both
categories of groups practice, are identified, with particular attention placed
upon the unintentional consequences of secularization and related institutional policies.

The remainder of the chapters concentrate upon the reactions, predominantly within the West, to acts of terrorism associated with Islam. Chapter 5
examines the impact of terrorism upon the perceptions of Western risk
through three theoretical perspectives: Beck's 'Risk Society', social con-
structivism and governmentality. It is argued that terrorism connects into
broader methods of calculating and perceiving risk associated with other
forms of 'uncontrollable' harm, all of which contribute to a further inflation
of the threat.

Consequences of the inflation of risk are explored in Chapter 6.
Particular attention is placed upon government and public reactions to the

September 2001 attacks on America and the subsequent 'war on terror' through the application of concepts like Durkheim's 'collective conscious-ness', Elias' 'decivilizing' processes, Furedi's 'culture of fear' and Weber's 'rationalization'. By connecting into feelings of uncertainty and suffering and pre-existing emotions of vulnerability and fear which became inflamed within heightened 'risks', it is argued that the American administration and to some extent other Western governments have introduced restraints upon freedom in the name of freedom.

Finally, Chapter 7 reviews the book's distinctive contributions to enhancing levels of knowledge and understanding about militant Islam and increasingly inter-related Western reactions. Despite these contributions, it is acknowledged that the book is far from definitive. Consequently, the chapter concludes with suggestions for future research.

1 The al-Qa'ida phenomenon and beyond

Myths and realities

Introduction

In this chapter, the nature of the phenomena under investigation is established. Important characteristics associated with militancy are identified and distinctions are drawn between Muslim interpretations to help clarify precisely what is being discussed. The significance of historical events and shifts in consciousness are outlined and the roots of contemporary theological influences uncovered. The chapter concludes with an examination of popular explanations for the causes behind the resurgence of militant Islam today. In so doing, it is intended to enhance levels of understanding about the complexities behind militancy and to provide the historical and discursive framework that subsequent chapters will seek to augment.

Establishing militancy

Because of the tendencies to categorize militant Islam under the all-encompassing al-Qa'ida umbrella and to concentrate upon events in the Middle East, the extensive range of groups, activities and ideological influences could be considered surprising. Halliday (2000) points out that there is no essential Islam and this point can be extended to militancy.

Militant groups like Hizb ul-Mujahidin in Kashmir, the Filipino Moro Islamic Liberation Front (MILF), Islamic Jihad in the Palestinian territories, the Islamic Movement of Uzbekistan, Lashkar Jihad in Indonesia, the Lebanese Hezbollah, Arakan Rohingya Nationalist Organisation in Myanmar and Southeast Asian Jemaah Islamiyah claim to draw their guidelines for life from Islamic scriptures that are viewed as disappearing, or have disappeared, from governance. This elimination is associated with concomitant oppression, corruption, immorality, pernicious and pervasive Western discourse and the loss of territories. Religious guidelines are considered to provide the basis for conduct and judgement, for ideas and practice, understanding life and the universe and the rectification of contemporary problems facing Muslims.[1] In so doing, contemporary problems would be eradicated. Islamic concepts should therefore embrace 'all aspects of life, culture, creed, politics, economics, education, society, justice and judgement, the spreading of Islam, education, art, information, science of the occult and conversion to Islam, and all the other domains of life' (Hamas 1988). How Islam as a way of life is to be implemented is a source of considerable debate that is outlined in Chapter 4. For example, even the rules and regulations for participating in the lesser *jihad*, associated with Holy War in the West, differ across and within the four schools of Islamic jurisprudence.[2] The lesser *jihad* is widely associated with 'self-defence' of the individual and religion but what this constitutes is the source of debate that draws upon a multitude of *hadiths*. Marranci (2006) points out that these sources are much more open to interpretation and modification compared with the *Qu'ran*. And like the *Bible*, *Torah* and Hindu *Vedas*, within *surahs* (verses) in the *Qu'ran*, there are numerous examples of a merciful and merciless, diplomatic and warlike God. Such exegesis inconsistencies require explanations that locate the *surahs* within contexts and a compatible theological framework. Khosrokhavar (2005) notes when confronting apparent incompatibilities it is necessary to provide a hierarchy with some *surahs* acquiring priority in certain conditions. Establishing this ranking and appropriate contextualization creates additional layers of interpretation and adds to further diversity. These vicissitudes allow Muslims to draw upon different *surahs* in support of their positions and, in the case of militants, to justify their violent actions according to selected religious sentiments.

A violent form of *jihad* can be considered to be justified as a form of reactive self-defence when the nation-state or Muslim country has been invaded. But for others it may involve the threat of attack, the suppression of Muslims or denial of the *shari'ah* in areas where there are large numbers of Muslims or in territories that are considered to belong to Muslims, usually stemming from historical control.[3] Inspirational figures like Qutb have adapted the concept, integrating political, social and individual religious aspirations, namely that social and political struggle towards an Islamic state must be an inherent feature of individual struggle towards virtue. Such interpretations can lead, as de Waal (2004: 8) suggests, to the application of transcendental logic where 'absolute *jihad* obliterates the division between the right to wage war and rights within war'. Despite the long history of Muslim humanity in warfare, this form of *jihad* does not place emphasis upon respect for the laws of war or restraint of actions upon victims. Yet, contrary to popular perceptions, this does not mean that such militant groups are undisciplined. De Waal (ibid.) notes that if *jihadis* are to survive and prosper they must be able to at least match adversaries, attract support, inspire loyalty and devise and implement strategies which requires discipline. The groups under investigation in this book are engaged in what they consider to be military actions and associated attempts at proselytism that involve individuals, institutions and the media. This definition does not include groups that are considered to be radical or fundamentalist like the *Tabligh* movement that was formed in India in 1926 and has become prominent in diverse places like Western Europe, Algeria, Mauritania, Somalia and Southeast Asia. For the *Tabligh*, *da'wa* activities are central to achieving change through a 'bottom up' approach that revolves around preaching and conversion. By 'calling' people to the correct path and a righteous life, it is intended both to increase membership and levels of religiosity through peaceful non-political processes. In this, connection is made to Muhammed's instruction that Muslims should learn from birth to the grave. Educationalists and the use of *da'wa* are central within this legacy. For such groups, processes of social change begin with individuals who spread their beliefs and practices beyond mosques into schools, factories, sport clubs and broader communities. Ultimately this approach is designed to result in the rejuvenation of the population's morals into a pious community and ultimately the implementation of an Islamic state. This is not to argue that violent militants are opposed to *da'wa*. In *Milestones*, Qutb (1991) outlines a preference for achieving popular support for the *shari'ah* through proselytism. Violence was, however, to be utilized when barriers and tyranny prevented people freely embracing (his interpretations of) Islam.

Another tradition associated with fundamentalism, the *salafiyya* and the Saudi conservative *Wahhabi*, is critical of political activism tending to focus upon individual behaviour and morality. The movement has gained popularity across the Middle East into North Africa, France, Sahelian and sub-Saharan Africa, South Asia and Southeast Asia. Across the Middle East, the Muslim Brotherhood is more engaged with political activism while remaining largely peaceful and heavily involved in *da'wa*-related activities. There are also numerous political parties[4] promoting Islamic discourse within democratic arrangements and attracting mass support which are often classified[5] with more militant groups. These Muslims aim to implement change within societies through existing mainstream political processes and are derided by violent militants. For example, Gerges (2005) details how *jihadis* are vehemently opposed to the influential Muslim Brotherhood. The Brotherhood is considered to have made irreligious concessions in the pursuit of political power. Yet they share some common goals and could have been allies. Indeed governments and academics often classify the two distinct factions within one category. However, for militants like al-Zawahiri, participating within the existing order is considered to be prolonging the state of *kufr* which is discussed in Chapter 4. In turn, non-violent Islamists have been extremely critical of the use of violence by groups associated with al-Qa'ida. For example, leaders like Mohammed Derbala and Nageh Ibrahim, of the formerly violent Egyptian group al-Jama'a al-Islamiya, have denounced the attacks on America in 2001. Zayyat (2004) has described the acts as a 'folly' lacking strategic clarity and foresight and which have had a detrimental impact on Islamist movements worldwide. He argues that the consequences of the attacks include the loss of many lives, networks and opportunities for political asylum in the West. In addition, the fractures within Islamism have deepened and governments have been able to repress legitimate opposition under the cover of the 'war on terror'. Religious texts have been used to counteract attempts to theologically legitimize the actions while highlighting examples of American support for Muslim nation-states and communities that contradict bin Laden's claim for a 'clash of civilizations'. The indiscriminate killing of civilians including women and children and sectarian violence have caused considerable consternation amongst groups like the Egyptian Islamic Jihad and Tanzim al-Jihad that have split with al-Zawahiri (Gerges 2005). Mainstream Muslims, including the *ulema*, denounce the killing of civilians as *haram*, forbidden by Islam (al-Zayyat 2004). Derbala accuses the al-Qa'ida 'hardcore' of misusing and over-concentrating upon the 'lesser *jihad*.'[6] The result is an imbalanced approach that results in un-Islamic behaviour with a detrimental impact on the *umma*. Finally, Ibrahim argues, the overwhelming tendency to hold the West accountable for the multitude of problems fails to acknowledge that Muslims are also responsible. By concentrating upon the West, he argues that the militants are hindering the abilities of Muslims to readdress the problems within.[7] But whilst these groups and parties have not been explicitly involved in the onset of violence, it will be argued in subsequent chapters that they are contributing to processes that are displacing ethnic loyalties and localized interpretations, especially *Sufi* traditions, which are being replaced by more radical practices and beliefs.

Contrary to popular perceptions, Islamic reformism also possesses a prominent recent history. Central reformist figures of the nineteenth century like Namik Kemal (1840–88), Sayyid Ahmed Khan (1817–98), Jamal al-Din al-Afghani (1837–97) and Mohammed Abduh (1849–1905) sought to bring about change within individuals and societies that would enable Western power to be challenged. Through modernist reconstruction of Islamic civilization, it was intended to reform Muslim societies and to eradicate the cultural, intellectual and spiritual decadence that was perceived to exist within communities. Islam was to be accommodated to the requirements of modernity, which enabled the reformers to utilize Islamic concepts to justify theologically the adoption of European institutions and practices. Similar reformist tendencies could be noted in other religions at this time. For example, van der Veer (1994) discusses reformist Hindu and Sikh movements that emerged in the nineteenth centuries, aiming both to defend society against 'foreign' influences, principally linked with British colonialism, and to address 'internal' weaknesses that had resulted in a decline from a preceding 'Golden Age'. For example, the most significant reformist nineteenth-century movement associated with Hinduism was the Arya Samaj. Its leader Swami Dayananda Saraswati wanted to return to the religion of the scriptures and to eradicate image worship, caste divisions and to change rites of passage. The Sikh reformist

Singh Sabha also sought to 'purify' the religion and eradicate 'Hindu' practices. Indeed van der Veer (1994) details that their main slogan was that Sikhs were not Hindus. Clear demarcations were established between interpretations of Sikhism and Hindus and Muslims. Religious groups that followed Sikh teachings but did not accept the brotherhood were not accepted as Sikhs. At the extreme of reformism were to be the Bhindranwale group[8] of nationalists who demanded the formation of Khalistan as a separate nation-state.

Reformers remain within Islamic debates, including most notably the former *Shi'ite* Iranian president (1997–2005) Mohammed Khatami and a range of ideological thinkers like Abdallah al-Hamid, Abd al-Aziz al-Qasim, Muhammed Arkoun, Hasan Hanafi, Muhammad Shahrur, Abdul Karim Soroush and Abu Zayd who personalize religion alongside popular political participation, seeking to integrate the central tenets of the religion with compatible components of modernity. Overall though there has been a shift from the modernist reformism, that became noticeable under Abduh's successor Rashid Rida (1865–1935) who placed greater emphasis upon resistance and anti-Westernism and brought the movement closer to developments within Wahhabism in the newly formed Kingdom of Saudi Arabia. Similar transmutations towards enhanced militant fervour can be noticed, to differing degrees, across Muslim societies and communities.

Discursive and historical influences within militancy

The immediate roots of transnational violent militancy can be traced back to the declaration issued by bin Laden in 1996. In the 'Declaration of War against the Americans Occupying the Land of the Two Holy Places', growing doubts about the potential of local *jihads* were expressed and Muslims were informed that they should kill Americans, including civilians, anywhere in the world. From this point, a broader strategy became conspicuous. The declaration outlines the expanding focus upon the main enemy and in particular the requirement to expel the Americans from Saudi Arabia. 'People of Islam should join forces and support each other to get rid of the main *kufr* who is controlling the countries of the Islamic world' (bin Laden 1996). Bin Laden cites Ibn Taymiyya in support of the approach being taken, that 'to fight in defence of religion and Belief is a collective duty; there is no other duty after Belief than fighting the enemy who is corrupting the life and the religion' (ibid.). At this stage though, the emphasis is still upon *jihad* as a defensive mechanism.

In 1998, the *fatwa* by the World Islamic Front for the Jihad against Jews and Crusaders changed this and *jihad* became globally aggressive, taking the fight to the 'far enemy'. Burke (2006) suggests that bin Laden acknowledged that attempts during the 1990s to rouse support for militancy on a nation-by-nation basis had failed. By transferring attention to a common enemy, it was hoped that allegiances could be established to overcome the parochialism that was apparent within militancy. It was at this stage in al-Qa'ida's development that the instruction was formulated 'to kill the Americans and their allies – civilians and military – is an individual duty for every Muslim who can do it in any country in which it is possible to do it' (bin Laden 1998a). By declaring the *fatwa*, the militants sought to mobilize and unite opposition around militancy and against the West. In this and subsequent announcements, bin Laden incorporated historical and contemporary events and images. In a manner recognizable in Huntington's (1998) thesis, a 'clash of civilizations' is portrayed of two religions in long-standing conflict. The West is considered to have caused death and misery in places like Palestine, Iraq, Bosnia, Chechnya and Kashmir. Global *jihad* had been declared the individual obligation of all true Muslims and was to become increasingly noticeable from this point. Shortly afterwards, on the eighth anniversary of King Fahd's invitation to American troops to defend Saudi Arabia from Iraq, US embassies in Kenya and Tanzania were destroyed and, in 2000, the *USS Cole* was attacked at Aden. In September 2001, the global *jihad* was taken into America.

Clearly events since the 1998 declaration have been fundamentally significant. But concentrating on related groups' activities will not enable the appeal or timeliness of militancy to be understood or fully explained. To help achieve this, a broader account is required that illuminates sources of inspiration, legitimacy and justification. These are rooted in a range of discursive sources and historical events, and, as the following chapters explore in greater detail, the actions of national governments and the failures of localized militant groups. Contemporary ideological influences are drawn historically from the 'Golden Age' of the four caliphs, Ibn Taymiyya (1263–1328) and more recently across Muslim societies. This is clearly noticeable within Qutbian discourse that emanated from the Egyptian militant Sayyid Qutb (1906–66). Qutb had been influenced by earlier figures like the Madhi of Sudan, Umar al-Mukhtar and Abd al-Hamid Ibn Badis and Abul Al-Mawdudi (1903–79) from the Indian subcontinent. All have become embedded to varying degrees in the synthesis within militancy. Groups draw upon the origins of Islam stemming from the revelations to Prophet Muhammed (670–732 AD) and the successful expansion of the religion from a small region, in what is now in Saudi Arabia, to cover large parts of Asia, Africa and Europe. Images of the global *umma* united in piety and devotion, governed by righteous leaders who implemented the *shari'ah*, originate from this period. Zayyat (2004: xiii) reflects popular sentiments within militancy when arguing that leadership during this period was 'guided by a prophetic understanding of divine justice, which enabled the wealth and greatness of the Islamic empire to emerge … in the time of *jahiliyya* (… ignorance). … Political rule by Islamic *shari'a*' is the only guarantor of prosperity and harmony on earth, and paradise after death.' The extent that this period of uniformity and purity actually existed amongst diverse religious and political practices and institutions across Muslim societies is a source of theological and historical debate.[9] From the militants' perspective, the emergence, implementation and success of Islam were factual and are the basis for the demand that the *shari'ah* should be reintroduced as a 'Golden Age' for the contemporary era. How, where and what exactly this will entail is a source of considerable debate within and between groups and is influenced by earlier responses to challenges facing Muslims. For example, inspiration is found within Ibn Taymiyya's reactions to 'impure' Muslim Mongol rulers. Ibn Taymiyya declared that rulers' refusal to implement the *shari'ah* meant that they were apostates and as such were legitimate targets to be eradicated in a top-down approach. By comparison, other influential figures like Muhammed Ibn Abd al-Wahhab (1703/4–92) focussed on the purification of Muslims' behaviour who he felt had internalized heretical practices associated with *Sufism* which needed to be removed, if necessary, through violence. Reactions against foreign rulers can be noticed in Hasan al-Banna's (1906–49) campaign in Egypt against the British occupiers while Qutb initiated the two pronged approach against local rulers and the international 'Jewish Crusaders'. These influences share a belief that the individual is subordinated to the collective identity associated with their religious interpretations. Other discourses have also been incorporated to differing degrees within conceptual and strategic development. Burke (2006) details some of the similarities between militant Islam and conversely both Marxism and fascism from the first half of the twentieth century. Qutb adapted the anarchists' role of the vanguard which has been further developed by groups associated with al-Qa'ida, alongside the classical anarchist tactic of propaganda by deed. The dialectical perceptions of history and the role of immutable texts have been instrumental within bin Laden's and Marxist rhetoric. With fascism, the militant Muslims have shared strong leadership, anti-Semitism, traditions of martyrdom and emphasis on morality and a purified, mythical past. As the following chapter explores, militant Islamic groups lack the complete originality with which they are attributed by Western commentators and governments.

In addition to ideological legacies, Abu-Rabi' (2004) points out that there have been distinct types of militancy associated with pre-colonial, colonial and post-colonial periods. Therefore, militancy is not new and preceding phases of militancy impact upon recent actions and beliefs. Throughout the history of Islam, there have been shifts and transformations in religious fervour and piety. Similarly, violence has been used at different junctures and legitimized by recourse to religion since the first battles of Muhammed and subsequent wars, defence of Empires and challenges to ruling elites, before, during and after colonialism. It is therefore important to discuss briefly the contemporary history of militancy to help ground the phenomena within historical processes rather than to consider acts of terrorism[10] in isolation. The development and interrelationship of militancy, Muslim societies and communities and the West are further explored in subsequent chapters where it will be argued that these relationships are central to understanding militancy today.

There have been a range of important movements and events since the decline of Muslim empires. Groups have been involved in civil wars, for example, the Lebanese Hezbollah during the 1980s, Armed Islamic Group in Algeria and Taliban in Afghanistan during the 1990s; nationalist struggles, for example, Hamas in the Palestinian territories and MILF and Abu Sayyaf in the Philippines; and revolution notably Iran in 1979. Other groups have been involved in forms of terrorism including kidnapping (Abu Sayyaf, Hezbollah[11] and al-Qa'ida in Iraq), bomb attacks (most notably groups associated with al-Qa'ida) and assassination (with the Egyptian President Anwar Sadat probably the most high profile victim when killed in 1981 by the Egyptian Islamic Jihad). Again it is important to stress the historical legacy of such tactics within Islam. Hassan Sabbah, who belonged to the *Shi'ite Ismaili* sect, developed a group that became known as the Hashshashins or Assassins. The order operated in Iran and Syria between the eleventh and thirteenth centuries and aimed to re-establish what they considered to be the rightful path of Islamic government. The Assassins quickly became notorious for their methods, concomitant terror and members' willingness to die for the cause. Their deaths, however, were not directly caused by their own actions. Instead, it was the manner in which they killed many of their victims in public which inevitably resulted in their own deaths. Victims were carefully targeted and killed by daggers to ensure no innocent bystanders were killed. Other methods that would have provided Assassins with opportunities to escape like bows or the covert use of poison were rejected. The public strategy would appear to have been driven by a desire to invoke fear in social environments, particularly amongst the *Seljuk* elite. Terror would be enhanced through the realization that the attackers were willing to sacrifice themselves for the cause. Hassan and his followers have remained embedded within elements of contemporary militancy because they fought against Christian crusaders. They specialized in covert actions that enabled them to gain clandestine entry into camps where they would execute Christians often using poisoned daggers. However, this form of terrorism was not restricted to Christians. The Assassins also fought against the Muslim *Seljuk* state and were responsible for the murders of a range of 'orthodox Islamic leaders, judges, teachers and prayer leaders ... together with countless state functionaries' (Taheri 1987: 33). The most high profile victim was the Seljuk sultan, Malek-Shah, who was 'ripped apart' by a knife attack with the assailant reported to have shouted 'the death of this Satan is the beginning of happiness'.[12]

Preceding forms of protest, struggle and rebellion could be found across Muslim societies. Lapidus (2002: 416) details the emergence of *jihads* in West Africa from the sixteenth century. These *jihads* aimed 'to turn small colonies into Muslim states by defeating corrupt and irreligious Muslim rulers, conquering the pagan populations, converting them to Islam and ruling them according to Muslim law'. Initially the struggles arose in isolation but gradually groups began to be influenced by actions within the region. And like contemporary militants, these earlier predecessors were informed by preceding reformists like Muhammad Abd al-Karim al-Maghili.[13] In turn, more militant leaders like 'Uthman Don Fodio (1754–1817) were to radicalize reformist ideas, strengthening the military component. He criticized rulers for, amongst other things, unjust leadership, polytheism, mysticism, pagan customs, free socializing of the sexes and dancing. Such tactics contributed to the Muslim protest being unified and the Islamic state of Sokoto was established in what is today north of Nigeria and Cameroon (Lapidus 2002).[14] Other *jihads* in the region took the form of rebellions undertaken by pastoral peoples, slaves and peasants against landowning and military elites. In other words, they were forms of social upheaval embedded with Islamic beliefs and behaviour. And like what occurred in the Senegambian *jihad* of the nineteenth century, participants would burn rival villages, killing pagans and enslaving enemies. However, as Lapidus (2002) points out, struggles became wars of expansion and conquest. Within these broader conflicts, religious fervour and symbols were utilized by leaders to mobilize support, primarily for pragmatic rather than theological purposes.

Across South and Southeast Asia, reform and militancy could be noticed. For example, in Bengal, the Fara-'idi led by Haji Shariat Allah (d. 1840) sought to eradicate Hindu customs and confronted corrupt religious leaders, Sayyid Ahmad Brelwi led military resistance in the nineteenth century and Tuanku Imam Bonjol, leader of the Padri in Indonesia, sought to purify local Islam and was involved in the struggle against Dutch colonialists. In the Middle East, the emergence of the Wahhabi in the eighteenth century is an obvious example of the long-term processes of militancy. Influences can be traced back much further. Ibn Taymiyya has central significance for contemporary violent militants. According to Qutb (2001 [1966]) and to some extent al-Zawahiri (2001), Taymiyya and the Mamluks are considered to have confronted the injustices and brutalities of the Tartars. The 'spirit of resistance' was subsequently retained by a number of figures like the Mahdi of the Sudan, Umar al-Mukhtar of Libya, and Abd Al-Hamid Ibn Ben Badis from Algeria.[15] Zawahiri has also praised the earlier contributions of Nur al-Din, who was instrumental in unifying Muslims and defeating the crusaders, and his successor Salah al-Din al-Ayubbi, better known as Saladin, whose victories included the capture of Jerusalem.

In some respects, militancy today is a continuation of these shifts which enables militants to draw upon the past to justify and explain their stance against local and global enemies. However, it needs to be stressed that while historical references are prominent within militant discourse, militancy today is much more than a rehashing of the past. Their diversity, references, means and methods highlight how the groups are very much products of their time (Milton-Edwards 2005). This study will be concentrating upon contemporary national and transnationalist groups while acknowledging the significant legacy of previous forms of militancy. Groups are often seen to share a hatred for the West, globalization and secularization. But again it is possible to notice important variations. Secularism is indeed contested but this is context driven. The level of theological influence is considerable in Saudi Arabia yet is inadequate for Saudi militants. By comparison, Turkey, despite a gradual penetration by Islamists, remains a secular nation-state. Militants within the country may consider the implementation of a Saudi system of government to be a positive development, if not a complete solution. Similarly, views on globalization differ, with many militants utilizing associated processes to connect with the reinvigorated *umma* and plan and undertake operations that were previously unimaginable.

By comparison with *Sunni* militants, there is less fragmentation within the smaller *Shi'ite* denomination.[16] This may be linked to *Shi'ite ulema* retaining credibility through closer ties to communities[17] and distanciation from non-religious forms of government witnessed by their central role within localized and global challenges. Across prominent *Shi'ite* communities like those in Iran, Iraq, Lebanon, Syria and Gulf states, there are leading religious political leaders whose influence exceeds their national boundaries. For example, Ayatollah Fadlallah in Lebanon is held in high regard in neighbouring Syria and Iraq and across into a number of Gulf countries. The Iranian Ayatollah Ruhollah Khomeini (1900/2–89) was hugely significant across the Middle East and beyond for *Shi'ites* and many *Sunnis*. In Iran where *Shi'ites* constitute around 89 per cent of the population, the involvement of *Ayatollahs* and *mullahs* was increasingly noticeable within a range of popular struggles from the 1891–92 Tobacco Revolt to the 1979 revolution. Similarly, the *Shi'ite* militant group and political party Hezbollah is controlled by Islamic figures and led by cleric Sayyid Hassan Nasrallah (Hamzeh 2004; Qassem 2005). *Shi'ite* religious figures may have retained a central position through the tendency to continue to practice *ijtihad* which was curtailed by *Sunnis* between the ninth and twelfth centuries (discussed in Chapter 4). This enabled them to develop theological interpretations and apply them to changing social circumstances. Keeping the 'gates of *ijtihad*' open has enabled the *Shi'ite ulema* to remain relevant and able to provide innovative solutions to contemporary situations. Ayatollah Khomeini in particular is noted for his insistence on the significant role of human authority in decision making within *velayet-e-faqih*, government of the Islamic jurist. Hezbollah in Lebanon and the *Tehrik-e-Islami Pakistan* party have also adopted this principle. This is in contrast to the militancy associated with Qutb where the emphasis is overwhelmingly placed upon sovereignty of Allah. Arguably the stagnation within the *Sunni ulema* that resulted from the 'gates of *ijtihad*' being closed has provided unqualified militants with an opportunity to reopen the gates to address contemporary concerns and issue their own reinterpretations. Due to its relatively marginal status, there is less emphasis upon the global *umma* within *Shi'ism* and consequently the International Crisis Group (ICG) suggests (2005) that there are closer ties to specific regions and nationalities.

Because the aims of *Shi'ites* are closely connected to specific territories, from a Western secular perspective, the actions of militants are easier to understand. Even the startling extent of Iranian soldiers willingly walking to their deaths in the war against Iraq (1980–8) resembles, in some respects, the nationalist sacrifices and massive death tolls on the French battlefields in the First World War (1914–18). Similarly, while there is widespread disagreement and even revulsion over the actions within Islamic *Sunni* nationalist struggles in the Palestinian territories, south Thailand, Kashmir and Chechnya, conflicts over territories are easier to comprehend. As Chapter 3 details, these militants have developed Islamic discourse both to help mobilize support and justify methods adopted and implemented. However, the discourse is intertwined with a nationalist struggle that is ultimately driven by the desire for liberation and ethnic independence. Within these struggles and across transnational groups, *jihad* is utilized as a method of waging war against enemies that include Jews, Westerners, secularists and apostates. Nationalists tend to declare *jihad* against nation-states like Israel, Russia, India and the Philippines that are viewed as obstacles to independence. These groups are circumspect about attacking 'lesser' Muslims or members of other religious denominations not directly engaged in the struggle without a related strategic outcome. By contrast, other factions, for example, the *Janjawiid* in Sudan, declare *jihad* against Muslims belonging to other ethnic groups. The *Janjawiid* are engaged in a practice of ethnic cleansing connected to control over Darfur, but actions of other groups seemingly driven by religious motives with vague and abstract ultimate objectives are harder to understand. Groups associated with al-Qa'ida have sought to establish themselves as the sole representative of true Islam, often viewing themselves as vanguards whose actions and example will inspire and awaken Muslims to challenge Western nation-states and overthrow national governments. Under this interpretation, other Muslims have lesser faith or are apostates who can be legitimately subjected to death, as discussed in Chapter 4. Their actions are still considered to be 'defensive' in a manner that is common across terror groups. As Taylor and Quayle (1994) observe in their study of different forms of terrorism, groups tend to consider their use of violence to be a provoked reaction that is required in defence against an aggressive enemy.

Groups operating in a manner that is most difficult for Western secularists to understand are more likely to be closely associated with al-Qa'ida. Despite acknowledged communication skills and awareness-raising through modern technologies, related groups are struggling to translate their actions into a meaningful alternative discourse. In other words, perceptions of the struggle need to be evaluated beyond 'good' against 'evil' to attain broader support against the contemporary equivalents of the Mongol, crusader and colonialist invaders. It is therefore instructive that al-Zawahiri (2001) also draws attention to the contribution of the twelfth century 'holy warriors' Nur al-Din Zangi and Salah al-Din al-Ayubbi who fought against perceived tyrants and colonialist rulers. In this manner, parallels are drawn with preceding periods of deviance and remediation suggesting that contemporary problems could be addressed through similar processes of moral purification and violence.

Clearly there is a relationship between Islamic devotion and militantism. However, this should not be construed to mean that there is an inevitable correlation between theological expertise, practise and violence. As the examples of Qutb, bin Laden, al-Zawahiri and al-Zawqawi indicate, leading *Sunni* militants are rarely qualified theologians. And many members, including those of recent cells involved in attacks in New York, Madrid and London, may have, as Marranci's (2006) research identified, intensified beliefs and *jihadi* rhetoric but often lack in-depth religious knowledge or allegiance to the specificities of particular groups. Analysis is further complicated by the tendency to attribute Sunni attacks in Iraq to al-Qa'ida-related groups. Yet Burke (2006) points out that, although the people are Muslims, many are not fighting specifically for Islam, indeed some are not devout Muslims. For these 'militants', religion proves a source both of unity within groups and ideological justification according to literalist interpretations, but the struggle is overwhelmingly about removing American forces and the ethnic nature of the Iraqi nation-state. And rather than being part of a coalition with al-Qa'ida, this has been an arrangement of convenience with some of their 'allies' actions causing revulsion, manifested by growing signs that the relationship is increasingly fractious and considered to be detrimental within this more 'nationalist' component. In some extreme instances, people involved in militancy have continued to be engaged in practices that are widely considered to be un-Islamic, for example, drinking alcohol. And as Rashid (2002) discusses with respect to Juma Namangani of the Islamic Movement of Uzbekistan, leaders also often lack Islamic knowledge and are influenced by both the actions and rhetoric of more influential militants, most notably bin Laden. Other people become involved within militancy for basic reasons. Burke (2006) identified members of the Taliban who had been attracted by the offer of food, money and security in exchange for their labour. It can therefore be misleading to assume that a Muslim involved in acts of 'terrorism' or a member of a militant Islamic group is inevitably deeply grounded within militant theology.

Explaining militancy

Analysis of 'Islamic' national and international terrorism tends to emphasize the significance of economic deprivation, and schooling and mosques as agents of brainwashing. However, it is argued that this only provides a partial account of the diverse routes into militancy and ultimately terrorism. In order to provide a broader picture, a range of economic, political, cultural and psychosocial explanations will be explored.

To this end, it is important to examine the structural processes and events at local and global levels that are seen to be transforming peoples' lives and their perceptions of these changes. As Crenshaw (1998: 250) comments, 'terrorism is not the direct result of social conditions but of individual perceptions of those conditions'. But it must be added that these perceptions are developed through social processes and interaction. Consequently, this research examines international, national and local processes and activities and their impact upon individuals. A range of academic research and militant sources including political discourse and biographical details are explored to help outline factors behind the radicalization of people. As Tilly (2004: 12) remarked, in respect to the work of Stern (2003a), 'no single set of cause-effect propositions can explain terrorism as a whole'. Yet, this overemphasis upon single causal analysis remains prominent, particularly within accounts that examine the relationship between militancy and materialism.

Economic development and materialism

'Islamic' militancy including terrorism is most widely perceived to be a consequence of poverty, absolute or relative, that results from modernization and development. Li and Schaub (2004: 236) exemplify this perspective when arguing that 'a primary cause of transnational terrorism is underdevelopment and poverty. ... Poor economic conditions create "terrorist breeding" grounds, where disaffected populations turn to transnational terrorist activities as a solution to their problems.' At a broader political level, the 'war against poverty' is strongly associated with addressing the conditions that are believed to contribute towards terrorism. In support, the former British Prime Minister Tony Blair argued that a combination of poverty, brutal dictatorship and fanatical extremism has resulted in terrorism.[18] Earlier President G. W. Bush (2002b) stated that 'we fight against poverty because hope is an answer to terror'.

There is considerable academic analysis that provides support for the causal relationship between poverty, modernization and militancy. For example, Mortimer (1982) analysed groups during an early stage in the formation of contemporary Islamic militancy and argued that people were attracted 'whose lives are in one way or another disorientated by rapid change: merchants and manufacturers being edged out by foreign competition or by the growth of a new capitalist class'. Roy (1994: 52) claimed, over a decade later, that Islamic movements were composed of 'the oppressed of all countries ... [who] dream of access to the world of development and consumption from which they feel excluded.' Sivan (1997: 11) argues on similar lines that Islamic fundamentalism 'is a reaction against a modernity that does not deliver even on its material promises. It creates a gap between Western style consumerist expectations and "Fourth world" production and per capita income.' And 20 years after Mortimer's observation, Paz (2002: 73) believes that the origins of 'Islamic' terrorism can be located 'in the inability of many individual Muslims to cope with the technological, cultural, social or economic aspects of Western modernization'. Finally, Butko (2004: 33) suggests that political Islamic 'movements have arisen in reaction to attempts at rapid development and modernization which have not fulfilled the expectations of a majority of their populations. Urbanization, higher education and the perception of relative material deprivation have led to feelings of alienation, frustration, and hence, a growing sense of powerlessness.' Throughout the 1990s, the rise of Islamists in places like Algeria and the subsequent civil war have been attributed to a mismanaged economy, declining hydrocarbon prices, rising population and unemployment (Maddy-Weitzman and Litvak 2003). Similar issues can be identified in the rise of militancy in Saudi Arabia (Hiro 2002) and across the Persian Gulf. And across Central Asia, the fracture of the Soviet Union in 1991 was accompanied by deteriorating economies and living standards and higher levels of inflation, unemployment, national and individual debt and social inequality. Alongside these materialist factors, the region has become associated with rising processes of Islamification and concomitant state repression (Rashid 2002). Many Muslim nation-states were simultaneously encountering both developmental crises and militancy with Islam considered, in an adaptation of one of Marx' famous sayings, to be not 'the opium of the people, but the vitamin of the weak' (Debray 1994: 15). And the impact of limited economic prosperity has other consequences which also connect with the appeal of militancy. Across Muslim societies, young men have been expected to gain independence through employment which enables them to obtain their own homes and to marry and have children. But as de Waal (2004: 58) points out with respect to Africa, but which also applies across Muslim experiences, with a combination of social breakdown and economic crisis, large numbers of young people, especially men, are condemned never to achieve this status, and must therefore spend most or all of their lives as 'social cadets'. Such experiences are not specific to Muslim communities. Similar patterns can be noticed in other 'developing' parts of the world. A range of religious and nationalist groups can offer solutions to the postponement or cancellation of the transition into adult independence that would establish individuals' social status according to cultural expectations. Consequently, the significance of economic matters to the appeal of militancy is not restricted to class situation in the classic Marxist sense. Instead, the Weberian concept of status is also applicable, helping to draw out the significance of lifestyles, consumption, tastes and related social esteem.

Hafez (2003) challenges the materialist argument more directly in his comparative analysis of Islamic militancy across a range of societies. He concluded that there is no correlation between levels of economic deprivation, demographics and insurgency. And in his comparison across nation-states, he argues that there is not a quantifiable relationship between level of national wealth and the extent of militancy. Instead, the issues extend beyond financial resources to incorporate political, cultural, social, legal and moral concerns. Yet there is, as the Egyptian militant Montasser al-Zayyat (2004) relates, a popular misconception that membership of radical groups is a result of poverty and lack of economic opportunity. This is not to argue that poor people or those unable to fully participate within consumerism are not engaged in acts of terrorism. However, many militants argue that rather than consumerism and materialism being appealing, they actually repel through their association with excessive individualism. As Hizbullah's Naim Qassem (2005) explains, materialism reflects an approach based upon life as an end in itself and not as militants believe, a trail to the hereafter. Gerges' (2006: 34–5) interviews with activists from the 1970s discovered people claiming that their involvement was not motivated by personal gain. As one respondent stated, 'we did not sacrifice the flower of our youth, the best years of our lives, in prisons to get jobs and earthly rewards. Our aim is to please God. The West cannot comprehend our spirituality and religiosity as long as it is blinded by materialism.' Similar reasoning is also highlighted in the following chapter when discussing some issue-based similarities between Western social movements and those associated with militant Islam.

Uneducated or unemployed people have been heavily involved across militant groups belonging to different religions. With respect to Islam, Kalpakian (2005) and Kepel (2004b) have both identified the number of people belonging to poor backgrounds who were involved in the Madrid bombings. In the Palestinian territories, poverty is endemic and services severely curtailed. However, Krueger and Malecková (2003a) report on opinion polls in the West Bank and Gaza Strip that identified no evidence to suggest that more highly educated people were less likely to support violence against Israeli targets. By comparison, the unemployed were less likely to be in support. Studies[19] of the socio-economic background of Palestinian suicide bombers indicate that people with higher levels of education and less experience of poverty are more likely to undertake attacks than the impoverished and uneducated. And crucially, while poverty and development are important factors for many people who become radical, they are not new phenomena. In many instances, the processes have predated terrorism by generations. The most prominent Muslim nation-states in relation to 'Islamic' terrorism like Saudi Arabia, Pakistan, Egypt and Indonesia have been undergoing modernization for generations. In addition, the 'poor' argument cannot account for the appeal of militant Islam across different socio-economic groupings, ethnicities, nationalities and gender, including educated, wealthy people. If, for example, the social backgrounds of suicide/martyrdom attackers beyond the Palestinian territories are analysed,[20] it is apparent that they have been organized and carried out by a wide range of Muslims from different countries, occupations, levels of educational achievement and gender.

Some explanations for militancy and acts of terrorism have acknowledged the diversity of socio-economic backgrounds but have tended to overconcentrate upon the exclusionary criteria noted above. The identification of educated supporters and members has also been noted across religious movements and terror groups and has led to a re-evaluation of the poverty thesis (Ayubi 1991; Kepel 2004a; Roy 1994). However, after acknowledging the existence of educated militants, the tendency has been to extend the poverty and frustration rationale to the better qualified, exemplified by Roy's (1994) description of the group as 'lumpen intelligentsia'. Emphasis is placed upon the tremendous expansion of educational opportunities and the inadequate job opportunities for graduates. People are seen to be reacting to nation-states' 'failure to fulfil the promise of increased employment and status' (Butko 2004: 34). Consequently, as the United Nations Development Programme (2002: 2) declared, in respect to Arab countries, 'there is a mismatch between aspirations and their fulfilment'. For many academics and government officials, the unemployed or underemployed graduates become radicalized. Gurr's (1970) theory of relative deprivation exemplifies this perspective, associating rebellious behaviour with economic deprivation. Certainly there are people who have joined militant groups as a result of these experiences but crucially others have developed successful careers post university. A number of studies[21] have shown that there is a diverse range of socio-economic backgrounds and educational attainment levels, and a preponderance of upwardly mobile middle-class individuals and professional backgrounds both within moderate groups and radical Islamist networks. For example, Hegghammer's (2006) study of recruitment and radicalization amongst Saudi militants identified an overrepresentation of middle-class and lower middle-class members. Very few were significantly overqualified for their jobs and therefore not anticipated to be encountering feelings of relative deprivation. Hegghammer (2006: 45) observes that 'on the whole the ... members were unremarkable in the sense that they were neither society's losers nor winners'.[22] Nor is this a recent development. As Ibrahim's (1980) study into jailed Islamists indicated, members of such groups tended to be highly educated, motivated, upwardly mobile and from middle-class backgrounds. In this respect, the terror groups' constituency is not dissimilar from movements associated with post-industrial politics and post-material values (discussed in Chapter 2).

Yet, despite this extensive challenge, Hafez (2003: xvii) observes that, 'Gurr's theory continues to prevail, explicitly or implicitly, as the leading explanation of Islamist violence and rebellion by area specialists, Islamic study scholars and journalists covering the Muslim world'. This misrepresentation becomes problematic when seeking to address the causes of terrorism. Explanations that concentrate upon materialist causes share, at least, an implicit belief that terrorism will disappear if developmental crises are resolved, income levels rise, relative deprivation disappears and unemployment is reduced. However, if the causes of terrorism extend across other social spheres that are not acknowledged and subsequently addressed, then terrorism is unlikely to be defeated. It is therefore important that the focus shifts beyond economics and employment to explore underlying causes that can help explain the diverse appeal of 'Islamic' terrorism in particular, and militancy more generally.

Repression and secularization

The role of opportunities for political engagement within decision-making and civil society, or to be more precise the repression of opportunities and indeed liberties, is also accorded significance within explanations for militancy and terrorism. For example, Hafez (2003) and Rashid (2002) have both argued that state repression is an important factor when combined with institutional exclusion. Anwar (2001) exemplifies this perspective when arguing that 'bin Laden and his protégés are the children of desperation; they come from countries where political struggle through peaceful means is futile'.[23] Certainly there is evidence to suggest that repressive threats to organizational resources and personal lives were contributing factors in Algeria, Egypt and Central Asia during the 1990s when militant challenges intensified. However, repression is much less prominent in places like Southeast Asia and Western Europe where Muslim radicalization is also noticeable. And in Malaysia, more radical forms of Islam have become noticeable. Ironically, the previous Mahathir government established itself as a defender of Islam which provided religious institutions with degrees of freedom of expression and protest that were not always possible through more mainstream politics. In this instance, religious institutions became forces of opposition. Conversely, as Hafez (2003) observes, repression has worked in Syria, Tunisia and Iraq (pre-2003).

Political domination is also important within explanations that emphasize the significance of secularization within Muslim nation-states. Through secularization, at various stages of the twentieth century, religion was formally removed from power, with theological influence no longer prominent within nation-states, and made subservient to secular governments. This exclusion of Islam from power is considered to be an important mobilizing factor in processes of radicalization. Again, it is important to note that secularization processes have varied considerably across Muslim societies and have often preceded contemporary terrorism by generations. Levels of political influence held by Islamic institutions also vary, ranging from the aggressive subjugation of religion in Turkey, to Islam being integrated within power relations since the formation of the nation-state in Saudi Arabia.[24] Yet, militancy can be found to different degrees in all Muslim societies and certainly is more prominent in Saudi Arabia than Turkey. Contrary to widespread opinion, it is therefore possible to argue that rather than the diminution of religious influence being central to the re-emergence of militancy, it is partly a consequence of concessions[25] (discussed below and in Chapters 3 and 4) being made to religious groups that have enhanced the prominence of Islam. By increasing the prevalence of Islam across societies, governments have unintentionally contributed to growing numbers of people being informed about more radical interpretations in conditions which are perceived to legitimize the challenging discourse. For example, in the oft-neglected North Caucasus region, the Islamic challenge to secular regimes has grown considerably following the demise of the rigid atheistic Soviet ideology[26] and the increasing prominence of religious institutions. In 'secular' Egypt, religious institutions like al Azhar have been increasingly accommodated within state power and have pervasive rights of censorship which extend across books, newspapers, civil service policies and publications and education (de Waal 2004). Across Muslim societies, concepts like *jihad* and martyrdom are now embedded within social and political discourse, and normative religious behaviour is less moderate, reducing the distance to be travelled to militancy and terrorism.

Economic and political exclusion is instrumental in processes through which people become militants. But as the above discussion has shown, many people do not experience these factors. Attention therefore needs to be placed upon other forms of exclusion, namely those associated with culture.

Cultural exclusion and allegiance

Analysis of the impact of culture upon religious behaviour generally and Islamic militancy in particular tends to follow two main avenues of thought. At one level, cultural changes are considered to impact upon individuals and religion becomes a resource to address a range of psychological requirements during times of upheaval, namely explanations, solace and social cohesion. And second, cultural elements within religions are attributed with causal power, most notoriously Huntington's *Clash of Civilizations* thesis.

Milton-Edwards (2005) details how Christian, Hindu, Islamic and Jewish fundamentalism are equated with a rejection of modernity in its many manifestations. Particular attention is placed upon perceived economic and political threats but many 'fundamentalists' concentrate upon dangers that modernity posed to their 'ways of life' and their self-identification. For example, the Christian Patriot movement in the United States places tremendous emphasis upon defending American lifestyles rooted in a perception of a purified past (Vertigans 2007a). Similarly, Islamic militants also hark back to 'golden ages' and stress discrepancies between ideal cultural behaviour and reality, most notably within debates over the role and visibility of women. In this example, many men appear to be reacting to changing socio-economic trends connected to modernization and globalization which are considered to threaten their patriarchal dominance. In response, some men are utilizing elements within Islam to try to protect and reinforce power within employment and familial relations.

At a broader level, religious resurgences are considered to be defensive reactions to globalizing forces of capitalism (Wallerstein 1980, 1983, 1984) or consumer culture (Robertson 1992; Waters 1998). However, it would be a mistake to consider militancy as inherently anti-modern. For example, in Chapter 2, numerous examples are provided that highlight how groups associated with al-Qa'ida are very much a product of modernity. Despite references to the past, the reliance upon globalization and associated processes of transportation and communication are central components of groups' strategies.

The tendency to stereotype militant Islam is noticeable within culturalist explanations. In such perceptions, Islam is the 'religion of the sword' and is the source for behaviour that is at odds with Western 'civilized' behaviour, for example, misogyny, dictatorships and terrorism. Huntington's (1998) *Clash of Civilizations* thesis is the best known account. In this thesis, Huntington argues that international conflicts will be between civilizations. Cultural distinctions that include religious beliefs and symbols become the most important sources both for identification and motivating factors for conflict. Underlying Huntington's (1998: 263) analysis is the consideration that Islamic civilization has a propensity for violence as a 'religion of the sword' that glorifies military virtues. Tensions cannot be attributed to extremism but inherent incompatibilities between the West and Islam. For Huntington (1998: 217), 'the underlying problem for the West is not Islamic fundamentalism. ... The problem for Islam is not the CIA or the U.S. Department of Defense. It is the West' ... Attacks by militants on the West, American-led invasions of Afghanistan and Iraq, rising Islamophobia in Western towns and cities, support for Huntington's thesis by bin Laden[27] and the rigid division of the world into *Dar al-Islam* and *Dar al-Harb* would appear to provide evidence for the thesis. And it is Islamic culture that is deemed responsible for the lack of democracy within Muslim nation-states, despite considerable evidence to the contrary in Turkey, Malaysia, Bangladesh and the Palestinian territories to name but a few. It is argued here that the thesis is heavily flawed, relying on unrepresentative selective examples, ignoring the multitude of cases that contradict the argument and ultimately only producing a partial picture of Islam.[28] Yet despite the initial inaccuracy of Huntington's argument, support for the thesis both within militant Islam and the West, and reliance upon unrepresentative images and actions by both sides, will contribute to a 'self-fulfilling prophecy'. In this scenario, the emotional commitments within both groups hinder a more accurate reading of the situation. Instead, events are interpreted and reinforced through stereotypical frames of reference. Through these processes, divides become further strengthened and areas of commonality shift further away. Consequently in some ways the original inaccuracy of the argument is becoming secondary to its potential contribution to reality.[29]

In addition to peoples' experiences of forms of exclusion, it is also important to establish how people become aware of broader concerns and equally how they are informed about militant Islam. In other words, simply being aware of poverty, injustice or repression does not inevitably result in people becoming terrorists.

Beyond brainwashing: the role of socialization

Within modernization theory, the widespread development of schools, universities and forms of media was considered conducive to progression. Today, the same socializing agents are also associated with processes of radicalization and, at the extreme, brainwashing. This form of explanation is prominent across studies of terrorism. For example, Hudson (1999: 32) believes that terror organizations 'attempt to brainwash individual members with their particular ideology'. The emergence of suicide bombers has also been strongly associated with brainwashing. But as the Israeli psychologist Ariel Merari observes, 'no group can just get someone to do that [be a suicide bomber]. At most, they can strengthen existing dispositions, but at the end of the day, it comes from the individual himself, from his experiences, from his beliefs.'[30]

Schools have been closely associated with 'brainwashing' militants. Government and militant groups across the Middle East, South and Southeast Asia have established a network of Islamic schools that disseminate radicalism and recruit members. During the 1970s and 1980s, religious content within states' curricula and the number of *medressas* (Islamic schools) increased tremendously, often aided by funding from the Gulf countries (Esposito 2002; Stern 2003a)). Many *medressas* combine classical religious education with a modern curriculum. Other *medressas* are controlled by more rigid Wahhabi ideologues and their pupils internalize dogmatic discourse (Byman and Green 1999; Esposito 2002). Most notably, Saudi Arabia has sought to utilize Islam to provide legitimacy for the nation-state and the Kingdom's status as guardian of the two Holy Sites. The Saudi regime is based upon a range of policies that have enhanced religious influence across society including education, law and economy. Islam within education has become increasingly noticeable. And within some prescribed textbooks, emphasis is placed upon *jihad*, meaning in this context, outer struggle against irreligious forces. Admon (2007) reports on a document titled 'Educational Policy' published by the Saudi Education Ministry. Amongst a range of goals are two that relate specifically to *jihad*, 'to prepare students physically and mentally for jihad for the sake of Allah' and 'to arouse the spirit of Islamic jihad in order to fight our enemies, to restore our rights and our glory, and to fulfil the mission of Islam'. The Saudi columnist Saud al-Balawi argues that the curricula provide 'fertile ground for teachers with extremist ideological tendencies to spread their views officially'.[31] Problems are not restricted to religious schools. Across many Muslim societies, Islam and radical teachers have become embedded within a range of educational institutions. And within different levels of learning, problems of over-crowding, inadequate resources, rote learning and lack of independent thinking are notable, creating conditions in which dissatisfaction and radicalization can arise (de Waal 2004; Vertigans 2003).

Clearly, there are many educational institutions involved in processes of radicalization. Yet their influence has often been overstated. Many militants, notably in the West, have not been educated at militant institutions or by radical teachers. They are assimilating the discourse from other sources. Mosques and religious leaders in particular have been closely associated with the rise in terrorism and methods of brainwashing. For instance, Kepel (2004b: 256) argues that 'the first stage of brainwashing occurs at the hands of a pietistic salafist imam'. Similarly, Rashid (2005) claims that 'the simple reason is the terrifying brainwashing suffered by most of the Arab youth at the hands of "religious clerics" and particularly at the hands of the extremists with backward views'. Across Muslim societies, the power and influence of the *ulema* has grown with governments increasingly utilizing religious legitimacy for political purposes. Yet conversely the close association of the *ulema* with governments has also contributed to them being de-legitimized as 'pulpit parrots' (Ibrahim 1980). This results in anti-establishment challenges frequently arising from outside established religious arrangements led by unqualified 'religious' leaders like bin Laden, al-Zawahiri and al-Zawqawi. And when examining links between religious institutions and perpetrators of recent bomb attacks and attempted attacks in the United Kingdom, there is apparently no direct association. It is believed that the group involved in the failed 21 July 2005 attack on London formed after meeting at the controversial Finsbury Park mosque in late 2002. But there is no evidence to suggest that any *imams*, including the notorious Abu Hamza, influenced the men. Similarly, research into the background of the four people considered to have been responsible for the 7 July 2005 suicide bombs in London has shown that as the group became radicalized they became estranged from local mosques which had no history of employing radical *imams* (Burke *et al.* 2005). Instead, as Hegghammer (2006) has argued with respect to Saudi militants, common recruiting grounds were informal religious study groups and gatherings, not formalized processes within mosques.

Within the West, Stemmann (2006) comments that mosques are losing their significance and are being replaced by personal contacts, private religious courses within informal settings and the Internet. This of course makes counter-terrorism much more difficult as groups adapt to evolving surveillance techniques and other agents become instrumental including technology and peers. The role of technology and the media has been well documented[32] but the role of groups is less well known. Individuals associated with bombings and foiled attempts in Bali, Singapore, Madrid, London and the Hamburg cell that attacked America became radicalized as part of a collective process within groups. As Hegghammer (2006: 50) comments, 'group dynamics such as peer pressure and intra-group affection seem to have been crucial in the process' of radicalization. Across Muslim communities, younger generations are sharing experiences, information and discourse and are collectively contributing to group radicalization or recruitment to existing groups (Burke 2003; Sageman 2004; Vertigans 2003). Salem and de Waal (2004) identify the significance of intergenerational conflicts for militant mobilization across Muslim societies in Africa, a point which can be extended across Muslim communities. In Africa, the problem is exacerbated by the dominance of gerontocratic political elites and the lack of opportunities for young people to attain their expected social positions, as discussed above. Younger Muslims living in the West can also be mobilized through events, experiences and discourse. Groups like Hizb-ut-Tahrir, al Ghurabee, the Saviour Sect and the now disbanded al-Muhajiroun have been connecting with young Muslims, contributing to the arousal of anger. Yet, despite opinions to the contrary, such groups do not explicitly provide immediate outlets for such emotions. Instead, it would appear that some members are impatient with these groups' long-term approaches to the recreation of the *umma* and decide to take more direct action within their self-formed smaller units. And for recruits, the sense of belonging to a group, sharing values, explanations and companionship, can be part of the attraction. As a former Egyptian member of al-Gama'a el-Islamiya, Khaled al-Berry (2005: 8) explains, 'I wasn't attracted to their brand of religion: I was attracted to them as people ... It's like a new group of friends ... and [I] want to be one of them because you like their courage and sense of donation'. Burke (2006: 176) explores this relationship in his research into militancy and believes that groups become substitutes for family, as 'fictive kin' instrumental in recruitment and progressive radicalization into terrorism.

Another aspect commonly identified is the vulnerability of individuals living in changing societies that transform reference points and undermine attachments on which peoples' identities are located.[33] Consequently, people who have undergone significant transformations in their lives, most notably migrants to cities, experience feelings of confusion, powerlessness, marginalization and alienation. In these contexts, religions like Islam, Hinduism, Judaism and Christianity can provide explanations, security and a sense of belonging that are attractive to the dislocated and disenfranchised.[34]

In order to gain a deeper understanding of the factors behind violent militancy, it is also important to examine the proclamations of radical groups in press releases, video and Website messages and personal messages issued by individual participants. Obviously such statements are biased, designed to try to enhance appeal. But as such they provide an insight into militant motivations and highlight factors that militants think will attract support and new members. Examination of communications issued by bin Laden, al-Zawahiri and acknowledged spokesmen reveals a range of predominantly non-materialist issues that are being raised to mobilize support. Instead of concentrating upon issues associated with poverty, which is rarely mentioned, bin Laden's pronouncements[35] cover a broad spectrum. Nationalist struggles are discussed in places like Palestine, Kashmir and Chechnya, as are problems with Muslim governments, especially Saudi Arabia and its association with corruption, irreligious behaviour and the decision to allow the American military on to holy land. Denunciations of America are common and include ongoing roles in Iraq and Afghanistan, association with Israel and Jews, cowardice, hypocrisy and perhaps, most surprisingly, the Kyoto Agreement. There is also considerable attention placed upon immorality, the behaviour of elites, most notably Saudi princes and associated corruption. Immorality is a common feature within militant rhetoric. For example, Burke (2003) reports on Imam Samudra, one of the Jemaah Islamiyah organizers of the Bali bombing in 2002, who had been disgusted by the 'dirty adulterous behaviour' of the 'whites'. His group targeted nightclubs as centres of such behaviour and also stressed the need both for Muslim unity within the *umma* (global Islamic community) and the essentiality of *jihad*.

When examining why individuals have become associated with al-Qa'ida, a multitude of factors can be discerned. These include events in their country of birth, for example, struggle for independence, opposition to governments, fights against oppression, cultural imperialism or Western military conquests. Feelings referred to by militants include anger, disillusionment and disgust.[36] When 'Islamic' terrorists in the West are examined, first-, second- and even third-generation immigrants often face a number of hardships including discrimination and racism. In these contexts, joining groups can be part of a common defence mechanism. And, perceptions of rising Islamophobia, discrimination and the impact of anti-terrorism laws are impacting upon loyalties. The four 7 July 2005 London bombers had experiences of deprivation and racism in Britain. But, as the narrator emphasized in Shehzad Tanweer's (one of the bombers) 'living will', these terrorists were not motivated 'because of poverty, unemployment and emptiness as some of the mercenary media try to portray it to us'. The acknowledged leader, Mohammad Siddique Khan is known to have expressed his dissatisfaction with the environment in which he lived.

But in his 'living will' he was vitriolic in denouncing Britain's foreign policy which was considered to be part of an onslaught against Muslims. Interviews with friends discovered frequent references to the war in Iraq and related suffering and injustices (BBC 2005b; Burke *et al.* 2005; Gerges 2005; Norton-Taylor 2006). Similar reasoning was provided by Salahuddin Amin and Omar Khyam at their trials for plotting to cause explosions in Britain. Both were British Muslims whose families emigrated from Pakistan, and the conflict in Kashmir was a defining issue in their radicalization. Another member of the group, Anthony Garcia, was born in Algeria, but influenced by his increasingly Islamic brother he became inspired by the situation in Kashmir, partly through exposure in videos that showed alleged atrocities committed by the Indian army.

The significance of 'virtual' events in regions that militants may not be familiar with can be noticed across socio-economic contexts. Through the increasingly penetrative media, people view images or listen to narrative that weakens secular discourse while strengthening the legitimacy of militancy. For instance, Gerges (2005: 61) interviews al-Bahri who left Saudi Arabia to join the *jihad* in Bosnia when aged 21. He was part of a generation that was much more aware of international political developments than older generations. Al-Bahri referred to the impact of 'a picture that is still printed in my mind to this day. It is of a Jewish soldier breaking the limbs of a Palestinian child with a stone, in front of the eyes of the world.' Another militant informed Gerges (2005: 60–1) that the trip to *jihad* was a consequence of 'watching the slaughter of children, women, and old people; the violation of honor and mass rape of girls; and the huge number of widows and orphans left by the war'. Similarly, a Libyan volunteer who went to fight the Americans in Iraq told Pargeter (2006: 8) that the 'media is what brought me. The pictures of Abu Ghraib ... the al-Jazeera and al-Arabiya channels and other TV channels like al-Shariqa and others.'

These examples highlight how the media, particularly television, videos, DVDs, MP3s and the Internet, has become a central feature within processes of radicalization. Devji (2005: 87) suggests that 'perhaps the most important way in which the jihad assumes its universality, however, is through the mass media. As a series of global effects the jihad is more a product of the media than it is of any local tradition or situation and school or lineage of Muslim authority.' Through international transmission by mainstream telecommunications and militant organizations, images and narrative are collectively witnessed. Devji suggests that these witnesses become part of the struggle as either friends or enemies of *jihad*. In this context, filmed acts of terrorism or 'living wills' seek to make connections and both unify supporters and reinforce divisions from the 'other'. And as Kepel (2004b) notes, this was part of a strategic approach adopted by al-Zawahiri designed to utilize modern communications as a new form of recruitment. Instead of the patient, gradual recruitment practices through Islamic associations and institutions that were previously adopted, al-Zawahiri has reasoned that televised images of successful attacks that resulted in large-scale deaths and injuries would both 'terrorize' the enemy whilst galvanizing support from Muslims.

Finally, the appeal of militancy is strongly correlated with the failures of other discourses. Western-influenced modernization and related secularization have raised expectations and resulted in the transformation of national landscapes; huge numbers of people have relocated, studied further and higher education, made tremendous sacrifices. Yet governments have failed to deliver promises, with many widely condemned for elitism, corruption and injustice.[37] These factors have contributed to forming opinions that ideologies and associated principles such as capitalism, socialism, communism, Arab nationalism and democracy had failed Muslims and should be replaced by the *shari'ah* (Islamic law). In these settings, militancy often has a receptive audience. Raising hopes within the population that are subsequently shattered seem to be particularly significant in processes of radicalization. This is exemplified by an Egyptian militant associated with the assassination of President Anwar Sadat in 1981, who informed Gerges (2006) of the long list of grievances that led to Sadat being killed. The foremost factor was when Sadat reneged on his pledge to implement *shari'ah*.

Conclusion

The contemporary development of different militant groups generally and violence in particular can be seen as a consequence of a range of social processes, associations and activities that connect to historical ideologues and activists. These include modernization, secularization and interrelationships with local, national and international histories and contexts. Many terrorists do not have personal experiences of the factors widely associated with 'Islamic' terrorism, namely absolute and relative poverty or brainwashing. Instead, interactions between individuals and socializing agents, militant Islamic discourse and local and global social relations and activities are creating a variety of different routes into militancy and terrorism. It is within these settings that socializing processes are helping to transform identities and contribute towards radicalization and ultimately political violence. There is not therefore a single track following brainwashing or economic deprivation. Militant messages are legitimized by local and global socio-economic, cultural and political events, and conditions that are encountered either personally or relayed by socializing agents. For some people, this happens through local issues and experiences. By comparison, for many transnationalists, a range of local and international issues are important including corruption, American attacks in Iraq and nationalist struggles in Chechnya, Kashmir and the Palestinian territories.

The variety of factors has tremendous significance for attempts to defeat terrorism, as Chapter 6 details. It is becoming increasingly clear that the

American-led military-based 'war on terror' is proving self-defeating. In other words, the 'war' is providing legitimacy for the discourse it is designed to defeat, and simultaneously weakening Western concepts and principles that were to be defended. Exposure to Western behaviour does not, as many believe, particularly in the West, necessarily result in widespread acceptance or imitation. On the contrary, it can contribute towards radicalization of opposing ideologies. And when examining the broad range of issues that include repression, racism, corruption, immorality and political and economic exclusion behind the appeal of militancy, it is also apparent that the 'war on poverty' can only be at best partially successful in explaining militancy. Consequently there is an urgent requirement for governments to reassess the causes of terrorism and to devise appropriate multi-layered strategies. To this end, greater research needs to be undertaken into different forms of militant Islam that exist in different contexts in order to be able to address solutions to unique problems. Equally, the tendency to hermeneutically seal 'Islamic' terror groups neglects crucial similarities and messages that are shared with other militant organizations and moderate movements. In other words, militant Islam is not as unique as it is widely perceived. The following chapter seeks to explore commonalities and differences between militant Muslims and Western 'New Social Movements'.

2 Militant Islam in local, national and transnational networks

Philip W. Sutton and Stephen Vertigans

Introduction

Interpretations of contemporary Islamic militancy have been heavily influenced by the al-Qa'ida phenomenon with its international cells, global discourse and anti-Western motivation. However, as Chapter 1 identified and Chapter 3 develops, Islamic militancy can be shown to have taken numerous forms with some groups operating locally or regionally, others nationally and yet more looking to create transnational connections. This chapter argues that at all these levels, but in particular the transnational, the sociology of social movements offers theoretical and conceptual resources which form a significant aspect of any comprehensive and satisfactory explanation for their emergence and development. The main problem with such a view, however, has been that the field of social movement studies has, until very recently, not shown much interest in religious movements including moderate or radical Islamic movements. Kurzman (2004: 289) rightly argues that, 'Over the past generation, the fields of social movement theory and Islamic studies have followed parallel trajectories with few glances across the chasm that has separated them.' Clear evidence of such parallel development can be seen in the lack of integration of Islamic movement studies, and religious groups generally, into the social movements' mainstream, as well as the recourse by many commentators to reductive psychological theories of Islamic brainwashing of vulnerable young individuals (Dawkins 2001; Hudson 1999; Rashid 2005).

In social movement studies, introductions to the field and edited collections of the last decade (almost) uniformly fail to cover Islamic movements. The collection of McAdam *et al.* (1996) draws on many secular movements but not Islamist mobilizations. Tarrow (1998: 185) identifies 'Islamic fundamentalism' as one of three 'transnational social movements', but does not pursue the characterization. Della Porta and Diani's (1999: 22) introduction is inspired by 'the experience of "new movements"' but these do not include religious movements and there are no indexed references to Islam or Islamic movements. Similarly, Crossley's (2002) introduction has no indexed reference to Islam and his representative list of social movements has no room for Islamic movements (p. 1). Finally, Goodwin and Jasper's (2003) recent volume includes just one selection on Islam, Kurzman's (1996) analysis of the Iranian revolution, the one 'Islamic' subject that has attracted the attention of social movement research, presumably because of its geopolitical significance.[1]

In all likelihood, the invisibility of Islamic movements in this field is not due to a lack of interest. Rather, it appears to be the consequence of a narrow definition of social movements rooted in the largely secular movements found in the West. Over the past eight years or so, there is evidence of an emerging interest in the application of theories and concepts from social movement studies to Islamic movements, though there is still some catching up to do (Clark 2004; Kurzman 2004; Lubeck 2000; Oberschall 2004; Wickham 2002; Wiktorowicz 2001, 2004). The relative neglect of religious movements from general reviews of social movement studies testifies to the widespread theoretical separation of the secular from the religious and the corralling of the latter into the specialized field of the sociology of religion, where studies of cults, sects and new religious movements mostly take place. Oberschall's (2004: 34) explanation for the marginal status of religious movements is that,

> Many Western academics are fixated on a poverty–social injustice–exploitation interpretation of discontent and grievance in the third world and [on] secular ideologies and justifications for action. They are confused and bewildered by religious crusaders who dedicate their lives to realizing God's will on earth, by violence if necessary.

Beckford (2003: 9) argues that this neglect within the social movements literature can be explained by the tendency 'to categorise religious movements as having little significance for an understanding of the major fault lines, grievances and conflicts of late modern societies'. In short, the study of social movements has been dominated by a general theoretical materialism that privileges economic inequality as a key motivator for challenges to the existing social order.[2]

However, the emergence of European New Social Movement (NSM) theory, which shifted away from this mainstream materialism to focus on some newer 'value-oriented' social movements, could have found room for religious movements and thus helped to fill the gap identified by Oberschall. Yet, with few exceptions,[3] research into NSMs remained primarily focused on secular Western movements such as environmentalism, student movements, gay and lesbian movements, feminism, disabled people's movements and others. This is unfortunate as some of the central 'new' features attributed to NSMs can be shown to characterize some moderate and radical Islamic movements, calling into question popular assumptions regarding the character of the latter. Of course, it would be a mistake to fall into a simple dualistic mode of thought at this point, with the orientation of NSMs seen as 'idealist' as opposed to the 'materialism' of earlier forms. This would be a mistake because all social movements are forms of collective action, which can never be reduced simply to ideas and beliefs. One of the benefits of a social movement perspective is that it helps to challenge the theoretical 'problems' of individual versus society and structure versus agency in sociology. Social movements emerge at particular historical moments (structure), but whether they are successful or not depends on how their campaigns are promoted, how strong is the resistance they face and whether the non-committed public can be moved to support them (agency). Movements are also networks of individuals, but invariably act collectively, and their action repertoires are learned and transmitted both across different movements and societies and over generations. Studying militant Islamic networks as types of violent social movement therefore helps to locate individual activists within the wider social groups and societies in which they are embedded. The argument developed below will suggest that when NSM theory is seen alongside previous social movement theorizing, Islamic militancy can be better understood and explained.

New social movements?

European NSM theory was designed to describe and explain the apparently unique wave of collective action that began in the 1960s. Several key characteristics came to be seen as evidence for such NSMs, primarily a post-industrial and post-materialist orientation, a core of middle-class activists, loose organizational forms, the widespread use of symbolic direct actions, a focus on the creation of new social and political identities, together with a 'self-limiting' form of radicalism. Strong claims to movement innovation were later criticized as somewhat exaggerated and historically naive. Nevertheless, the integration of key NSM elements into wider social movement studies has led to changing definitions of what social movements actually are and has opened up new opportunities for the integration of religious movements into the social movement mainstream.

Although NSM theories are not homogeneous and there are disagreements amongst those working with the thesis, six elements stand out as commonly recognized features of NSM activity across the differing accounts. We can deal with these in turn.

First, NSMs are seen as products of post-industrialization and the emergence of a new form of post-material politics (Steger *et al.* 1989; Touraine 1971). In Western Europe, the emergence of a group of new movements amid a wave of collective action was seen as reflecting macro-social and economic change. Compared with industrial, welfare-based and labour movements whose central concerns were class inequality, wealth distribution and lobbying the state for reforms (Habermas 1981; Offe 1990),

NSMs represented an emerging post-industrial society and the displacement of class-based movements (Melucci 1985, 1989; Touraine 1981). NSMs reflected the rise of post-material values and goals related to the quality rather than the quantity of life (Inglehart 1977, 1990). In doing so, NSMs demonstrated an expressive form of political engagement centered on the formation of identities that posed new challenges to existing political systems and parties (Dalton and Kuechler 1990; Kitschelt 1990). Arguably, this link to post-industrial change was the central theoretical claim of strong versions of NSM theory.

Second, NSMs defied a simple class analysis. Their activist core was drawn primarily from the new middle class; those people were employed in welfare, creative and educational sectors (Mattausch 1989) which had expanded significantly since 1945. From the time of the 1960s student movements, a variety of social groups have engaged in movement activity, generating forms of political activity around quality of life issues in everyday life, rather than materially self-interested campaigns rooted in workplaces. Beyond the core activists, large-scale demonstrations and collective protests brought together supporters in socially-differentiated so-called rainbow coalitions, not easily accounted for by social movement perspectives tied to mainstream materialist assumptions. Such mobilizations suggested a form of politics emerging outside of the formal, institutionalized, representational political system (Offe 1985) that was not reducible to working-class interests.

Third, NSMs seemed to have little or no internal coherence or organization, appearing to be intentionally and explicitly anti-hierarchical. NSMs therefore represent the emergence of a type of social movement characterized by loose networks, anti-hierarchical structures, and participatory approaches to politics (Melucci 1985; Olofsson 1987). NSM activists operated in the sub-political world of everyday life in contrast to the hierarchical and tightly organized trade unions and mainstream political parties. Even within the new Green political parties, for example, attempts were made to prevent the accretion of power, including regular rotation of the leadership and participatory rather than representative policy-making. A form of 'anti-political politics', that is opposed to business as usual, seemed to be emerging as a challenge to representative democratic systems (Havel 1988).

Fourth, NSMs engaged in striking campaigns built on symbolic direct actions, targeting problems directly at source, creating varied action repertoires. Relying on mass media attention to bring new issues before the public, direct action symbolized in the present the wider changes NSMs sought to bring about in the future. Newly formed groups such as Greenpeace quickly became adept at creating 'eco-dramas' (Harries-Jones 1995), symbolizing the struggles of relatively powerless groups against states and multinational corporations. Working outside established political processes and interest representation, NSM actions were committed to non-violence and this was itself symbolic of their attempts to bring about cultural change rather than attempting to take political power. Again, this contrasted with an older materialist politics and revolutionary ideologies.

Fifth, NSMs set their face against violent revolution, thereby opting for a self-limiting radicalism that stopped short of militaristic adventures in favour of cultural transformation (Cohen 1985). Whilst socialist, fascist and communist movements sought state power to shape societies according to their ideological programmes, NSMs eschewed such grand schemes. Instead, the radicalism of NSMs was limited by their focus on the defence of civil society against state encroachment, or as Habermas (1981) put it, NSMs defended the lifeworld – that everyday taken-for-granted world in which people make themselves at home. Similarly, NSM organizations' attempts to combine radical aims with reformist strategies and to reconcile new-middle-class interests with those of marginalized groups distinguished the new movements as a collective (Papadakis 1988). Their coherence consisted of a shared 'ideological bond' centred on, 'a humanistic critique of the prevailing system and the dominant culture ... and a resolve to fight for a better world here and now with little, if any, inclination to escape into some spiritual refuge' (Dalton and Kuechler 1990: 280). This new form of political–cultural engagement encouraged the construction of new social identities.

Finally, those new identities were created via an expressive politics that promoted self-realization and the right to autonomy, rather than the assimilation of movement demands into mainstream politics. Living out the lifestyle changes they sought for the future gave credence to the 1960s feminist slogan, 'the personal is political'. However, the NSM focus on the right to difference was at odds with the older assimilationist equal rights movements that fought for inclusion into mainstream society. Expressive identity politics flowed directly from the weakening of class identification in an emerging post-industrial society, thus befitting a society increasingly dominated by people-centred, service-sector employment.

This characterization of post-1960s activism makes a strong case for the emergence of a genuinely new type of social movement. However, by the late 1990s, the weight of criticisms against NSM theory suggested that the linkage of specific movement characteristics to post-industrial change could not be empirically sustained. Tarrow (1998: 202) summarized the views of many, arguing that NSM challenges to existing social movement theories 'have paled as these movements went through life cycles much like their predecessors'. In short, NSM theory failed to take account of the cyclical processes of movement formation, development and establishment, mistaking the features of an early formative stage in the development of movements for the emergence of a distinctively new type of post-industrial social movement (Brand 1990). Other critics noted that loose networks of activists, nonviolent direct actions, post-material values and expressive identity-based politics can all be found within much earlier 'old' social movements (Bagguley 1992; Calhoun 1995; D'Anieri *et al.* 1990; Gould 1988; Sutton 2000). Hence, the argument that NSMs provided evidence for the birth of a new type of movement in a new type of society lost much of its force. NSMs did not seem quite so 'new' after all.

Nevertheless, even if the thrust of such criticisms is conceded, it can still be argued that the 'bold conjecture' represented by NSM theory has been enormously productive. It has contributed to new lines of research in some of the previously underresearched or neglected aspects that characterize many social movements. The theory also focussed attention on some key features of movement mobilizations since the 1960s. Social movement scholars were alerted to the role of changing social values in the shaping of movement activity, the 'horizontal' movement networks underlying public demonstrations and protest, the use of direct action and cultural symbols together with processes of identity construction. These elements constituted the spine of NSM theorizing. Therefore, an important caveat needs to be added to Tarrow's conclusion. NSM theory *has* in fact made a significant contribution to social movement studies, including leading to revised definitions of what social movements actually are in the first place. Diani's (1992: 13) synthetic definition illustrates this point (see also della Porta and Diani 1999: 14–16);

> A social movement is a network of informal interactions between a plurality of individuals, groups and/or organizations, engaged in a political or cultural conflict, on the basis of a shared collective identity.

While this definition looks for common ground across American and European approaches, it clearly owes much to the influence of NSM theorizing. With its inclusion of central NSM features (networks, informal interactions, a plurality of organizations, shared identities), Diani's revised definition also fits Militant Islam very well. Militant Islamic movements are organized through networks of interactions between a plurality of activists and organizations that are engaged in both political and cultural conflicts on the basis of radical Islamic identities. In addition, some of these groups engage in symbolic direct actions linked to a strongly held religious ideology. They are also focussed on post-industrial concerns rather than wealth distribution and social class-based issues. With these features in mind, it may be that 'new' movement activism will not be restricted to the secular, non-violent and 'self-limiting' activities of Western NSMs, but will also include the growth of religious movements that are quite prepared to use violent methods in pursuit of their aims. But to what extent might such a conclusion fit the whole range of Islamic militancy at local, national and transnational levels?

Local, national and transnational Islamic militancy

When examining Islamic militancy beyond the populist rhetoric and forms of violence, a remarkable array of differences that undermine attempts by governments to establish a common enemy and hinder transnationalist aspirations for unification. Different theological interpretations and practices combine with ethnic, tribal, regional and national distinctions and language barriers to prevent unity on both discursive and pragmatic grounds. Groups within the radical movement seek a greater role for Islam within social relations and institutions but vary in their religious interpretations and strategic approach. For example, some groups, including Tablighi Jamaat focus on improving individual faith and practice, predominantly in South Asia. Hamas and Islamic Jihad in the Palestinian territories seek to bring about an Islamic Palestinian nation-state, whilst the 'hardcore' within al-Qa'ida and groups that have been associated – including Islamic Jihad and al-Gamaat al-Islamiyya from Egypt, Harkat al Jihad in Bangladesh and Jamiat-ul-Ulemae-Pakistan – emphasize achieving a global Islamic community, the *umma*, and adapting divine law to the modern world.[4] Within the wider radical Islamic movement are social movement terrorist organizations (SMTOs), that include the latter groups, which use violence as a means to achieve their aims. Many participants and groups have, as Hafez (2003) has identified, originated in nation-states with restrictive or repressive measures that do not permit popular participation through mainstream political parties, social movement organizations (SMOs) or even more informal channels within civil society. Consequently, without democratic outlets and with peaceful forms of protest frequently banned, mass arrests and imprisonment commonplace, militants, in these contexts, face considerable structural restraints and have frequently utilized resources for violent collective action. And as the subsequent discussion on the evolution of al-Zawahiri and Egyptian Islamic Jihad indicates, suppression of militancy within national settings has been instrumental in the shift towards transnationalism. In Chapter 3, distinctions between national and transnational groups' ideologies, aims and targets are explored. For the remainder of this chapter, it is intended to concentrate upon transnational groups, frequently and lazily referred to as 'al-Qa'ida' because it is argued that important similarities exist with other SMOs. Applying social movement theories and concepts assists in illuminating commonalities in processes, organization and methods which contribute to the later discussion in the book about the consequences of militancy. Of particular relevance are the implications for Western societies and governments if SMTOs are seen to be sharing issues of fundamental discontent with SMOs.

Transnational militant Islam: applying NSM concepts

Within the transnational militant movement, perceptions of al-Qa'ida's preparedness to advocate violence to bring about revolutionary change has been instrumental in establishing the group and its associates as the most prominent group in the wider movement. Its methods and objectives can be distinguished from the more moderate and popular Islamic resurgence. The prominence of al-Qa'ida, its participants' ability to attract media attention, oversimplified media reports and political opportunism on the part of some governments, have all contributed to a popular misunderstanding that militant Islam simply is al-Qa'ida, which is then held responsible for all acts of 'Islamic terrorism'. However, drawing on social movement theories and concepts, particularly those elements drawn from NSM theory, helps to place al-Qa'ida within the wider radical movement and bring into view the group's relations with other SMOs.

In Chapter 1, the emergence of al-Qa'ida was traced to ideological transfusions, problems and militant failures within Muslim nation-states, and inspirational events like the Soviet invasion of Afghanistan and the ensuing war (1979–89). From an initial focus on welfare provision, the group sought to overcome divisions within Islam and then to provide an international army capable of defending Muslims from oppression (Bergen 2001; Burke 2003; Reeve 1999). Following the end of the war, the 'Arab Afghans' left Afghanistan trained in armed combat with higher levels of religiosity and the basis of an emerging international network, the cornerstone of al-Qa'ida before 11 September 2001. Fighters returned to countries with secular cultures and/or religious regimes widely considered to be corrupt, with which they quickly became disenchanted, reinforcing their radical interpretation of Islam. This radical religious interpretation of world affairs has arguably become more significant after the disintegration of communism and represents one possible configuration for post-industrial politics.

Non-material and post-material values

We also saw in Chapter 1, discursively, the roots of al-Qa'ida reflect an internal international coalition and can be traced to the growing militancy of radical Islamic thinkers and organizers. A range of both ideological and organizational influences, including Ibn Taymiyya (1268–1328), Wahhabism from the Arabian peninsular, Deobandis across the Indian subcontinent, the Pakistani Jamaat-i-Islami and the Muslim Brotherhood across the Middle East, have been brought together in a unique fusion. Al-Qa'ida's ideological position is therefore grounded in earlier radical thought that has been synthesized and adapted to contemporary events, providing a framework for life across economic, political, social, cultural, philosophical and legal spheres. Radical groups' non-material motivations are similar, though not identical, to the rising post-material values identified by NSM theorists, in so far as these stand behind or form the backdrop to collective action, and are not easily explained as purely economic grievances. Bin Laden's statements often exemplify this. Rejecting Western materialist explanations for the rise of militant Islam, bin Laden (1998b) stated that,

They [Western commentators] claim that this blessed awakening and the people reverting to Islam are due to economic factors. This is not so. It is rather a grace from Allah, a desire to embrace the religion of Allah. ... When the holy war called, thousands of young men from the Arab Peninsula and other countries answered the call and they came from wealthy backgrounds. ... We believe that this is the call we have to answer regardless of our financial capabilities.

Bin Laden's deputy, al-Zawahiri (2001) also pointed out that the values radicals hold exceed material interests and personal loyalties as they 'have abandoned their families, country, wealth, studies and jobs in search for jihad arenas for the sake of God'. In 2002 bin Laden criticized modern materialism, stating, 'I urge you to seek the joy of life and the afterlife and to rid yourself of your dry, miserable, and spiritless materialistic life' (bin Laden 2002a). Though they cannot be entirely separated from material issues, such religious motivations cannot easily be reduced to these either. Clear links can be drawn with Qutb's (1991) declaration that whilst Muslims were not in a position to compete materialistically with the West, this was unimportant when measured against achieving Allah's will and the afterlife.

The development of the radical movement is also connected to political, economic, social and cultural changes associated with post-industrialism and post-material values, and the interrelated processes of modernization and globalization. In this respect, there do not seem to be any conclusive reasons why the religious orientation of radical Islamic groups should prevent a mainstream social movement analysis. Tarrow (1998: 112) notes that, 'Because it is so reliable a source of emotion, religion is a recurring source of social movement framing. Religion provides ready-made symbols, rituals and solidarities that can be accessed and appropriated by movement leaders.' Framing protest and collective action in strongly religious terms, deferring to a higher power and tapping into highly significant culturally embedded ideas of 'holy war' may even lend a stronger legitimacy to ideologically committed violent actions than that available to secular movements.

Militant constituencies

Though social movement theories have previously neglected Islamic movements, this does not mean that the social sciences have ignored the Islamic resurgence or the rise in national and international terrorism. On the contrary, a large amount of research has been undertaken which has tended to be dominated by explanations grounded in the secularization paradigm. From this perspective, both the broad Islamic resurgence and minority Islamic terrorism are widely considered as short-lived phenomena related to economic exclusion (e.g. Ayubi 1991; Hiro 2002; Mehmet 1990; Paz 2001) and thus amenable to a materialist explanation as discussed in

Chapter 1. Certainly some members of radical groups are unemployed or have businesses and occupations threatened by modernization, and many want a greater share in national wealth. But one of the surprising findings in recent studies of radical Islamist networks is the preponderance of middle-class individuals and those from professional backgrounds. For example, Sageman's (2004) study of biographical data of 172 Islamic militants has identified the overrepresentation of the well-educated, upper and middle classes. This is noticeable in the socio-economic backgrounds of Al-Qa'ida's pre-9/11 leadership, which included bin Laden (a multimillionaire), al-Zawahiri (a surgeon), Mohammed Atef (a police official), Khalid Shaikh Mohammed (an engineer) and Saif al-Adel (an army colonel). al-Qa'ida has also garnered considerable financial backing from other wealthy donors. As outlined above, this is a similar finding to earlier surveys of West European NSMs. The element of surprise stems from previous neomarxist or materialist assumptions that the structural location of the middle class does not predispose it to radical politics, much less so to violent and terrorist activity. Such considerations also neglect the involvement of middle-class professionals and students in 'red' terror groups within America, West Germany, Italy and Japan (Vertigans 2008).

At the level of operational management, the group relies on knowledgeable, educated and skilled recruits who provide communicative, technological, administrative and organizational qualities that are essential to their continuing international militancy.[5] Membership of al-Qa'ida and the wider radical movement is much broader, drawn from across Eastern Africa, the Middle East, Central, South and South Eastern Asia, and the West. Many militants join the movement in countries different from where they grew up, while others belong to the second and third generation of migrants to the West. Sageman's (2004: 92) study of international *jihadis* found that 'seventy-eight percent were cut off from their cultural and social origins'. The movement also covers different socioeconomic groupings, ethnicities and nationalities and, in the case of Hamas and Islamic Jihad in the Palestinian territories, involves many women activists. In this sense, the combination of a largely middle-class leadership and socially differentiated groups of movement supporters is similar to the structure of many other social movements, including NSMs (Bagguley 1992).

Organization: fluid networks

The transnational character of al-Qa'ida and the wider radical movement can be seen in the networks and coordinated actions directed at local and international targets across the world. Diverse organizational forms and an international emphasis have also been enabled by the ways in which activists have 'embraced the artifacts of globalization' (Bergen 2001: 21) by using satellite phones, computers, fax machines and modern methods of transportation to communicate, attract support and carry out direct actions (Vertigans and Sutton 2001). Al-Qa'ida 'does not have a permanent central command center'. Individual cells have a 'great deal of autonomy in choosing their targets and organizing their planning' (Orbach 2001: 10). There is 'no "top-down" organizational structure' (Martin 2003: 194). Such descriptions contrast with the documentary evidence from the abandoned Afghan training camps that showed 'a bureaucratic organization with administrative lines of authority and an insistence on budgeting', leading insiders to refer to al-Qa'ida as 'the company' (Kurzman 2002: 17). Following the closure of the Afghan camps, Reuter (2004: 146) has argued that 'al-Qa'ida has reorganized ... exchanging the relative stability and openness of a Taliban-dominated Afghanistan for a vast, clandestine, decentralized underground operation with cadres based in cities and towns across Asia and Africa' and, of course, Europe and North America too. Such a transformation may be partly a consequence of the destruction of the Afghan camps with their militaristic structure. And as the International Institute for Strategic Study (2003) notes, 'the counter-terrorism effort has perversely impelled an already highly decentralized and evasive transnational terrorist network to become more "virtual" and protean and, therefore, harder to identify and neutralize'. This re-emergence in diverse organizational forms demonstrates the commitment of activists to pursue 'al-Qa'ida's' goals.

In recent years, a more decentralized and loosely organized activist network of militants has grown up with a polycephalous power structure in which local autonomy is becoming a key element. At the centre of al-Qa'ida is what Burke (2003: 13) calls the 'hardcore', around 100 highly motivated and trained activists who have remained physically and ideologically close to bin Laden since the end of the Afghan war. Burke suggests that the 'hardcore' operated as trainers and administrators in Afghanistan, fought in Bosnia or Chechnya (and in the latter case continue to do so), act as recruitment agents, deal with other radical Islamic SMTOs and, very occasionally, run terrorist operations themselves. This group is part of a 'vanguard' aiming to lead by example, providing direct and indirect support, guidance, financial assistance and training. The 'hardcore' provide the link between the organized training camps and covert, decentralized operational cells. Beyond the hardcore, the composition of al-Qa'ida is less well defined. Through the Afghan training camps and relations with other radical groups, al-Qa'ida has recruited volunteers through the religious associations, mosques, community centres and charities of the moderate Islamic movement to undertake activities on their behalf. Although al-Qa'ida is just one group within the radical movement, it has been able to tap into the wider movement through establishing 'associate members' (Burke 2003: 207). Associates undertake activities and act as intermediaries or links to the 'vast, amorphous movement of modern radical Islam, with its myriad cells, domestic groups, "groupuscules" and splinters, joining the "network of networks" to the hardcore itself' (ibid.).

Since the onset of the so-called 'war on terrorism', groups within the radical Islamic movement have become more autonomous as the al-Qa'ida hardcore has become weaker through deaths, imprisonment, disappearances and disrupted communication channels. The loss of hardcore members has not prevented the continuation of the al-Qa'ida network though and there are signs that lower level members and recruits are now becoming more prominent (Johnston and Sanger 2004). Despite increasing financial restrictions on al-Qa'ida, terrorist attacks organized by other SMTOs have also continued. The loose, decentralized arrangements within the movement have meant that people who consider themselves part of a single overarching movement but have no known connection to existing radical groups have often initiated attacks. Some may have requested and received some funding and training from al-Qa'ida, but remain operationally autonomous. In this sense, al-Qa'ida has employed a bottom-up approach with contacts, recruitment and attacks initiated by individuals and groups wanting to join or carry out operations (Burke 2003; Sageman 2004). A case in point is the 1999 'millennium plot' to attack sites in California and Jordan. This relationship may seem in line with al-Qa'ida's earlier strategy in which activists put ideas to the 'hardcore' who then decide whether to give permission for a plot to develop before allocating funding and support. However, the hierarchical relationship implied here seems no longer an adequate description. Of particular importance was the Bali bombing of 2002, which involved 'sophisticated techniques and [was] motivated by a profound hatred of anything that represented the West. ... [It] was an attack in the style of al-Qaeda [sic], but apparently not involving the group itself. ... As there was no one, in Afghanistan or elsewhere, to go to for training and support, the Bali bombers did it on their own' (Burke 2003: 237). Attacks on Western targets in Pakistan, Jordan, Kuwait, Yemen, Saudi Arabia, Spain and England have also been undertaken since 2001, and there is no conclusive evidence to suggest that these operations involved al-Qa'ida. As bin Laden's former bodyguard, Nasser Ahmad Nasser al-Bahri notes, 'those who carry out operations are not necessarily Al-Qa'ida members. People without an organizational connection to Al-Qa'ida are perfectly capable of carrying out operations.'[6] And as Khosrokhavar (2005) has remarked, terror networks enable cells to be involved with different aims. In organizations with traditional pyramid structures, members are expected to be in agreement with the hierarchy. By comparison, networks restrict contact between members and differences between cells are easier to accommodate, providing unity exists within the smaller units.

Several commentators have recognized the internal transformation of al-Qa'ida and its lack of 'normal' organizational form, but fail to provide adequate explanations of this transformation, relying instead on extrapolating from descriptions of the current position. Gunaratna (2004: 93) argues that after 11 September 2001, 'the drastic increase in the terrorist threat has been a result of Al Qaeda's transformation from a group into a movement', while Al-Bahri (Middle East Media Research Institute, 2004) observes that, 'today Al-Qa'ida is not an organization in the true sense of the word but only an idea that has become a faith'. Such descriptions of al-Qa'ida as a 'movement', a 'faith', or an 'idea' are ways of grappling with al-Qa'ida's loose and flexible networks from theoretical positions outside social movement studies. In fact, this way of describing al-Qa'ida was also used much earlier in social movement studies to convey something of the novelty of many post-1960s NSMs (Dalton and Kuechler 1990). These accounts may help to identify al-Qa'ida's impact but do not locate the group within the wider radical movement of which it is a part. The transnational radical Islamic movement is composed of networks and their relationships with other groups and loose associations. Although the movement is not the same as al-Qa'ida, it has been influenced and inspired by the SMTO's violent direct actions, ideas and religious values that have now transcended the group. Bringing radical Islam within a social movement framework holds out the potential to better understand the way that SMTOs like al-Qa'ida have developed over time, as a result of adapting to the opening up and closing down of political and organizational opportunities, as in Afghanistan, and how the context is instrumental in producing the type of structure which ranges from loose networks of activists to much tighter, hierarchical organizational arrangements. It also helps explain why their action repertoire has become increasingly violent, given the symbolic value of successful attacks against a more powerful enemy in emboldening potential supporters and participants.

National and international symbolic violence and images

NSM theory alerted scholars to the significance of symbolism within social movements for movement activists, supporters and the uncommitted public. Using direct actions to create dramatic and often theatrical demonstrations, NSMs forcibly made their point by adopting non-violence as their touchstone protest style. This then allowed NSMs effectively to draw attention to the state security forces' monopoly of the means of force and violence and to ally their own actions with peaceful action for change. In a similar vein, SMTOs such as al-Qa'ida have learned how powerful symbolic actions are. The key difference is that they use violent direct actions against carefully chosen targets to convey a symbolic message reflecting their interpretations of radical Islam. This marks them out as engaging in a unique form of direct action combining key elements of the NSMs with tactics that are highly meaningful to their own potential pool of support. Many violent terrorist actions undertaken by al-Qa'ida and associated SMTOs have targeted highly symbolic sites; they are not simply opportunistic acts of violence. Abu Ayman al-Hilali, closely linked to bin Laden (cited in Paz 2002), argues with respect to the nature of *jihad* that, 'our solution is organized Jihad that sets at the head of its priorities the attack against American and Zionist interests. It should not just boycott their goods, but explode their headquarters, centres and industries, and everything that symbolizes them, such as MacDonalds, etc.' Targets have included exclusive hotels, business centres, religious institutions, military complexes, foreign embassies and residential compounds across North America, Europe, Asia and Africa. These attacks have enabled small, internationally active groups of terrorists to gain global media coverage that has increased levels of support and provided the inspiration for similar attacks. Such targeted attacks have a double symbolism, which bin Laden (1998b) recognized when lauding the suicide bombers who attacked sites in Riyadh, Saudi Arabia in 1995 and Al-Khober in 1997: 'they have raised the nation's [*umma*] head high and washed away a great part of the shame that has enveloped us as a result of the weakness of the Saudi government and its complicity with the American government'. Hence, in addition to hitting the target itself, there is high symbolic capital in the nature of the attacks by the 'underdog' against overwhelmingly more powerful forces, particularly when committed by suicide bombers who are seen as martyrs. First used in contemporary Islamic militancy by the Lebanese group Hezbollah, suicide attacks are theologically justified as ways of dying for the cause of Islam and the greater good, and as a way to improve the individual's salvation chances,[7] thus combining altruistic and egoistic motivations, and are increasingly associated with fatalism within the Palestinian territories (Sutton and Vertigans 2005).

Changes in symbolic violence are connected to the evolution of militancy. New types of leader, discourse, aims and strategies have been designed to re-energize peoples' religiosity and combat the 'near' and 'far' enemies. There are strategic and tactical reasons for committing acts of violence against individuals, groups, nations, organizations or buildings. In other words, similar processes of impact and outcome assessment are undertaken by militant Muslim groups to other ideological groups like the urban terror groups, the West German Red Army Faction and Italian Red Brigades, and nationalists associated with *Euskadi ta Askatasuna* (ETA) and the *Irish Republican Army* (IRA) (Vertigans 2008). The determining of localized or international targets for Muslim groups is closely connected to whether they are focussing upon the 'near' or 'far' enemy and who is a legitimate target. This is a long-standing strategic choice that can arguably be traced back to Ibn Taymiyya's argument that Muslims should not be controlled by infidels. Habeck (2006: 154) points out that Taymiyya's declaration that the 'people of Islam should join forces and support each other to get rid of the main *kufr* [unbelief] who is controlling the countries of the Islamic world' has been used by bin Laden in his famous 1996 declaration of war against America. As this quote implies, Ibn Taymiyya supported the use of armed struggle and has since become known as one of the foremost proponents of *jihad*, widely considered to have extended the activity to incorporate Muslims who sought to avoid participation. Once the Mongols were removed, the *jihad* would focus upon other non-believers. There are clear similarities between the situation that Taymiyya sought to resolve and the conditions perceived by militant Muslims today, namely imposed irreligious leaders. By comparison with Taymiyya's interpretation, the eighteenth-century religious leader Muhammad Ibn Abd al-Wahhab sought to purify Islam and targeted Muslims who were considered to be heretics through their adaptation of practices like *Sufi* rituals and the veneration of saints and sites. Today, groups' national or transnational focuses translate into targets for attack. National groups will focus upon the enemy within or nearby enemies, for example, irreligious Muslims, *Shi'tes* or *Sunnis* and other religious groups, or nation-states like Israel or Russia in the case of Chechens. Divisions between supporters of attacking the 'near' and 'far' enemies have, Gerges (2006) suggests, been solidified by the 2001 attacks which led to governments repressing both national and transnational groups. The significance of these examples is further explored in Chapter 3.

Radical Islamic groups therefore adopt symbolic direct actions as a key part of their action repertoire, but unlike many other social movements, they are able to make the most effective symbolic statements through violent actions against Western targets. The careful selection of targets shows that SMTOs like al-Qa'ida have quite a sophisticated understanding of the media-saturated social life of modern societies. Their use of violent actions is certainly very different in degree and extent to the non-violent NSMs, though the animal rights lobby, radical environmentalist fringe and pro-life groups have all used aggressive fear-inducing tactics to intimidate opponents. In some recent terrorist attacks, a more arbitrary and less symbolic approach to targeting has become evident. Indiscriminate attacks on Muslims in Saudi Arabia (2003 and 2004), Muslims killed in the Istanbul bombings (2003) as well as the ongoing sectarian violence in Iraq and the targeting of commuters in Madrid and London may be evidence of the reduced involvement of the al-Qa'ida hardcore in the planning process. These attacks have produced considerable revulsion across Muslim societies and communities, and seem unlikely to generate support for the radical Islamic movement.

Awareness of the significance of symbols can also be seen in the simple, austere clothes and lifestyles of the al-Qa'ida hardcore that can then be compared with the 'decadence' of the Saudi princes or the corruption within many Muslim governments. Bin Laden's presence with the Afghan Arabs in harsh conditions 'sitting with us and eating rice and potatoes'[8] despite his immense wealth has been an important image contributing to his popularity (Bergen 2001; Reeve 1999). Such a portrayal has contributed to the perception across radical groups of 'bin Laden as a heroic figure, symbolic of their collective struggle' (Burke 2003: 14). And as Burke (2006) observes, modern technology has been carefully utilized to create and reinforce this iconography.[9] Though his practical involvement has significantly diminished, this iconic status remains, even amongst some Muslims who disagree with his ideas or associated actions (Marranci 2006).

Goals of Islamic militancy

As al-Qa'ida has developed, particularly after bin Laden returned to Afghanistan in 1996, it has become increasingly international and multifaceted in the attempt to rouse and unite Muslims in militancy against the West and corrupt Muslim governments. Martin (2003: 234) argues that al-Qa'ida 'has two overarching goals: to link together Muslim extremist groups throughout the world into a loose pan-Islamic revolutionary network and to expel non-Muslim (especially Western) influences from Islamic regions and countries'. Such goals could hardly be described as 'self-limiting' in the same way that NSMs restricted their activity. Hence, once again, the al-Qa'ida network seems to draw selectively on the experience and successes of NSMs whilst at the same time pursuing its own global political agenda. Early al-Qa'ida pronouncements concentrated on the Saudi regime and its departure from the *shari'ah*, corruption, economic weakness, poor social services and the presence of US forces on the land of the two holy places. After the Soviet withdrawal from Afghanistan in 1989, militant Muslims concentrated upon liberating former Muslim territories in places like Kashmir, defending Muslims against attack (as in Bosnia) and attacking regimes considered irreligious and corrupt, predominantly in the Middle East. In the mid-1990s, there was a shift in strategy with attention shifting from attacking the 'near enemy' (local regimes) towards the 'far enemy' (principally the United States). This occurred for a number of reasons, discussed in more detail in Chapter 3, including the growing belief within the militant movement that attacking local leaders was having limited impact. This is, they argued, because the West is instrumental in the problems within Muslim societies and is the main obstacle to the creation of an international *umma* (Burke 2003; Sageman 2004; Saikal 2003). As a consequence, the international militants believe the West has to be confronted.

In interviews from 1996 and 1998 (declaring the formation of the World Islamic Front), bin Laden (1998a) signalled a move towards a more international or global perspective, taking in Israel, war against the Iraqi and Bosnian people, the deaths of innocent Muslims and the use of nuclear weapons in Hiroshima and Nagasaki. The increasingly broad range of issues raised within the wider movement now includes the American refusal to sign the Kyoto agreement and the claim that natural surroundings are being destroyed and the environment polluted with industrial waste, 'whilst leaving a world barely inhabitable for our children' (bin Laden 2002b). The breadth of coverage highlights the all-encompassing radical Islamic ideology that is critical of any aspect of social life not considered to be conforming to religious tenets. But as Halliday (2002: 50) observes, the issues of wealth distribution, poverty reduction or tackling the problems of the 'world's poor' are not addressed. Since 11 September 2001, al-Qa'ida has become more vociferous in its anti-Western rhetoric, seeking to broaden its appeal through identification with populist issues such as the Palestinian and Kashmiri struggles (bin Laden 2001a), extending the focus to Bosnia, Chechnya, East Timor, the Philippines, Somalia and Sudan (bin Laden 2001b). These are issues with considerable resonance across Muslim societies, particularly the United States' perceived unconditional support for Israel (Davis 2003) and negative aspects of 'the civilization of the disbelievers' (stated in the letter left behind by the September 2001 terrorists).[10] This is an effective strategy because, while there are many disagreements within the movement, there is a shared hatred of America which holds out the possibility of uniting a diverse range of views.[11]

Based on the statements of associated groups, it can be inferred that these goals should be set within the wider context of achieving the *shari'ah* or divinely sanctioned law. The goals reflect the praxist character of radical Islam with its fusion of theory and practice (Vertigans 2003) aiming 'to inspire a movement of purifying, cathartic community rebirth' (Calvert 2004: 13). In this sense, similarities can be noted with movements associated with post-material values, a focus upon civil society and attempts to reconcile the interests of middle-class and marginalized groups. However, al-Qa'ida and other groups also share similarities with Asbat ul Ansar in Lebanon, the Filipino Abu Sayyaf, the Islamic Movement in Uzbekistan, Indonesian Lashkar Jihad and al Ansar al Islami and 'al-Qa'ida' in Iraq (including al-Zarqawi's former al Tawhid al Jihad) in seeking to reshape social relations. The broader movement therefore consists of multiple associations and networks of support. Participants may agree (although this is by no means inevitable) with al-Qa'ida and bin Laden's statements and groups may undertake actions that contribute towards international *jihad*. But these groups also have their own concerns which may seem local or parochial in comparison with the internationalism of al-Qa'ida, to whom they refuse to cede control (Burke 2003). In this sense, radical Islam is not 'self-limiting' in the same way that some Western NSMs have been. Some groups and networks do seek to take over states and to create a global Islamic revolutionary network to facilitate this, which is explored in Chapter 3.

Militant identities

The NSM focus on processes of identity formation also provides an effective starting point from which to approach the study of radical Islamic identities. Militant internationalist Muslims do not share nationalist or nation-state centred ideologies (unlike groups fighting for national independence such as Hamas) and are opposed to many of the practices undertaken and principles held by non-Islamic governments. As a consequence, it is unlikely that the movement will be assimilated into mainstream national political life. Instead, like NSM activists, they aim to live out lifestyle changes and implement their religious interpretations within existing societies. But how they seek to do this varies across organizations. Some, like the Tablighi Jamaat, concentrate on proselytizing and living according to their interpretation of the key Islamic precepts and standards. By comparison, groups associated with al-Qa'ida, while also practicing what they believe in (within the constraints of secular societies), see this as too slow or ineffective in uniting the international Muslim community. Hence, they turn to acts of symbolic violence to force through change.

Like NSMs, militant groups emphasize their difference from others and espouse an expressive identity politics that provides clear behavioural guidelines. However, this emphasis is not a celebration of difference but an exclusionary approach based on their monopoly of truth and insistence on conformity. This does not make militants reactionary traditionalists though, as their construction of Islamic identities is very much a product of the contemporary era, developing in a variety of socioeconomic backgrounds through diverse socializing processes which synthesize the historical and contemporary, the secular and religious, and their global and local influences and experiences (Burke 2003; Sageman 2004; Vertigans and Sutton 2001).

The norms, values, behavioural parameters and guidance transmitted by socializing agents including friends, teachers and family are proving attractive to those encountering directly, or witnessing through the mass media, experiences and events that radical Islamic ideologies explain. Radical identities are then developing, often over a period of years, based around religious norms, values and behaviour that contribute towards self-realization, attempts to live authentic Islamic lifestyles, and increasing social isolation from outsiders. Sageman's (2004) study of international *jihadis* discovered that the beliefs of many militants were gradually formed within friendship groups that became collectively radicalized over time. The dynamics within groups contributed to a growing intensity of belief and practices and led to group solidarity and collective identity transcending individual characteristics. At a political level, radical 'Islamic' solutions to the long-standing corruption and weakness of Islamic states and the cultural, economic, and political threats seen to be posed by the West, especially the United States (Wiktorowicz and Kaltner 2003: 80), are internalized. Having accepted these praxist values, such identities orientate much more around radical interpretations of beliefs and activities with people becoming more willing to undertake violent actions.

Conclusion

Militant Islamic movements pose a challenge to social movement studies. Can such religiously oriented forms of activism be analysed using theories and concepts from the social movements field? The assimilation of key NSM elements into the general social movements toolkit has opened up this possibility. If contemporary militant Islamic movements emerged alongside Western NSMs and are amenable to analysis using concepts designed to study the latter, then instead of withering away, we may see rising levels of support for religious movements and ideologies which are able to tap into post-Cold War fears and anxieties associated with post-industrial and post-modern conditions. al-Qa'ida-related groups organize in ways not dissimilar to secular NSMs, and are flexible enough to adapt to changing situations and national locations. Connections to the wider radical Islamic movement are not fundamentally different to the networks that make up other social movements, though they are necessarily more clandestine than most. Its critique of the emerging US-dominated international order bears similarity to that of anti-globalization mobilizations, whilst the planning of symbolic direct actions and use of modern information technologies rivals that of well-established but non-violent secular SMOs. However, unlike many NSMs, the radical Islamic movement is not self-limiting, but pursues the transformation of global social relations. Al-Qa'ida should be studied as a SMTO that is part of this wider movement, rather than as simply an aggregate of individual terrorists. This does not mean that the wider movement is tightly organized or consistently acts in concert. Rather, it is a loosely organized 'network of networks' connected by a shared ideological position and the identification of a common opponent.

The religious orientation of militant Islam has served to keep it outside the mainstream of social movement studies, which strongly suggests that the development of the latter has primarily been through the analysis of secular movements. If so, then the post-materialism of NSMs is a reminder that people can be spurred to action by intangible moral and religious values and perceived threats to these, in addition to material grievances. Bringing some of the central elements of NSM theory to bear on radical Islamic movements offers the potential to better explain their emergence and development as an alternative to currently popular, individualistic explanations of violence in the name of religion as the consequence of brainwashing by irrational madmen or the last resort of the materially deprived.[12] The popular acceptance of such 'explanations' may tell us something though about the way that modern societies try to dehumanize violent terrorist activity as a way of coping with the rising levels of social fear and perceived risks that such actions create. When extreme acts of individualized violence and brutality can be brought into the living rooms of modern populations via the Internet and TV broadcasts, then their pacified, civilized and predictably rationalized everyday life faces a new challenge that nation-states and civil societies seem ill equipped to protect them from. This dilemma is explored in more detail in Chapters 5 and 6. At this juncture, it is important to reiterate that not all militant groups can be productively examined within an NSM framework. Militancy is also integrated within nationalist struggles and consequently groups like Hamas and MILF share more commonalities with groups like ETA and the IRA than environmentalism and anti-global movements. In Chapter 3, the roots of national Islamic groups and distinctions from transnational groups are established both to further challenge perceptions of a homogenous militant movement and to acknowledge similarities with other forms of collective cultural, social and politicized identities.

3 Reinterpreting the *umma*

Islamic nationalism and transnationalism

Introduction

Integral to the resurgence of Islam have been the growing significance of the *umma* (Islamic 'community') and the perceptions of a global Muslim community or nation. Reasons for these transnational feelings and loyalties include changing patterns of communication and transportation associated with globalization and the perceived movement towards supranational and subnational collectivities identified across nation-states.[1] Clearly, globalization is central to understanding both the processes by which attachments to Islam globally are established today and the networks within which they are expressed. Through globalization universal affiliations between Muslims and common loyalties are strengthened. Less attention has been placed upon how the *umma* has been adapted by militant Muslims to engender transnational support. Similarly, the reasons why Muslims have become attracted by this wider form of allegiance at the expense of localized ethnic and national identities require further exploration.

To this end it is important to examine the factors behind the growing popularity of a concept that cross-cuts nation-state boundaries and the failure of secular institutions in Muslim societies and the West to embolden particularistic, localized attachments. Transnational and localized processes that have contributed to the significance of Islam within collective identities across the generic Islamic resurgence are explored. This is because militant Islam emerges from within the broader growth in religiosity and shares commonalities with less radical interpretations. All the groups within militancy are, to varying degrees, aiming to implement an Islamic state within society governed by purified Islamic discourse with peoples' primary loyalty being to Allah. Yet, the boundaries of the 'Islamic nation' and the processes through which it should be achieved are sources of considerable disagreement. Thus, nationalist groups like Hamas, Kashmiri Jaish-e-Mohammed and Moro Islamic Liberation Front (MILF) seek to achieve national independence and introduce localized Islamic governments. By comparison, groups associated with al-Qa'ida strive to attain fundamental global changes. Both national and transnational groups within militant Islam are explored here to attain a greater understanding of both collective identities that are part of their appeal and the processes that contribute towards their formation. Adopting McCrone's (1998) view that studies of nationalism (and, by extension, transnationalism) need, wherever possible, to bridge the structure/agency dichotomy, this chapter seeks to identify both relevant global and national events and processes and to analyse individual militant perceptions and group discourse. By using individual explanations and biographical accounts to supplement structural analysis, a more composite picture should emerge about the interaction between global and local processes and their impact upon collective identities. Finally, the significance of the fractures within militancy is explored and it is argued that, despite al-Qa'ida's emphasis upon transnationalism, national loyalties remain that influence the behaviour and interests of members. A useful starting point is the sociology of nationalism which has, however, tended to neglect the significance of religion within nationalist movements.

The sociology of nationalism

The impact of the sociology of nationalism has tended to follow political developments and perceptions. During the discipline's early development, nationalism was rarely accorded significance. Among the founding fathers, only Weber acknowledged the importance of a 'community of sentiment', albeit viewed unproblematically. By comparison, Marx and Engels were dismissive of nationalism as a capitalist ideological tool. Indeed the persistence of national identity has continued to be problematic for Marxists, who have associated such particularistic allegiances with the development of industrial capitalism. Consequently, these forms of collective loyalties would dissolve within broader processes of historical transformation. Durkheim was also opposed to nationalism for very different reasons. Perturbed by events in French society, he denounced it as 'an extreme and morbid form of patriotism'.[2] Social scientists did not become fully interested in the potentialities and consequences of nationalisms until the latter part of the twentieth century. It was not until the 1980s that the sociology of nationalism attained prominence through the debate about the nature of nations and nationalism and the extent to which these are products of modernity. The subdiscipline was given further legitimacy following the end of the Cold War and the emergence of new forms of nationalism and nations, highlighted most dramatically by the breakup of Yugoslavia, the emergence of Bosnian, Croatian and Serbian violence, ethnic genocide in Rwanda and ongoing conflict between Palestinians and Israel. And despite the emergence of supranational collectivities like the European Union, national identities remain prominent and the nation remains a primary source of allegiance.

Throughout this period, nationalism and nations have been widely viewed as a Western construct. Kedourie (1960: 9) exemplifies the Eurocentric approach, arguing that 'nationalism is a doctrine invented in Europe at the beginning of the nineteenth century', although there are arguments that the concept emerged much earlier.[3] And as with much development, Western processes have been taken as the templates with which to compare other parts of the world. As Kohn (1944) noted, liberal nationalism was associated with democracy, civic rights and universalism and was considered to be typical of the West where the cultural nation was seen to coincide with the state's political territory. By comparison, illiberal nationalism was found in the East and was particularistic and ethnic, based in part around conflict over state boundaries that did not accord with cultural perceptions.

Arguably, the focus upon secular political ideologies and movements, the ongoing prominence of the secularization thesis within sociology and reluctance to apply concepts and theories across subdisciplines has contributed to the significance of religion being relatively neglected within studies of nationalism.[4] While both Anderson and Gellner acknowledge that religious symbolism and liturgy are retained, religion is portrayed as a traditional social resource that was believed to have been lost in the 'progressive' transition of societies. By comparison, nationalism is aligned with modernity. Yet, extensive interrelationships exist between religion, ethnicity and nationalism, most notably within recent conflicts in the Palestinian territories, Sri Lanka, former Yugoslavia, Kashmir and the partition of India. Equally similarities between the forms of discourse are neglected. As Kinnvall (2002) and Rieffer (2003) point out, religion, like nationalism, provides a sense of security, universalism, unity, symbolism and explanatory discourse and is based on the notion of an imagined community. Both often involve the construction of the 'other'. Turner (2001: 135), when analysing the rise of citizenship identities, observed that 'nationalism required negative images of outsiders, and as a result modern politics became a politics of friend or foe'. He points out that nation-building ideology usually assumed a religious character. Kedourie (1971) also explores the interrelationship between religion and nationalism, identifying nationalist leaders who aroused emotive support from the populace in part by associating their slogans, actions and symbolism with religious prophets like Jesus, Moses and Muhammed. Significant religious dates were adopted for national festivals. The intertwining of religions like Islam, Judaism, Sikhism and Hinduism within collective senses of identity, nation-states, national and international movements suggest that the exploration of nationalism needs to be more inclusive. Consequently, while this chapter primarily aims to utilize the sociology of nationalism to enhance levels of understanding about militant Islam, it is also hoped to contribute to the extension of the subject matter incorporated within the subdiscipline.

Origins of nations

Within the sociology of nationalism, considerable attention has been placed upon the origins of nations and the central dichotomy between primordialist and modernist approaches. These different perspectives influence the definitions that are developed and applied for ideological concepts like nationalism, and associated terms like nation, that often refer to geographical boundaries that overlap with the state. For example, Anderson (2006: 6), who is viewed as a leading modernist, considers the nation to be 'an imagined political community – and imagined as both inherently limited and sovereign'. The numerical scale of the nation means, he suggests, that individuals can never personally know all other members and must imagine the wider community and social interconnections that attach them to the national entity. In this sense, individuals imagine themselves to be part of a wider entity, the nation. This connection is incorporated within a sense of identity, a personal characteristic that incorporates cultural and national identity and as such is the basis for allegiance within the nation.

For Anderson, nations are a modern construction. He traces the emergence of the nation, and by extension nationalism, to the formation of nation-states based upon secular rationality associated with the Enlightenment, the French Revolution and industrialization. For this to happen, hierarchical dynasties and the 'divine right of kings' to rule as direct intermediaries and representatives of deities had to be challenged and ultimately rejected. However, the removal of rulers' infallibility, divinity and the usage of sacred texts and languages that gained the support and submission of the populace had to be replaced. And in a manner associated with Tönnies' (1965[1887]) *Gemeinschaft und Gesellschaft*, a shift occurred that replaced communities based around blood and localized territory with associational ties between individuals; in the context of the nation, then, larger swathes of territory could be added. In other words, if unity was to be developed and maintained within the national boundaries, a new form of consciousness had to be nurtured.

The development of Western societies and subsequently other nation-states[5] is associated with industrial modernization and the associated processes of technological advancement, growth of commerce, urbanization, rapid expansion of bureaucracy, the division of labour and increased literacy. National consciousness was, Anderson (2006) argues, heavily influenced by the emergence of what he refers to as 'print capitalism' and which connected to the growing rates of literacy through expanded educational programmes. Developments in printing and transportation considerably improved the availability of information and destroyed the monopoly of the written word held by the *anciens regime*. Books, novels and newspapers were published and raised awareness about senses of time and space in which readers were located. Such forms of media also provided the mechanisms to challenge perceptions of divinity and fatalism through growing confidence in scientific discovery and methodology. And through the formation of a popular language, print capitalism was able to provide a common narrative for the populace, helping to engender national consciousness which provided the basis for shared institutions and laws. Similar processes are identified in other parts of the world. van der Veer (1994) examines the role of print, radio, television and film within nationalism in colonial and post-colonial India. However, instead of eroding the sacred languages and associated communities, as Anderson claimed, at least some of these languages were reinforced with Hindi and Urdu becoming increasingly significant for Hindus and Muslims respectively. Equally, Arabic has grown in importance across the world through similar processes.

For the potentialities of print capitalism to be maximized, large numbers of the population would have to be capable of reading the new materials. This was achieved through the widespread introduction of schools, curricula and other forms of socialization that emphasized components central to the 'diffusion of a state ideology of national identity' (Halliday 2000: 115). The development of an educated populace also had unintentional consequences. Gellner (1983) argues that most susceptible to the lure of nationalism were the educated and relatively economically privileged who felt politically underrepresented. Rarely were the poor identified as its cornerstone. And as the following sections indicate, a range of Islamic nationalisms emerged in reaction to colonialism, across a broad spectrum of the population, both educated and unschooled. But in Chapter 4, it is argued that the tremendous increase in Islam within education has contributed to contemporary militant collective consciousness.

From these modern origins, people shared a sense of belonging that was solidified through the printed history of the nation; they were connected to this civic model of the nation through the past and in the present, even though much of the former was not factually correct. Halliday (2000: 7) suggests that,

> the pretense of both nationalism and religion is that they represent a true reading of a given, the past or the doctrine; the reality is that different groups, in power or out of it, in the region or in exile, constantly redefine and reselect to serve contemporary purposes.

History is important, as primordialists argue below, but Halliday (2000) asserted that there is no continuity with pre-modernity. Instead, symbols and narratives from the past are selected, reformulated and fabricated. National consciousness therefore emerged as individuals imagined that they belonged within discrete parameters, shared with the living and dead. Adopting a teleological position, Anderson argues that nations can only be formed when humans have the ability and means for construction and, as these only existed within modernity, nationalism can only be a modern phenomenon.

Pre-modern roots

Primordialists are a useful counterpoint to the modernist approach. Arising with the work of Shils (1957) and Geertz (1963), primordialists argue that although nations may appear to be modern constructions, they 'may have pre modern precursors and can form around recurrent ethnic antecedents' (Smith 1999: 11). Consequently, the nation as a concept should not be reduced to modernity but instead can be traced to the pre-modern era and the cultural realm. Smith, while critical of both approaches, has been associated with primordialists and certainly provides illuminating explorations of pre-modernization. However, he also recognizes the importance of processes associated with modernity and introduces a broader definition of a nation that reflects this. For Smith (1991: 14), a nation is 'a named human population sharing an historic territory, common myths and historical memories, a mass public culture, a common economy and common legal rights and duties for all members'. Nationalism is 'an ideological movement for the attainment and maintenance of autonomy, unity, and identity on behalf of a population some of whose members deem it to constitute an actual or potential "nation"' (Smith 2003: 24). These definitions seek to incorporate the interplay between the past and present and Smith's belief that nations are historical products that orientate around shared descent and ancestry. He argues that 'no enduring world order can be created that ignores the ubiquitous yearnings of nations in search of roots in an ethnic past, and no study of nations and nationalism that completely ignores the past can bear fruit' (Smith 1986: 5). And while he acknowledges that the languages used to describe nations may be products of modernity, this did not prevent ethnic communities with collective identities from forming, embedded within and transmitted across generations of, popular culture. Actions, beliefs and affective emotions are integral to understanding the long-term processes rather than overconcentrating on the actions of the elite, an approach associated with the modernists. Certainly, nations are imagined but must also be willed and felt. Imagination alone cannot explain, Smith (2003: 22) argues, the 'exercise of collective will and the arousal of mass emotion'. Within this perception, the 'ethnie', or ethnic community, is integral, providing a sense of solidarity that is connected to a shared culture that includes myths, traditions and historical memories and links with territory. For Smith, this highlights that collective consciousness and loyalties to larger units predate modernity.

Guibernau (2004) argues that Smith's account places inadequate attention upon the role of the nation-state and consequently is unable to explain nationalism in the twenty-first century. History, it is argued, cannot explain the present. What people or movements 'do in the present is dictated by present concerns, and the past is the source from which legitimation, justification and inspiring examples can all be drawn' (Halliday 2000: 38). Halliday (2000) is also critical of primordialists and, by extension, elements of Smith's work; namely while cultures and social allegiances existed prior to industrialization, this does not mean they were nations as they are understood today. Smith is also criticized for overestimating the robustness of nationalism and placing insufficient attention upon the Enlightenment culture (Llobera 1994).

However, while Smith identifies the legacy of pre-modernity in modern national consciousness, he also acknowledges the contributions of processes engrained within modernity and identifies two methods through which nation-states formed. Within what he describes as 'the lateral route', aristocracies associated with West Europe and the newly formed centralized states incorporated the frequently disparate populace and regions through bureaucratic processes. By utilizing the judiciary, military and administrative systems, a composite community was formed based upon cultural traditions and ethnic norms and values that formed civic or state nationalism. As Hutchinson and Smith (1994) point out, this required an intermingling between the peoples and a subsequent broadening of cultural identity. Alternatively, nations emerged as part of a challenge to the established foreign, namely colonial, rulers through a vertical route. Demotic ethnies who shared religious values and traditions were mobilized by educator-intellectuals and emphasis shifted from looking backwards and inwards to activist opposition demanding liberation. For Smith (1991: 64), intellectuals were able to politicize the ethnies through vernacular mobilization that drew upon historical traditions and 'the poetic space and golden ages of the communal past' within ethnic nationalism. By emphasizing components of history that individuals and groups shared, common support was mobilized in defence of a cultural legacy, national characteristics and associated territory. For many Muslim militants, the golden age of the communal past stems from the time of Muhammed and the formation of the *umma*.

Religious nationalism

The concept of religious nationalism is defined as 'a community of religious people or the political movement of a group of people heavily influenced by religious beliefs who aspire to be politically self-determining' (Rieffer 2003: 225). Religious beliefs, ideas and symbols are integral to the movement and are often closely connected to attempts to enhance levels of religiosity within communities. Despite the widespread belief that nationalism had replaced religion, as the above examples indicate, religious influence and loyalties have continued to permeate throughout nations, and indeed have often become the most prominent form of collective identification. Conversely, secular nationalisms often reject many central religious tenets and practices. But, as Smith (2003: 17–18) comments, if examined beneath official discourse, the nation binds its members through selective ritual and symbolic practices and mythologies that stem from deeper cultural resources and sacred foundations that connect both to 'chosen' people and holy land through memories, sacrifices and memorials. Thus, when seeking to explain the durability and strength of national identities, Smith (2003: 77) focussed upon nations' collective beliefs and sentiments and their relationship with older beliefs, symbols and traditions associated with religions. Myths associated with religion have a 'capacity for mobilizing and motivating communities and states, and underpinning a sense of national identity through a sacred communion of the elect'. Using the example of Zionism, but which could also be applied to other religious nationalisms, Smith (2003) argues that the connection with the past and ethnic election is essential to understanding the mobilization of Jewish people and the aim to return to spiritual roots. And within nation-states, religious cultural resources and sacred foundations have been entwined with contemporary ethnicity.

However, the tendency to overconcentrate on Western processes and crude division between East and West has resulted in analysis frequently being overgeneralized and important trends overlooked. Even Smith's exploration is restricted to European societies, although he does express the hope that a similar analysis can be adapted to other religious and cultural traditions, in particular within southern and Southeast Asia. In many parts of the world, religion remains embedded within the nation, religious activism is increasing and secularization is less dominant than in many parts of the West. For example, Chatterjee (1993) examines the struggle for national independence in India and argues that the movement integrated religion within national identity. And van der Veer (1994) explores the programmes instigated by the radical Hindu party, Shiv Sena, in 1993. Religious images were utilized that had recently been reinforced within popular Hindu culture, for example, the widely popular television dramatization of Hindu stories. In Poland, throughout communism, Catholicism was intertwined with national identity (Zawadzki 2005). Anderson (2006) acknowledges that religions like Islam and Buddhism cover large swathes of territory. But when applying the example of Islam, he argues that different languages meant communication was impossible beyond ideographs to be located within the sacred classical Arabic texts, with the *Qu'ran* until recently untranslatable. This made the communities distinct from today's imagined communities because, Anderson (2006: 13) suggests, the linkage with sacred languages provided the older communities with greater 'confidence in the unique sacredness of their languages, and thus their ideas about admission to membership'. However, it is also important to avoid overstressing the role of language which, in isolation, does not result in nationalism. Indeed, as Weber (1978: 395–6) pointed out, many nation-states have more than one language.

Although Smith concentrates on processes through which predominately Western nation-states utilized religion, there are more explicit religious adaptations. Zawadzki (2005) observes that not only do nationalist movements appropriate religion, but religious movements have reconstructed nationalism. Juergensmeyer (1993) examines the processes through which 'religious nationalists' use the corruption and alienation associated with modern societies as factors to mobilize the 'return' of the community to righteous behaviour. Religion is also utilized by secular nationalist leaders to help solidify support, strengthen collective consciousness and legitimize behaviour, particularly during times of crisis. Contrary, therefore, to popular perceptions, religion was integral to the emergence of nationalism and remains influential individually, ethnically and within nation-state discourse, often providing a moral benchmark upon which current behaviour is measured by 'religious nationalists.'

It is also important to acknowledge that conflicts commonly associated with religion are not purely religious but also incorporate nationalist sentiments and intentions. In the 1979 Iranian Revolution and aftermath, Halliday (2000) identifies a range of sentiments that drew upon the concept of the nation and Persian traditions. In other countries like Egypt, it is possible to note political leaders seeking to connect to Egyptian, Arab and Islamic loyalties according to the issue (Zubaida 1989). Halliday (2000: 45) also points out that religious transnationalism cross-cuts and predates nations and from which it is distinct: 'All three Middle Eastern monotheistic religions allow for arguments that deny the legitimacy of particular states, often on the grounds that the establishment of such a state does not meet the ethical or scriptural expectations which the religion lays down.'

The rise and fall of the 'Islamic nation'

In a manner akin to other more 'orthodox' nationalists, religious groups also utilize the past. Smith (2003) points out that perceptions of the past are instrumental in people making sense of the present and the ways in which members were bound into communities sharing common history that revolves around memories of battles, poets, heroes and heroines. 'Golden Ages', when the community was powerful, prosperous and creative, contributing to culture, religion, moral purpose and knowledge, are drawn upon in the present. This belief in the glorious past underpins the sense of national identity held by many, encourages virtue, provides feelings of collective dignity, especially in periods of oppression or division, and often inspires emulation. The fact, as Dieckhoff (2005) remarks, that aspirations to restore lost cultural purity are largely illusionary with their origins rooted in myths and cultural crossbreeding overlooked should not detract from the social effectiveness of invoking the 'Golden Age'. By emphasizing components of history that individuals and groups share, common support has been mobilized in defence of a cultural legacy, national characteristics and associated territory. This is clearly apparent in militant Muslims' emphasis upon the exploits of Muhammed and the time of the four *caliphs* when Islam was the dominant global discourse. During this period, Muslims were believed to be pure, devout practitioners governed by righteous leaders through the *shari'ah*. A Yemeni veteran of the Afghan conflict against the Soviet Union encapsulates these sentiments within religious nationalism:

> Afghanistan reminded Muslims of all colors and races that what unites us is much more important than the superficial differences wrought by colonialism, secular nationalism, and other material ideologies. We felt we were on the verge of re-enacting and reliving the Golden Age of our blessed ancestors.[6]

The golden age of the communal past stems, for most Muslims, from the time of Muhammed and the formation of the *umma*. Across denominational interpretations, the *umma* retains a significance that has arguably increased in importance. The perception of this community is highly contested and has led to the *umma* being considered by Khosrokhavar (2005: 61) to be an 'imagined community', because although 'Islamic *societies* exist in the real world ... there is no such thing as *an* Islamic society'. Crucially for militants, the *umma* is achieveable and indeed contactable. The leading ideologue, Sayyid Qutb (1906–66), for example, considered the *umma* to be

> a collectivity of people whose entire lives – in their intellectual, social, existential, political, moral, and practical aspects – are based on Islamic ethics. Thus characterized, this *umma* ceases to exist if no part of the earth is governed according to the law of God any longer.[7]

Drawing upon the seventh and eighth centuries when Islamic control spread beyond the Middle East into North Africa and Spain, Qutb argued that the Islamic community could only be restored through the leadership of a vanguard of the *umma*. Throughout this period and beyond, the religion continued to spread and Islam became both politically and numerically dominant in many areas. Yet, Lapidus (2002) suggests that by the eighth and ninth centuries, the *caliphate* was already evolving into a colonial and secular regime. In the new era, which Lapidus dates between AD 950 and 1200, Islam went from defining the political elite to expressing 'the communal identity of the masses of Middle Eastern people' (ibid.). Consequently, the religious and ethnic characteristics of the region that are commonly associated with the emergence of the religion developed over 600 years and have continued to evolve. Since the emergence of the *umma* under Muhammed's leadership and the onset of the Muslim conquests, followers have belonged to a multitude of communal groups and loyalties. Their roots stem from family, tribal and ethnic ties, rural and urban societies and preceding civilizations, religions and paganism that were dominant prior to the emergence of Islam. In other words, like other forms of collective allegiances, 'Islamic identity' has always been heterogeneous, interwoven with local influences like ethnicity, culture, gender and socio-economics.

Islam within the Middle East, and the religion more generally, became influential in other parts of the world, but again important vicissitudes can be noticed. The military conquest of the Indian subcontinent began in the eighth century and Islamic regimes became dominant in the region by the end of the twelfth century. Sub-Saharan Africa encountered Islam through a range of trading and teaching networks and processes of migration. The spread of Islam slowly permeated southwards. Muslim communities developed in parts of Somalia and Ethiopia from the ninth century and had become integral in parts of Sudanese towns by the twelfth century but did not become influential in the Ivory Coast and Guinea until the nineteenth century. After Southeast Asia first encountered Islam in the seventh century, the religion was not established until between the thirteenth and fifteenth centuries in a similar manner to sub-Saharan Africa (Rubenstein 2002). People were often introduced to Islam through Sufis, commercial activities and the conversion of leaders for realpolitik purposes but not through military conquest. China provides an example of the introduction of Islam being both violent and peaceful (Esposito 1999). From the seventh century, the religion was encountered through the 'Silk Road' trade and militarily through Turkic and Arab invaders. In these different contexts Islam was localized. For example, the conversion of leaders and their maintenance of power resulted in the continuity of pre-Islamic values and practices in Southeast Asia. Similar processes can be noticed in the latter conversion of the Muslims of Central Asia, where large-scale conversion among many groups like the Kazakhs did not occur until the eighteenth century (Lapidus 2002). In neighbouring Dagestan, however, Islam was introduced in the seventh century and had spread across the region by the sixteenth century (Roschin 2006).

The emergence of the majority of today's recognizable Muslim nation-states generally commenced throughout the first half of the twentieth century. Legitimation for the formation and continuation of separate defined Muslim territories for moderate Muslims, in particular, can be found in the breakup of the early *Caliphate*. Certainly, today an examination of Islam and associated frontiers details a lack of a generic transnational approach. Instead, some countries like Turkey and Tunisia subordinate religion to state control; although the balance is slowly shifting, Malaysia, Indonesia and Mauritania promote what Lapidus (2002: 837) refers to as 'Islamo-nationalist identity' and Afghanistan, Iran, Pakistan, Saudi Arabia and Sudan have all declared themselves Islamic states over recent years. There is therefore a strong argument that connects identity formation with ideological dominance within communities and defined territories. A central component, a point echoed by both militants and to a lesser extent Western academics like van der Veer (1994), is that colonialism has been instrumental in the formation of modern nationalism in Muslim societies.

Impact of colonialism

Today, nationalism is largely opposed and viewed by transnational militants as either a Western imposition or the outcome of struggles for independence against colonialism. In some respects, there is historical evidence that supports this perspective. Habeck (2006: 101) reports on the view that nationalism was introduced to weaken the Muslim community by splitting it into racial and ethnic groups. Concepts like 'integration' and 'multiculturalism' 'are specifically designed to reduce a Muslim's attachment to the community and Islamic ideals, while convincing Muslims that other religions and cultures are the equal of Islam'. Yet at the same time, colonialists were promoting more moderate forms of Islam and collaborated with religious leaders who defended the regimes and even helped recruit military support.

European domination was frequently associated with conflict as local ethnic Muslim groups fought against the colonial invaders. For example, across East and West Africa, the Madhists in Nigeria, Tuaregs in Niger and Sufis in Mauritania and Somalia fought prolonged struggles. Ultimately, however, foreign domination was generally enforced. In Turkistan, opposition to Russian control also included militant Muslims, most notably Muhammad al-Khailifa Kabir (1856–98) who led a short-lived campaign. The impact of the *jihad* spread to neighbouring regions until they were finally defeated. More substantive challenges were noticeable in the aftermath of the 1917 Russian Revolution when, during the fighting between Russian Reds and Whites, Muslims in Azerbaijan, the Caucasus and Kazakhstan sought independence. Finally in Indonesia, the first nationalist mass movement, Sarekat Islam, was formed in 1912 and quickly split under the pressures of internal conflicts. Two groups emerged out of the religious anti-colonial struggle, Muhammadiyah and Nahdlatul Ulama, that were to remain influential long after independence had been attained (Cederroth 1996). During the 1920s, nationalist and Islamic groups developed political and cultural networks that cut across regional, ethnic and discursive differences to achieve a common challenge to the Dutch colonialists.

For transnational militants, the influence of the Indian born Sayyid Abul Al-Mawdudi within the challenge to British colonial control of India is embedded within perspectives of nationalism. Al-Mawdudi opposed the formation of the Pakistani nation-state, arguing that nationalism implied the sovereignty of the people. By comparison, the true Islamic state was founded on the principle that sovereignty belongs to God. He therefore considered nationalism to be a process through which ignorance (*jahiliyya*) was instilled in the populace. Ayman al-Zawahiri,[8] when arguing that the establishment of a global *caliphate* was the duty of all Muslims, stated 'we do not recognize Sykes-Picot [the 1916 agreement that resulted in the division of the Middle East]'. Kepel (2005) reports on the comments of the *Jama'at Islamiyya* member, Isam al-Din al'Aryan, who declared that nationalism in post-independent Egypt was simply a new form of westernization. But as Pappé (2005) notes, nationalism is now an integral component of non-Western societies, *albeit increasingly interwoven with religion.* At the level of Muslim nation-states, Halliday (2000:130) explains that while they may be involved both in rhetorical threats to the West and individual acts or strategies, 'Muslim states are incapable of mounting a concerted challenge, let alone of redrawing boundaries'. Arguably, the strategic weakness of Muslim nation-states is fuelling transnationalism and asymmetrical conflict by other forces operating outside government control.

The militant critical dismissal of nationalism also overlooks the manner in which religion was intertwined within opposition to colonialism and provided a unifying discourse for otherwise disparate groups to enable popular mobilization. The strengthening of national identities was often invigorated by the formal division by the colonisers of the indigenous populations into religious groups, like the Hindus and Muslims and Buddhists and Hindus, in India and Sri Lanka respectively. For example, in response to British rule, Shah Abd al-Aziz declared a *fatwa* in 1803, demanding that Indian Muslims fight against the colonialists in Holy War.[9] In the Senegambian region of Africa, the *jihad* led by a *Qu'ran* teacher, Ma Ba (1809–67) sought to achieve independence while attacking indigenous enemies and perceived pagans and seeking to conquer other areas and peoples. 'Throughout West Africa Islam had come to be the almost universal language of political ambition and moral reform. … In many cases Islam provided for the unification of heterogeneous peoples and the creation of states.'[10]

Rise of state nationalism and decline of religious influence

For modernists like Ernest Gellner (1978), nationalism strongly correlates with nation-states. It is the ideological cement that connects people to the nation-state and civil society and protects state culture. In this sense, Gellner has been criticized for his assumption that nationalism as a challenging discourse is over. Nations became embedded within West European territories and competition between them for influence and resources led to the pursuit of land to colonize a variety of ethnic groups, which were divided and controlled through the establishment of maps and boundaries. Post-Second World War, Anderson (2006) argues that the 'last wave' of nationalisms possess their own characteristics but these can only be understood in terms of the success of Western nations. While modernists have examined the impact of colonialism, Chatterjee (1993) suggests that Anderson in particular overconcentrated on processes within the West and failed to fully identify the role of colonial systems. The imposition of foreign governments made a huge contribution to the emergence of nationalism within the colonial territories that sought independence. For example, Anderson (2006) dates the emergence of nationalism in Malaysia and Indonesia, when both were subjected to colonial rule, to be 1938 and 1928 respectively. In the latter example, Anderson explores the formation of nationalism across a large population that was fragmented across some 3000 islands and numerous religious allegiances and ethnolinguistic diversity. The establishment of government schools, he suggests (ibid.: 121), and 'uniform textbooks, standardised diplomas and teaching certificates, a strictly regulated gradation of age groups, classes and instructional materials, in themselves created a self-contained, coherent universe of experience'. Anderson tended to concentrate upon these policies as an extension of dynastic governments, a point he acknowledged in the 2006 edition of *Imagined Communities*. In this edition, he added that across Southeast Asia, accommodation was made with different religious affiliations that had 'served as the basis of very old, very stable imagined communities not in the least aligned with the secular state's authoritarian grid-map' (Anderson 2006: 169). Why these religious imagined communities were not considered to be nations was not explained. Nor was the significance of universal processes in contributing to anti-imperialist movements fully explored.

The formation of Muslim nation-states is also contentious. Milton-Edwards (2005: 73) comments that in many instances,

> new nations and new peoples who were subject to statehood were declared with little evidence of consultation with the leaders of pre-existing religious and other communities in these areas. It was little wonder that the legitimacy of such states and their locally appointed leaders were called into question by the fundamentalists.

The majority of today's Muslim nation-states formed through independence in the first half of the twentieth century. Previous local elites, family, tribal or community membership had to be replaced. New allegiances were built 'upon a fusion of historical lineage, ethnic, linguistic, and Islamic symbols recast in linguistic-ethnic and nationalist terms'.[11] Processes designed to achieve modernization were embedded with slogans and symbols designed to appeal to a common collectivity. Gershoni and Jankowski (1987) detail the long-standing attempts within Egypt to introduce a well-developed pre-Islamic history that stressed distinction and separation. In Turkey, Atatürk initiated a similar scheme with a fictitious Turkic past which became a template for adaptation by many modernizing Muslim governments. Iran emphasized a pre-Islamic past that identified unique national characteristics. Arab nationalists reciprocated and a process evolved that contributed to wider cultural and political divides. In Egypt, nationalists failed to embed the Pharaohic past within twentieth-century nationalism because there was a distinct lack of continuity across language, symbols and culture. Across Muslim societies, these attempts at 'imagined pasts' were only partially successful.

This can be partly attributed to the interrelated processes of secularization and modernization that have been adopted across Muslim societies and, as Chapter 4 details, have had only limited success. Education has been central within attempts at modernization and the strengthening of national consciousness across Muslim societies. In Chapter 4, the impact of educational schemes is examined in more detail. It is important here to note that the role of schooling upon national consciousness is mixed, with education paradoxically instrumental both in the formation of secular and Islamo nationalism.

At a structural level, nationalism is present within Muslim cultural, political and economic institutions in a 'top-down' approach. But McCrone (1998: 40) suggests, 'the everyday affirmation of national identity is an active process, reinforced by the banal symbolism of national identity'. The successful transmission and acceptance of nationalism is therefore dependent upon people identifying with both the discourse and 'imagined' community. In turn, it could be argued this identification feeds into broader social processes and the reproduction of historical memory. Within many Muslim societies, these processes have failed to overcome the imposed origins of the nation-states that did not connect to popular sentiments and attachments. And, national governments have failed to integrate their 'top down' approach within civil society, with many people disengaged or disillusioned with the failure of nationalist discourse to deliver promises. Equally, other broader social identifications like Arab nationalism have also been seriously undermined through association with failure, most notably defeat for a coalition of Arab nation-states in the 1967 war against Israel.

National and transnational identity

Despite considerable efforts to embed nationalist loyalties within territories, identities remain diverse. This is not unusual. McCrone (1998: 183) suggests that 'the power of nationalism in the modern world lies in its capacity to reconfigure personal identities and loyalties in a way more in tune with the social, cultural and political realities'. But this is not to state that nationalism is inevitably the paramount form of identity. Instead, McCrone acknowledges that nationalism may not have priority over multiple identities, other forms of social identity like socio-economic class or gender. Today, other economic, political and cultural forces have eroded the universalism of the nation-state for many. Interpretations of the nation, what it means, the boundaries and the selective use of history are, as Halliday (2000) points out, contingent and ever changing. The internalization of nationalism and level of accordance will therefore depend on the extent to which it accords with individual identity and other collective consciousnesses in rapidly transforming contexts. In this sense, national identity is not fixed and immutable but, like identity more generally, 'always in process' (McCrone 1998: 138). Again, the interaction between discourse and identity is an inherent feature of the internalization of religious values generally and militancy in particular. Islamic movements are therefore subverting 'the principle of not only the nation-state, but also, possibly, of nationalism' as Dieckhoff and Jaffrelot (2005: 266) argue. Instead, Islamic militants are promoting a form of nationalism that challenges the dominance of Western forms of nationalism.

Alongside geographical boundaries, the globalization-related transformation of media, communications, transportation and migration have contributed to new forms of identity that transcend national, racial, ethnic and socio-economic barriers. Factors identified by van der Veer (1994) in the mobilization of religious nationalism among Hindus and Muslims in India, like religious travel, pilgrimage and migration, became accelerated through global processes. There has been a proliferation of transnational and global Muslim movements that include 'such diverse groups as publication and propaganda organizations, missionary (*da'wa*) societies, Sufi brotherhoods, banks, youth associations, emigrant communities with international ties and others (Lapidus 2002: 868). However, despite the greater interlocking between Muslims, and shared experiences, there is little evidence to support Lapidus' (ibid.) claim that there is a 'universalistic identity'. This overlooks the tremendous variations within identity formations, beliefs and other cross-cutting loyalties. Lapidus does acknowledge that there are other forms of loyalty that root people within particular communities. And certainly there are some similar practices and beliefs, but the variations of implementation, behaviour and accommodation with political discourse result in religion varying from being a small component on which to base individual identity to an all-encompassing framework. Prior to the latest burst of globalization, Milton-Edwards (2005: 29) observed that 'pre-fundamentalists' like al-Afghani, Abduh, Sayyid Khan and Rashid Rida responded to fears of foreign domination and the need for enhanced religiosity and utilized 'technological development in communications, travel and culture to get their message across to a wider audience'. In some respects, the 'pre-fundamentalists' provided an early template for later generations to adapt.

Militant Islamic nationalism

Although ethnic identities remain important in localized conditions for groups like Kurds, Berbers and Chechens, Lapidus (2002) outlines how many people within other ethnicities like Indonesians, Malaysians, Bangladeshis, Turks and Algerians now place greater emphasis on religion as their primary source of collective identity. This process is being aided by encroaching religious influence within government relations, ranging from the introduction of the *shari'ah* in Mauritania and in several Nigerian federal states to the incorporation of Islamic parties within political processes across the Middle East, North and East Africa, South and Southeast Asia. For example, Sudan is divided according to geography, religion and ethnicity, with northern territories populated by Arabic-speaking Muslims and the south controlled by non-Muslim Africans. Lapidus (2002: 781) suggests that in Africa it is only where substantial numbers of Muslims claim Arab descent that 'national identity is expressed in Islamic terms'. The brutal attacks on 'African' Muslims by 'Arabs' Muslims in Darfur that are justified on racial and religious grounds would seem to support this. 'Despite their claim to be supranational, most Islamist movements have been shaped by national particularities. Sooner or later they tend to express national interests, even under the pretext of Islamist ideology' (Roy 2004: 62). Similarly, processes of rising Islamic nationalism are identified by Schwartz (2005) who points out that extremists in the northern Muslim states of Nigeria want to install the *shari'ah* but as the form of government within a separatist state.

The struggle for national independence is noticeable in places like the Palestinian territories, Chechnya, Philippines, Thailand and Kashmir where large numbers of Sunni Muslims feel they are being suppressed. Militant groups operate in these identifiable boundaries like Palestinian Islamic Jihad, Hamas and MILF. All these groups have specific objectives orientated around the attainment of independence and/or an Islamic nation-state within a localized geographical region. Seesemann (2006) notes that Islamic groups, like these, are focused on internal social and political transformation; the global *umma* is subordinate within their priorities.

In other regions, religious nationalism has become noticeable in different circumstances. Unlike many post-independent regimes that initially relegated the role of religion, the demise of the Soviet Union was accompanied by a noticeable rise in religious fervour across the Islamic spectrum, from moderation to militancy. The demand for an Islamic state within Kazakhstan, Tajikstan, Turkmenistan and Uzbekistan has been noticeable from the point at which Soviet repression was lifted. For millions of Central Asians the break-up of the Soviet Union provided them with greater freedom to develop and express different forms of collective identities. They explored ethnic and internal and international religious associations that had been suppressed following the communist revolution and the subsequent division of the territory into socialist republics (Rashid 2002). Islamic awareness was aided with the arrival of Islamic educators, advisors and funding for mosques and Qu'ranic translations. Religious nationalism therefore increased markedly in these regions and transnational fighters are known to have located to the region (Rashid 2002). Yet there is little evidence to suggest any significant contributions from Central Asian Muslims outside the region.

Perceptions about, and the attempts to mobilize on behalf of, and defend, the *umma* therefore vary between and within groups. Transnationalists refer to religious obligations to defend Muslims across the world and to implement international change. Militants operating within national contexts will focus upon mobilizing a localized *umma* while seeking to utilize the globalized neo-*umma* to attract wider support. Hamas' (1988) Covenant provides illuminating examples of a localized group that utilizes the global *umma*. Reference is made to the Islamic world being on fire, fighters who 'have sacrificed their lives on the soil of Palestine', to support from the 'vast Arab and Islamic world' with the liberation 'bound to three circles: the Palestinian circle, the Arab circle and the Islamic circle' and the duty of every Muslim wherever they maybe. The Islamic Resistance Movement (Hamas) is described as 'a distinguished Palestinian movement whose allegiance is to Allah, and whose way of life is Islam. It strives to raise the banner of Allah over every inch of Palestine' which has been consecrated by Muslims 'till the Day of Judgement'. 'Nationalism, from the point of view of the Islamic Resistance Movement, is part of the religious creed. Nothing in nationalism is more significant or deeper than in the case when an enemy should tread Moslem land'.

Many other less well-publicised nationalist groups adopt similar tactics. For example, foreign intervention, mutual misgivings and mistrust between Hindus and Muslims in Kashmir have led to both groups increasingly considering the 'other' as a growing threat. The perceived lack of integration into the Indian nation-state has contributed to Kashmiri identity steadily becoming synonymous with Kashmiri Muslim identity (Blom 2007; Rao 1999). Inequality, repression and feelings of injustice have Islamized Muslim national identity while contributing to the Hinduization of the Kashmiri conflict for Hindus. James and Özdamar (2005) point out with respect to Kashmir, and which can be applied to other nationalist conflicts, that the rise in Islamic identity causes tensions between different interpretations within communities and solidifies perceptions of difference between Kashmiri Muslims and Indian Hindus, and in the process reinforces ethnic antagonisms. Similar, if more complicated yet condensed, processes can be observed in the spiralling of violence between orthodox Serbs, Catholic Croats and Muslim Bosnians. Despite long-standing historical grievances and ethnic disputes, the Tito government had been able to enforce security and some cohesion through federalism. However, after the death of Tito in 1980 and rising economic and political insecurities, ethnic solidarities fractured and old disputes were inflamed by political nationalists. Religion became the most immediate method of identifying and ultimately attacking the 'other'. In turn, attacks and threats of attack strengthened group loyalties around the social identity they held in common and which was ironically being used as the grounds for their 'otherness' (Iveković 2002; Milton-Edwards 2005). In other words, this multiple reciprocal process quickly spiralled into greater religiosity and violence. For the Bosnian Muslims, this meant that their previously secular beliefs were replaced by religion and Islam became more dominant during the conflict. However, as Berger (1999) points out this did not mean that the conflict was inspired by religion. Instead, religion became a source of identification and in some instances a source of justification for actions. The involvement of religion in the conflict is further complicated by the participation of transnational Muslims. For the wider militant movement, Bosnia became symbolic of Western inaction and indifference to Muslim deaths. However, many foreign fighters were dismayed by what they considered to be the lax practice of the Bosnians. And following the creation of the Bosnian nation-state in the mid 1990s, Islam has gradually diminished in significance with politics dominated by secular parties.

A different example of the relationship between national and transnational militancy can be found within another underreported example of

Islamic militancy in Libya where the Libyan Islamic Fighting Group (LIFG) seeks to overthrow the Qadhafi regime. This is in order 'to save the Libyan Muslims from the oppression, tyranny and even more importantly, from the deviation of Qadhafi from true Islam'.[12] LIFG also attempts to mobilize support for the conflict amongst Muslims within Libya and across Muslim societies and incorporates theological influences from global figures like Qutb, Azzam, al-Shankiti and al-Uthaymin with local martyrs like Umar al-Mukhtar who was hanged by the Italians (Terdman 2005). But within Libyan militancy, there are also Muslims who advocate a duty to other *jihadis* and conflicts, witnessed by the discovery that some Libyan nationals had been arrested or killed fighting in Iraq.[13]

The breakup of the former Soviet Union has also contributed to the resurgence of Islam and greater integration between religion and nationalism. Mili (2005) and Wang (2003) argue that this impact has permeated outwards to neighbouring states and has influenced Muslim sentiments amongst the Uygurs who comprise more than seven million of the Xinjiang region of China's 17 million population (Rubenstein 2002). Changes in neighbouring countries, involvement of some Uygurs in the fight against the Soviet Union in Afghanistan and the relaxation of transport restraints contributed to enhanced links with surrounding Muslims and greater religious awareness. Alongside these factors, long-standing economic failure and corruption resulted in growing demands for Islamic political involvement, which have developed into demands for independence and the imposition of the *shari'ah*. The East Turkistan Islamic Movement has used terror tactics to try to achieve this. In the North Caucasus, after becoming riddled with ethnic divisions, the Pan-Caucasus movement failed to attain independence and the Confederation of the Peoples of the North Caucasus (KNK) became more explicitly Islamic, aiming to unite around religion and install an independent Islamic state in Chechnya. At the time, one of the leaders, Zelimkhan Yandarbiyev, declared that 'all the Moslem countries should participate in the Chechen *jihad*, providing it with both military and humanitarian support'.[14] The participation of Arab mujahideen within the Chechen conflict indicates a transnational component. Until his death in 2002, the Saudi Emir Khattab sought an Islamic state in the North Caucasus. Islamic government in Chechnya was to be the first stage in the process of regional development. Consequently, conflict in Chechnya was a means to broader ends but, as Tumelty (2006) points out, the focus remained regional with the American 'far enemy' not featuring in military or even rhetorical attacks. Following the succession to leadership of Abu Walid and then Abu Hafs al-Urdani, this changed and attacks against the United States were advocated. Yet, the conflict in Chechnya includes Chechen religious nationalists who may fight alongside the transnationalists for shared outcomes, blurring distinctions between groups. But many Chechens led by Shamil Basayev, are ultimately fighting for self-determination[15] and can be considered to be part of the evolution from nationalism to Islamic nationalism with roots in the nineteenth-century struggles against Russia (Larzillière 2007; Milton-Edwards 2005; Thornton 2005). Jemaah Islamiyah (JI) provide a further localized example, aiming to impose an Islamic government initially in Indonesia before the formation of a unified Southeast Asian Islamic state that stretched from southern Thailand across the Malay Peninsula and the Indonesian archipelago and into the southern Philippines (Shuja 2005).

Religious nationalism can also be prominent where Islam is not the dominant religion or other religions are considered to be too influential and/or are responsible for moral denigration. In countries like the Philippines and Thailand, Muslims are a minority and undertake violent nationalist struggles against the Catholic and Buddhist majority respectively, while also attacking the perceived decadence of local Muslims. These are, as Chalk (2002a) mentioned in respect of the Malay districts of Thailand, localized and nationalistic conflicts led largely by the Pattani United Liberation Organisation. In the Philippines, MILF fight for localized issues but have links with JI and a commitment to a global agenda including a religious obligation to assist other *jihadis* (Abuza 2003, 2006; Chalk 2002b). By comparison, another leading terror group, the Abu Sayyaf Group, is more militant than MILF advocating no coexistence with other religious groups who are considered to be the legitimate target of attack, including the beheading of women and children. The group is considered to be closer to the global transnational networks. Another Southeast Asian nation, Indonesia is the most populous Muslim country, with a greater aggregate population than the Arab Middle East, and confronting tremendous pressures to maintain unity across a multi-ethnic nation that JI seeks to exploit. And in the Moluccas, there is ethno-religious fighting between Christians and Muslims, supported by the militant Lashkar Jihad (Houben 2003; Noorhaidi 2002). It should be stressed, as identified in Chapter 1, that the national against transnational chasm which is found within *Sunni* Islam is much less noticeable within the smaller *Shi'ite* denomination with its closer association between groups and nation-states.

Militant Islamic transnationalism

Groups associated with al-Qa'ida have sought to establish themselves as the sole representative of true Islam, often viewing themselves as vanguards whose actions and example will inspire and awaken Muslims to challenge Western nation-states and overthrow national governments. By comparison with the nationalist militant Muslims, *Sunni* transnationalists outline religious obligations to defend Muslims across the world and to implement international change. Some groups have been associated with a range of attacks that have been undertaken towards this end, including *Sunnis* attacking *Shi'ites* who are deemed infidels in Pakistan and Iraq. Processes behind the emergence of these groups connect closely to the debate about transnationalism and interconnect with the experiences

Muslims are encountering across the world. In some respects, these groups, like millions more moderate Muslims, appear to be what Appadurai (1996: 169) has described as 'postnational' and 'divorced from territorial states'. Recently within studies of nationalism, there has been a growing emphasis placed upon transnationalism which, Basch *et al.* (1994: 7) argue, is the process 'by which immigrants forge and sustain multi-stranded social relations that link together their societies of origin and settlement'. They undertake 'actions, make decisions, and develop subjectivities and identities embedded in networks of relationships that connect them simultaneously to two or more nation-states.'

Developing upon Anderson's 'print capitalism', Appadurai (1996) suggests that new forms of 'electronic capitalism' inherent within globalization can have a similar, if not stronger, effect that enables the transmission of cultural features, values, symbols and meanings that extend beyond nation-states to transnationalism. Appardurai is not, however, arguing in support of McLuhan's 'global village'. Instead, he suggests that the vernacular and domestication of globalization at local levels results in hybridization rather than homogeneity. These cross-cutting loyalties, while a feature of diasporas, can also incorporate indigenous people. For many individuals though, this form of nationalism is not directly about the demand for self-determination. Nationalism often involves living in a stateless nation and is not therefore inevitably territorial. Clearly these relations have particular resonance within diasporas while conversely often contributing to a reformulation of defensive national identity within societies: for example, the resurgence of the extreme right within Britain, France and Germany and its correlation with migration and perceived threats. Anderson (1998) describes the multi-stranded relations and loyalties within diasporas as 'long distance nationalism' which is a consequence of evolving capitalism. Like other forms of nationalism, the long distance version is also formed and reformed in relation to the 'other'. But Anderson argues that rather than long distance contributing to a weakening of resolve, space can contribute to greater radicalism because individuals in the West and their immediate family are freed from the fear of prison, torture or death. The example of migrants highlights that the attachment to nation is not restricted to those living within territories, nor even specifically is it about land.

For Roy (2004: 38), processes of migration interact with other factors like the collapse of the Soviet Union, closer political and economic ties between Muslim nation-states and Western governments and associated processes of globalization, to contribute to what he describes as 'deterritorialisation.' This happens when

> religion and culture no longer have a relationship with territory or given society ... It means that religion has to define itself solely in terms of religion: there is no longer any social authority or social pressure to conform. ... It has to define itself in comparison with all 'other' – other religions, other values, other environments.

Solace for a minority within transnational communities feeling ill at ease, humiliated and stigmatized in societies, where materialism dominates and is the benchmark of success, can be found within the neo-*umma*. And for Roy 'deterritorialisation' can be experienced without the individual leaving their own country. In these localized settings, Westernization and globalization have challenged local values and are considered to threaten ethnic cultures and marginalize Islam.

Again this is not to stress a uniformity of experience or collective identity. The 'Muslim community' within Europe, North America and Australasia consists of a multitude of values, beliefs, customs and languages. In other words, religion can provide a unifier amongst neighbours, although even here practices and beliefs may be unidentifiable necessarily. Migrants and Western-born Muslims often have little in common and certainly do not share a communal identity. These processes are noticeable among many migrants to the West and subsequent generations. In different countries, Muslims share experiences of racism and forms of covert discrimination that provide barriers to integration and strengthen existing social and cultural networks. The rise of Islamophobia has resulted in many Muslims uniting around that which leads to their exclusion, namely their religion, which becomes the basis for the formation of communal and status groups.

Despite Muslims being born in the West, their loyalties are being questioned. Yet, the overwhelming majority have not given any cause for nation-states to be concerned, but government and societal reactions are contributing to processes of exclusion and the re-examination of identities. Marranci's (2006) research discovered that many Western-born Muslims, rather than feeling lost in between the West and their familial country of origin, stressed their individuality allied to the *umma* which was considered to be shaped in a 'community of emotion' rather than Anderson's 'imagined community'. Within these perceptions, Marranci discovered that Muslims were part of a spiritual community and people shared their experiences and emotions. Many rejected nationalist and ethnic divisions. He reports on Western-born Muslims' perceptions being heavily influenced by global media through which many attained Islamic education. Their perceptions of the *umma* differed from their parents with greater emphasis placed upon shared identity and humiliation. For example, a respondent from Paris suggested that 'Islam is one and we should behave as one nation only' while another based in Italy commented 'when you see what Palestinians and other Muslims around the world are suffering, you feel as if your family has been attacked and your brother or sister killed ... the *umma* is like ... when you go to a concert of pop-music, you don't know anybody but feel part of the group' (ibid.: 107). For in-migrants the *umma* is very much a 'community' within which differences, including religious, nationalism and prejudice against other ethnic Muslim groups, can be observed. Emotions also play an important role in facilitating unity beyond the locality to the wider community. Khosrokhavar (2005) suggests that migrants share a sense of 'non-belonging'. In addition to problematic experiences in Western societies, migrants also share the sufferings of societies they have left, feelings strengthened by enhanced media coverage. For these people, he argues, the *umma* provides a sense of certainty and allegiance. In other words, many Muslims are refusing to compromise their beliefs in order to integrate with the incompatible perception of the Western nation and associated processes of Westernization. They are experiencing either individually or collectively perceived Western neo-imperialism and are reacting in defence of the Islamic nation and sense of honour that comes from addressing the shame that the allegiance is feeling. As the following discussion identifies, this is clearly apparent in the experiences of many migrant and Western-born Muslims and is resulting in the 'near' and 'far' distinction being lost; Muslims in Britain are targeting their home country for attack, most notably in the London 2005 bombings.

The most obvious example of militant transnationalism that attracted fighters and supporters from all over Muslim societies and communities can be found in the war in Afghanistan against the Soviet Union during the 1980s. A fighter informed Gerges (2006: 112) that the war 'internationalized and militarized the jihadist movement further'. Success against the Soviet Union gave confidence and legitimacy in the possibility of a global *umma* and the term became prominent within al-Qa'ida-related pronouncements from an early stage. For example, in December 1994, bin Laden declared 'the banner of *jihad* is raised up high to restore to our *umma* its pride and honor, and in which the banner of God's unity is raised once again over every stolen Islamic land, from Palestine to al-Andalus and other Islamic lands that were lost because of the betrayals of rulers and the feebleness of Muslims'.[16] After attacks in Riyadh and Khobar, bin Laden expressed his admiration, declaring the perpetrators had 'removed the shame from the forehead of our *umma*'.[17] Denouncing the feebleness, degradation and corruption of the *umma* and the Crusaders' invasion of Muslim lands were to become regular features of public communications. In 1996, bin Laden draws attention to massacres considered to be occurring against Muslims around the world. Yet 'the greatest disaster to befall the Muslims since the death of the Prophet Muhammad – is the occupation of Saudi Arabia, which is the cornerstone of the Islamic world'.[18] Rectifying events in the 'Islamic' world generally and in Saudi Arabia specifically were early declared aims.

A useful indicator of the transnational nature of groups associated with al-Qa'ida lies in the wide-ranging membership across geographical boundaries. Khosrokhavar (2005: 61) suggests that al-Qa'ida members 'belong to a variety of communities … are involved in a plurality of cultures without belonging to any one of them'. Hiro (2002) mentions that notebooks discovered after the fall of Kabul in 2001 identified al-Qa'ida-associated representatives who originated from 26 different nationalities, while Bergen (2001) refers to 25 different ethnic nationalities involved in Afghan training camps. Breadth is also noticeable in the range of conflicts that transnational militants engaged in after 1989. Gerges (2005: 57) refers to *jihadis* defending co-religionists in 'Bosnia-Herzegovina, Chechnya, the Philippines, Kashmir, Eritrea, Somalia, Burma, Tajikstan and elsewhere'.

The geographical issues promoted by transnational groups unsurprisingly differ from the specific geopolitical focus of Hamas, Hezbollah, and Kashmiri Jaish-e-Mohammad and Lashkar-e-Toiba. A study of statements by bin Laden shows that following the 2001 attacks, attempts were made to rationalize the actions and broaden the appeal of this strand of militancy. References were notable to 'the *umma* of 1200 million Muslims' that 'is being slaughtered, in Palestine, in Iraq, Somalia, Western Sudan, Kashmir, the Philippines, Bosnia, Chechnya, and Assam'.[19] Greater attention is placed upon the plight of the Palestinians; yet ironically in light of the centrality of the Palestinian struggle to militancy today, during the 1990s the appeal of other conflicts led to a downgrading and relative neglect of the Palestinian–Israeli dispute. Even today bin Laden argues, the Palestinian cause must be subordinate to the global struggle. In response to a question that the spate of references to the Palestinians was relatively new, bin Laden replied that 'sometimes we find the right elements to push for one cause more than the other. Last year's blessed *intifada* helped us to push more for the Palestinian cause. This push helps the other cause.'[20] He then argues that there is no conflict between attacking America and the Palestinian cause. By comparison, Chechnya and other conflicts, while occasionally referenced, do not attract the same vocal or pragmatic support amongst militants. This may be due to the lack of familiarity of Muslims with the region, language, history and the lack of symbolism that Chechens and the territory holds within transnational identities. In other words, familiarity helps to strengthen international bonds and loyalties. As McGregor (2006) observes, the struggle in Iraq has mobilized international *jihadists* at the expense of Chechnya for cultural, linguistic and possibly climatic reasons.

Bin Laden sought to connect with Muslims everywhere through the use of the concept of the *umma*. He has stated, 'our concern is that our *umma* unites either under the Words of the Book of God or His Prophet, and that this nation should establish the righteous caliphate of our *umma*'.[21] However, the *caliphate* as a concept had largely been dormant since 1924[22] and had not been popular in many regions prior to that time period because it imposed Turkish rule over Arabs. This leads Devji (2005) to suggest that the *umma's* primary role is in deterritorialized space with no centre or periphery. Later in 2003, the *umma* is explicitly described as a physical entity, with bin Laden hoping 'that God blesses our *umma* with a state that includes all Muslims under its authority'.[23] Such comments connect to Qutb's[24] belief that a 'Muslim's nationality is his religion'. Khosrokhavar (2005: 52) suggests that the modern discourse is addressed to individuals and not the community. 'It is addressed to creatures of flesh and blood, rather than to restricted groups of religious believers who have already been shaped by the religious tradition and who do not have to be convinced of Islam's legitimacy.' As Khosrokhavar (ibid.: 61) acknowledges when discussing Qutb's contributions, the emphasis upon individualism is considered in relation to community, a neo-*umma* is promoted that transcends national boundaries based upon beliefs rather than ethnicity, race or existing nation. In the place of existing geographical barriers 'a mythical Islamic community' is promoted.

By comparison, *Shi'ite* transnational sentiments have been influenced by clergy rooted within a nation-state. For example, the Iranian leader Ayatollah Ruhollah Khomeini's approach is instructive in reconciling divergent interests. After declaring that Islam has no frontiers, Khomeini then sought to utilize religion to legitimize the new regime within the Iranian boundaries. Reference to Islamic traditions and perceptions of ideological commonality were also embedded within transnationalism and helped arouse broader support. Through existing religious links, the Iranian government were able to establish organizational networks in order to export their revolution. Hezbollah, the *Shi'ite* group in Lebanon supported by Iran, have sought to promote cross-sectarian unity between *Sunni* and *Shi'ite*. This is noticeable in the emphasis placed upon the liberation of Jerusalem and Palestine, factors introduced earlier by Khomeini to try to mobilize, declaring that 'Israel is a cancerous goiter that occupies the liver of the *umma*: Palestine'.[25]

A route from Islamic nation-state to transnational Islamic nation

When seeking to understand the militants' expansion into transnationalism, al-Zayyat's account of Zawahiri's transformation from leading Egyptian militant into a central figure within the wider movement is illustrative. Initially, Zawahiri considered the internal enemy to be the main source of confrontation, arguing 'fight those of the disbelievers who are close to you'.[26] In this, he and Islamic Jihad were not alone. Gerges (2005) examines *jihadis'* writings between the 1970s and early 1990s and found an overwhelming nationalist emphasis upon local affairs. Global issues and the Palestinian–Israeli conflict were neglected beyond the territories and Lebanon. Localized militants were vehemently opposed to American actions, Western values, its perceived global dominance and neo-colonialism. However, they felt that this was happening because of the collusion and/or weakness of secular Muslim leaders. If the leaders could be overthrown, then the relationship with the West would be transformed and societies would become Islamic. This is not to claim that there were no attacks against the West or its representatives. As Gerges details, Egyptian militants killed tourists and the Algerian GIA attacked targets in France. But these were not part of a concerted campaign, were connected to localized issues and caused tremendous consternation within the respective militant groups and supporters. Zawahiri's participation in the International Islamic Front for Jihad on the Jews and Crusaders in 1998 indicated a philosophical and pragmatic break in his approach. The attack shifted from the Egyptian government to the West, and in particular the United States and Israel. On reflection, however, it was apparent by late 1997 that Zawahiri was shifting focus, emphasized by the title of an article published at that time 'Muslim *Umma,* Unite in Your *Jihad* on America'.

A number of reasons have been provided for Zawahiri's transformation. These include the failure of violence to undermine the Egyptian government, widespread arrests and detention of members and supporters which had weakened the militants, financial shortages, internal divisions, state infiltration and closer relations with bin Laden which had originated in the war against the Soviet Union. Zawahiri explains in *Knights under the Prophet's Banner* that following the victory in Afghanistan against the Soviet Union, expectations were high that *jihadis* would be able to mobilize the 'masses' to overthrow corrupt government. However, across Muslim nation-states like Algeria, Egypt, Indonesia and Saudi Arabia, governments remained firmly established and a fundamental shift in strategy was required, namely shifting attention to the 'far enemy'. As the militant Kemal informed Gerges (2006: 114) 'Islamists overestimated their real strength and felt overconfident. ... They miscalculated'. Therefore, failure against one target led to a redirecting of attentions to a different enemy that had long been hated by militants and now became the principle focus of attack. By attacking the United States, Israel and the West generally, it was felt that co-religionists across the *umma* would rally to their support. Through the allegiance with bin Laden, al-Zayyat (2004) suggests that Zawahiri and Islamic Jihad members were able to attain sanctuary and new credibility while retaining the capability of attacking Egyptian targets. In other words, a multitude of largely pragmatic factors resulted in the change in approach.

Nations within the 'Islamic nation'

Today there is contradictory evidence about how extensive transnationalism actually is. For example, despite the strong association of Somalia and Sudan with al-Qa'ida, Seeseman (2006) argues that militants in these countries seek to deliver local and national agendas that aim to purify social relations and politicize religion. Few people become actively engaged in international terrorism. Hamas' strategic targets are localized, overwhelmingly associated with Israel and selected specifically for the purposes of national liberation. By comparison, transnationalists associated with al-Qa'ida are considered to be rootless, aiming to implement the *shari'ah* across Muslim communities but without a specific locality to fight (and die for in the case of Palestinian and Iranian 'martyrs') and a less clearly defined enemy.

Transnational militants argue against national territorial allegiance exemplified by al-Zarqawi's claim that 'I am global, no land is my country'.[27] The challenge to geographical boundaries is accompanied by religious transnationalism. As one *jihadist* told Gerges (2005: 63), 'we realized we were a nation [*umma*] that had a distinguished place among nations. Otherwise what would make me leave Saudi Arabia – and I am of Yemeni origin – to go and fight in Bosnia'. Yet, even within the actions of the most prominent figures associated with al-Qa'ida, there are discrepancies. bin Laden's roots in Saudi Arabia and the strong association of al-Qa'ida with other Saudi members, exemplified by fifteen of the nineteen September 2001 attackers originating from the kingdom, appear at odds with the transnational approach. Similarly, although pronouncements associated with al-Qa'ida cover a range of issues in different locations, the Saudi regime attracts a disproportionate amount of attention.[28] As Gerges (2006) remarked, many of those located in the Afghan camps on behalf of al-Qa'ida had already internalized nationalist sentiments. These resulted in suspicion and resentment about the numerical dominance of Egyptians[29] within the inner circle and led to bin Laden broadening the leadership's geographical representation. Steinberg (2005) comments on the approach that transnational groups like Zarqawi's former network in Iraq must adopt to incorporate actions that appeal to potential multinational members. Recruitment is easier if the group includes targeted regimes in potential members' home countries. Zarqawi himself was a good example of this, retaining an active interest in Jordanian affairs and seemingly heavily involved in the 2005 suicide bombings in Amman. Roy (2004: 62) encapsulates the tensions within militancy generally, and al-Qa'ida in particular, when stating 'despite their claim to be supranational, most Islamist movements have been shaped by national particularities. Sooner or later they tend to express national interests, even under the pretext of Islamist ideology.'

Trans/national allegiance and sacrifice

A central question raised by Anderson relates to the extent of the attachment that people felt for the imagined communities that meant they would be willing to die for it. For Anderson, this is the outcome of the perceptions of the purity and inherent goodness that people feel for the nation. In other words, they possess a strong conviction in the virtue of the nation and would sacrifice themselves for the wider entity. In this sense, Anderson (2006 [1991]) compares this faith akin to religious imaginings, although he failed subsequently to develop these similarities, as Smith (2003) points out. For Smith, individual and collective sacrifice is essential to understanding nationalist mobilization. Sacrifices for the nation become part of common memory, remembered and celebrated, but Smith suggests this is not unique to modernity. Throughout history people have died for broader communities, with their actions immortalized. In regions that were not nations according to contemporary definitions, holy places became the destination for pilgrimages, like the Wailing Wall for Jews and Mecca for Muslims, fostering solidarity and cultural consciousness. Defeat and sacrifice is particularly emotive for believers and is widely commemorated on particular dates and at certain locations. The crucifixion of Jesus, fall of Jerusalem and battle of Karbala where Hussein, the prophet's grandson, was killed continue to resonate throughout religious sentiments and reinforce loyalties. Clearly, nationalism not only relies on sacrifice but also on the use of violence on its behalf. Hassner (2005) notes that nation-states have sought to monopolize violence and implemented processes designed at internal pacification. People are therefore only encouraged to commit acts of violence on behalf of the nation, frequently through interstate war. And as McCrone (1998) notes, warfare between 1870 and the First World War was instrumental in the formation of national consciousness within Europe. For militant Muslims, Islam 'legitimises sacred death in the service of the community or umma by making it part of the fabric of a war that enjoys religious legitimacy, namely *jihad*' (Khosrokhavar 2005: 52). A recent notable example of this link between sacrifice and religious nationalism can be found in the Iran–Iraq war (1980–8). At the commencement of the conflict, Khomeini utilized religious discourse and the significance of sacrifice within *Shi'ism* stemming from the martyrdom of Hussein, in a massive mobilization of the population to defend the Iranian nation. This is exemplified in Khomeini's claim that 'the more people die for our cause, the stronger we become'. Reuter (2004: 34) describes the sounds of the 'human waves' of the Iranian army, shouting 'Ya Karbala! Ya Hussein! Ya Khomeini!' as they walked towards machine guns and death. The willingness, even desire, of the largely youthful recruits to die in the cause of Iran had a huge symbolic significance both within the country and the opposing Iraqi army. Similar attitudes on a much smaller scale were also noticeable within the protests against the Shah before the revolution, when unarmed demonstrators would confront armed military personnel resulting in the 'martyrdom' of many.

Conclusion

Despite the obvious disagreements within the sociology of nationalism, there is a general consensus that nationalism emphasizes similarity, and by implication, difference. Islamic nationalism and/or transnationalism discourse provides a sense of identity around an 'imagined community' for supporters that places emphasis upon shared similarity with others. These loyalties are very much products of their time, associated with processes of modernization, state formation and globalization that have contributed to closer allegiances within and across geographical regions. However, as Smith would point out, these relationships are built upon religious values, symbols, perceptions of historical events and interplay between the past and present which help provide the legitimacy for religious nationalism today. Within nationalist struggles, contested territories frequently share religious perceptions of sacred space. The collective loyalties that are prominent today within militant Islam are partly a consequence of recent developments within societies, international relations and processes of globalization. But they are also the outcome of long-term processes that can be traced to the heroes, sacrifices and purity of the 'Golden Age' and the immemorial qualities of the 'nation' that in turn provide the 'maps' for the road to national destiny and 'moralities'.[30]

Today, the struggle over strategy remains deeply divisive within the militant movement culminating, Gerges (2005) argues, in a civil war within *jihadism* between transnationalists and religious nationalists who have considerable numerical supremacy. For the former, the failure of the latter proved the need for broadening the attack. But for the latter, the actions of the former are self-defeating, proving detrimental to militancy generally and localized struggles specifically. Certainly the conflict is noticeable within oral and written communications, with components of both strategies vehemently denouncing the other through speeches, Web sites, books, journals and pamphlets. Groups like al-Jama'a have been vitriolic in their statements about the transnationalists' misinterpretations and distortions of Islamic texts. Gerges' (2005: 229) study of *jihadis* led him to conclude that 'there is a general realignment within the jihadist current against, not in favour of, Al Qaeda and global jihad'. Equally, groups associated with al-Qa'ida are bitterly critical of the nationalist focus and in particular alliances with 'near' enemies. For example, Al-Zawahiri has strongly denounced Hamas signing the Mecca agreement, an act which he suggests shows a 'loss of leadership' and the fact that the group has 'sunk in the swamp of surrender', joining 'Sadat's [procession] of humiliation and capitulation ... ' and of 'abandoning not only the [Islamic] land but, more importantly, shari'a law – and all for the sake of securing a place in the Palestinian government' (Middle East Media Research Institute 2007).

Considerable disagreement within the militant movement about what constitutes the essence of nation and nationalism raises issues about where Islamic government/s should control and which groups and symbols are legitimate targets towards achieving those ends. A range of Islamic sources is utilized to try to support opposing viewpoints. The picture is further blurred by the range of actions that are undertaken that support both national and transnational objectives and, conversely, the extent of sectarian attacks between Muslim groups. By implication, emphasis upon similarities as the basis for collective solidarity excludes the different 'other', people, groups and 'nations' that do not possess the requisite characteristics. This process is also accompanied by explicit denunciation of the 'other', whether Jews,

Christians, Hindus, people from the West or even moderate Muslims and other denominations. Yet this behaviour is consistent with nations and competitive nationalism and shares similarities with the earlier involvement of Islam in struggles against colonial control.

The territorial demands of Muslim groups seeking independence are easier to understand according to Western precepts. Religion and nationalism are integral to struggles against 'others' in the pursuit of freedom and territory. Groups associated with al-Qa'ida are more difficult. They need to be considered as part of a transnational movement that aims to utilize the *umma* concept and unite Muslims around the world in their struggle against the West and localized associates. Militant transnationalism has been formed through broader processes of global communications and improved and more comprehensive education systems, often sponsored by secular nation-states. These have contributed to Muslims being more cognizant about Islam and militant interpretations and national and global events that these perceptions draw upon. Exposure to the concept of the *umma*, and supranational communities within the West and Muslim societies, provide a framework for behaviour and help to provide security and sense of purpose and collective identity that contributes towards greater empathy for Muslims in (other) troubled parts of the world. In these circumstances, where local nation-states are seen to be failing, secular nationalism is not firmly embedded and international systems appear overwhelmingly oppositional, many people are attracted by transnational militant Islam and the idea of a superstate and associated collective identities. Ultimately this transnational conflict is driven by a desire to replace Western military, political and cultural influences in Muslim territories with Islamic tenets based upon a synthesis of contemporary and historical discourse, images and symbols. The discussion connects into an 'imagined community' and is inspired by the 'Golden Age' of Muhammed and the early caliphs. In a number of ways, this transnationalism is similar to more 'conventional' forms of nationalism and the greater application of theories and concepts from the study of nationalism may help to further enhance levels of understanding about the phenomenon. The interrelationships between secular and religious, national and transnational processes are further explored in Chapter 4 through the adaptation of Max Weber's concept of social closure.

4 Social closure and *takfir*

The interrelationship between secular and militant 'switchmen'

Introduction

In this chapter, it is argued that Weber's usage of the concept of social closure can make a valuable contribution to enhancing our understanding about the processes that result in the formation and reinforcement of distinct secular and militant Islamic groups. The origins of the respective forms of closure and interrelationships between methods of exclusion and usurpation involving national and Western governments and militant groups are examined. Particular attention is placed upon processes of secularization, especially the role of education, that have contributed, ironically, to the contemporary resurgence of militancy and the adaptation of Islamic concepts like *tawhid, takfir* and *jahiliyya* as codes of closure.

The concept of social closure is commonly associated with Max Weber. Yet, although Weber introduced the concept, it was arguably underdeveloped. For Weber, social closure is a process through which social groups sought to maintain and enhance their position by excluding others from access to particular rewards and privileges. Certain social or physical characteristics, which other groups possessed, would be singled out as the basis for boundary closures. Virtually any feature identifiable within a group could be chosen as the criterion for exclusion, including race, religion and social origin. The process of exclusion is designed to ensure 'the monopolisation of specific, usually economic opportunities. This monopolisation is directed against competitors who share some positive or negative characteristics; its purpose is always the closure of social and economic opportunities to outsiders' (Weber 1978: 342).

In traditional societies, Weber argues closure was based upon descent and lineage and was used to retain and reinforce resources across generations. By comparison, systems within modern societies appeared to be more egalitarian, with educational qualifications determining access to positions of power. This apparently more open system was nearly as effective as traditional methods of exclusion. The modern methods denied the majority of the population participation in power because they did not possess the necessary qualifications. Ownership of qualifications therefore became as important as the possession of property. According to Weber, common identification can become the source of group closure and the monopolization of goods, qualifications and skills. Social class became the main cleavage in society, legitimized by inclusion and exclusion and orientated around perceptions of egalitarianism. Crucially, for this study, Weber explained that group status closure could occur outside the market situation and it is this acknowledgement that will be further explored for militant Muslims. Through the application of an ideal type of 'status groups', Weber was also able to extend the rules of domination and exclusion to include cultural and social facets. These characteristics are based upon a shared quality. A claim to social esteem and honour and 'above all else a specific *style of life* is expected from all those who wish to belong to the circle' (Weber 1978: 932). Relations within these groups will vary according to the extent that commonalities are shared, whether the relations are 'communal', based upon affectual, emotional or traditional bases, or 'associative', based upon rational judgement and assessment of individual interests. The length of time in which status-driven characteristics become embedded within the group are also instrumental in the intensity of the association. Race, ethnicity, religion, sex and credentials could all provide the basis for status and subsequently closure. However, Weber's application of social closure is not without criticism and there have been a number of attempts to apply and extend the concept's applicability.

Surprisingly in light of the attention Weber places elsewhere, the role of the state in the closure process is understated. As Parkin (1982) commented, Weber seemed to perceive the struggles and conflicts associated with closure to be occurring within civil society. Different status groups included and excluded according to their experiences in the market-place, which could be seen to be determined by (non) ownership of property and qualifications. The role of the state in legalizing and enforcing these monopolies is acknowledged by Weber but not explained.

Parkin also challenges Weber's argument that groups exclude others according to any characteristic or attribute that could be most easily seized upon to achieve exclusion. On the contrary, Parkin (1982: 102) suggests, the grounds for closure had already been defined by the state: 'The communities singled out for exclusion – blacks, Catholics, Jews or other minorities – are curtailed by the forces of law and order. Such groups become the target for exclusionary practices precisely because their capacity to resist has been undermined by the state powers.' The exclusion of these groups can often be linked to colonialism or forced migration and the deliberate denial of their social and political rights by the state according to lineage, race, religion or gender and so on, and which subsequently become the basis for exclusion by dominant groups. Equally, however, it is important to avoid adopting an overly structured approach. Blau (1977) and West and Zimmerman (1987) highlight how exclusion also needs to be examined within the context of everyday interaction and the use of language, symbols, control and violence.

Finally Murphy (1988: 66) challenges Weber's (and Parkin's) overemphasis upon education in accessing the elite and concomitant neglect of the market and property classes in determining 'the necessity, value and nature of the credentials required for positions, thus structuring the very nature of credentialed groups.'

Closure beyond Weber

Since Weber, the concept of social closure has been underutilized. Today, a cursory glance at indices within many of the authoritative texts about Weber finds the continuing neglect of the concept. This has been partly rectified by a number of studies, particularly Frank Parkin and Raymond Murphy who have developed social closure to help explain social formations and processes. The majority of the studies have tended to apply social closure to the development of the ruling class, employment processes associated with occupational practice and labour markets (Brown 2000; Kreckel 1980; MacDonald 1985) and race and sex discriminatory practices (Roscigno *et al.* 2007). Parkin (1974, 1979) sought to refine and enlarge upon Weber's usage. By concentrating on the interaction between class stratification with other forms of social division like gender, race and religion, Parkin (1974: 4) aimed 'to extend the notion of closure to encompass other forms of social action designed to maximize collective claims to rewards and opportunities'. Drawing upon Weber's (1978) acknowledgement that people may react against the class structure through acts of both irrational protest and rational association, Parkin includes the social reactions of the excluded within his bi-polar model based upon exclusion and solidarism.

Parkin (1974: 5) explains the two forms. Exclusion is 'a form of closure that stabilizes the stratification order, solidarism is one that contains a potential challenge to the prevailing system of distribution through the threat of usurpation'. Therefore, 'modes of closure can be thought of as a different means of mobilizing power for purposes of staking claims to resources and opportunities'. But without state support, the 'usurpers' have to mobilize opposition if they are to be successful in their range of goals, which Parkin (1974: 10) suggests range from 'marginal redistribution to total dispossession'. The excluded are also subdivided according to what Parkin refers to as 'dual closure'. Some intermediate groups are both denied opportunities and resources while establishing practices that prevent those in different subordinate positions from progressing at their expense. Examples include the White working class who have prevented Blacks from benefiting from their collective resources and the exclusion of the Catholic working classes from particular industries and occupations by Protestants in Northern Ireland.

The distinctions between exclusion and solidarism are not without criticism. Murphy (1988) argues that both practices are seeking to exclude other groups from the available resources and involve monopolistic practices. Therefore, the differentiation between the two concepts is less clear-cut, with both processes primarily being modes of exclusion with usurpation a subtype for the intermediate groups.

The dual closure relationship is also open to criticism from Murphy. He points out that contrary to Parkin's supposition, intermediate groups do not necessarily determine the exclusionary criteria. Citing examples from the labour market and the apparent segmentation around race, gender and religion, Murphy argues that the dominant class has the power to impose the rules of closure.

Through the identification of differences between exclusion practices, Parkin distinguished between individualist and collectivist forms of exclusion. Collectivist exclusion is based upon communal characteristics which are used as the basis for determining the transmission of advantage to a group or groups while simultaneously being responsible for other groups' exclusion, for example, gender, race, religion and lineage. Individualist monopolization is based upon protecting advantages through concepts like achievement and credentialism (Collins 1979; Bourdieu and Passeron 1977). Access to rewards and privileges is increasingly achieved through the acquisition of qualifications which, Parkin (1974, 1979) suggests, is not as effective in restricting access. In modern societies, rules of exclusion have shifted from collectivist to individualist and represent the triumph of the bourgeois in the nineteenth century against the lineage practices of the previously dominant aristocracy. Consequently, exclusionary power does not emanate from one source, like ownership and the means of production for Marxists. Instead, Parkin argues attention must also be placed upon credentials which provide the basis for monopoly and exclusion. Yet, this stress upon credentialism has led, as Murphy (1988) points out, to the impact being overstated at the expense of property which retains an integral role in the transmission of resources. For Murphy, this stems from Parkin confusing the rules of exclusion, according to individual and collectivist criteria, with the means of power, for example, through production, destruction and so on. This led Parkin to neglect differences 'between the rules of exclusion as well as obscuring their interrelationships' (Murphy 1988: 67).

Finally, Parkin concentrated upon processes within the 'developed world' where considerable importance is undeniably placed upon both credentialism and property. However, the prominence of such individualist criteria is less noticeable within other parts of the world where collectivist rules remain in place and people are denied access to Western resources on the grounds of their place of birth. And the overwhelming majority of people born outside the West remain, through Western processes of closure, excluded from its values, resources and opportunities. However, it would be a mistake to support Murphy's (1988) claim that the 'Third World poor' want to become incorporated into Western societies and cultures. Instead, as the analysis of global anti-Americanism indicates, many people are actively imposing closure mechanisms against Western cultures, including most notably militant Muslims.

Murphy's social closure

Raymond Murphy's exploration of the social closure concept is probably the most extensive. He analyses both market monopolization (by property holders) and other forms through the power and opportunities held by status groups. For Murphy (1988: 18–19), 'at the root of closure theory is the perception of the parallel between the processes of monopolisation, such as those based upon race, ethnicity, sex, religion, the Communist Party, credentials and knowledge'. Social closure is therefore about the processes of monopolization and exclusion in the pursuit of power and the study of domination and the responsive struggle it provokes. Dominance is achieved through mechanisms of power and control that are located within the rules of exclusion. People belong to a range of groups which contribute to a multitude of experiences of both dominance and exclusion according to gender, race, property and religion; relationships that fracture stronger associations among particular excluded groups.

The 'switchmen'

In developing a more extensive theory of closure, Murphy incorporates a range of Weber's other important sociological contributions, including one of the most famous concepts, that of the switchmen.

'Not ideas, but material and ideal interests, directly govern men's conduct. Yet frequently the "world images" that have been created by "ideas" have, like switchmen, determined the tracks along which action has been pushed by the dynamic of interest' (Weber 1958: 280). Murphy (1988: 1) interprets the tracks as 'none other than codes of social closure: formal and informal, overt and covert rules governing practices of monopolisation and exclusion'. These codes include capitalism, state socialism, patriarchy, racism, religious beliefs and meritocracy. All are forms of monopolization that seek to exclude other groups from available resources and privileges. Contradictions begin to develop when the exclusionary codes become visible, leading to ideas forming which create contradictory 'world images' and ultimately opposing rules of exclusion or tracks. Particular ideas can create certain world images which result in specific forms of closure. The dynamic of interest then drives the determined action along the tracks, seeking to install the new world image. For Murphy (1988: 4), this is 'Weber's dialectic of material interests and ideas, the dialectic of constraint and creativity'. Social closure is therefore a dynamic, conflictual process seeking to maintain or enhance groups' shares of power and domination. Because rules of closure invariably create contradictions leading to changes, there will be reactions against perceived injustices and the rules of exclusion will shift.

Smith (2003: 259) has also identified the impact of switchmen within forms of nationalism. Although arguing that older belief systems cannot give rise to nationalist movements, he suggests they provide resources and images that nationalists can utilize for attracting support. They also 'frequently act as switchmen of the tracks along which the material and ideal interests of those who seek to create nations push through their objectivities – and, we may add, as the grounds of popular mobilization to those ends.'

Ranking the rules of closure

A common deficiency that Murphy finds in the work of Weber, Parkin and also Randall Collins' (1979) credentialism is their failure to adequately evaluate the structure of rules of closure or establish the primacy of some rules over others. They have identified domination relationships via particular exclusion rules, for example, property, race, gender and religion and the ensuing reactionary struggles which Murphy (1988: 80) terms 'first order structural relationships of closure'. But relationships at a second-order level of structural association have been neglected. Believing this to be a central weakness within the closure framework, Murphy sought to extend his conceptual and methodological framework to incorporate investigation between codes of closure and to analyse their relative importance.

In order to achieve this, Murphy developed three main types of exclusion: *Principal* which examined closure rules supported by the state's legal and military apparatus orientated around private property; *Derivative* forms which were rules that enabled the monopolization of societal opportunities but were dependent upon the principal form, for example, credentialism, race and religion; and *Contingent* codes that were based upon skills and attributes which are not directly controlled by the principal forms but which are contingent upon them. Again gender and credentials are included.

An accompanying three-fold classification of exclusion structures was devised. First are tandem structures with derivative and contingent sets of rules that depend upon one principal rule found within capitalist and state socialist systems. Second, dual or paired structures provide two relatively complementary sets of rules, for example, the pairing of apartheid and property in South Africa. Third is the polar structure which is based upon two principal opposing sets of exclusion codes. This is best exemplified by the global opposition of structures based upon private property and communism. Conflict is 'characterised by the paradoxical dependence of each of the principal forms of closure upon the opposition of, and usurpation of, usurpation by, the other' (Murphy 1988: 75).

Strategies of closure generate conflict, with the excluded, as Parkin identified, involved in reactive usurpatory action. Murphy develops a further distinction between inclusionary and revolutionary usurpation. In the former, groups seek incorporation within the existing system, promoting a shift from collectivist to individual processes of inclusion and exclusion. Revolutionary forms aim to change the structures of positions in society from which they are excluded and some demand change to state structures.

Within these closure processes, Murphy argues an excluded aggregate will emerge, formed around a consciousness that is based upon the same structural experience. These experiences act like a centripetal force, pushing people together. However, in a point that is used to criticise Marxists, Murphy argues that simultaneously the aggregate is also fractured by a centrifugal force, namely members' other structural relationships. Thus, different experiences within the aggregate of other forms of exclusion weaken group unity and frequently prevent a unified, stronger challenge to the rules of exclusion. Using the example of the women's movement, Murphy points out that although the movement was united by experiences of exclusion on the grounds of gender, other experiences related to class, race, credentials, religion and ethnicity were the source of division. By bringing in these cross-cutting experiences, Murphy extends the focus of closure theory and in detailing aggregates' organizational forms incorporates other Weberian concepts; status group, communal and associative relationships.

1   Status group – The concept of the status group was developed by Weber (1978: 932) in his analysis of the social and cultural composition of groups and their relationship with domination and exclusion. In the process, he distinguished between class and status as separate dimensions of stratification. The former is defined by market position and the latter is derived from aspects outside the market and revolves around lifestyles, consumption, taste and esteem. Status groups, Weber believed, 'may be connected with any quality shared by a plurality ... [and which] is normally expressed by the fact that above all else a specific 'style of life' is expected from all those who wish to belong to the circle'. They are often amorphous and make an affective claim to social esteem and social honour. Examples include groups based upon race, religion, gender and ethnicity.

Typically, Weber's definition is an ideal type. Actual status groups ranged from tight-knit communities based upon a common lifestyle and social esteem, and groups who base associations on shared lifestyles and esteem, to loosely connected, unorganized groups who will also share a particular lifestyle and social esteem. Status group monopolies were, Weber believed, in conflict with property monopolies, with the latter appearing dominant under particular conditions. Market competition was considered to be undermining a number of monopolies including race, religion and gender contributing to gradual secularization.

2   Communal relationships – These relationships occur if 'the orienta-
     tion of social action ... is based on a subjective feeling of the parties,
     whether affectual or traditional, that they belong together. ...
     Communal relationships may rest on various types of affectual, emo-
     tional or traditional bases' (Weber 1978: 40–1). Examples include the
     family, religious brotherhood, a national community, an erotic rela-
     tionship and a military unit.

3   Associative relationships – These relationships refer to social action that

> rests on a rationally motivated adjustment of interests or a simi-
> larly motivated agreement, whether the basis of rational judge-
> ment be absolute values or reasons of expediency ... The purest
> cases of associative relationships are ... the purely voluntary
> association based on self-interest, a case of agreement as to the
> long-run course of action orientated purely to the promotion of
> specific ulterior interests, economic or other, of its members; the
> voluntary association of individuals motivated by an adherence
> to a set of common absolute values, for example, the rational
> sect, insofar as it does not cultivate emotional and affective inter-
> ests, but seeks only to serve a cause
>
> (Weber 1978: 40–1).

Rationalization of closure

For Weber, rationality revolved around structural and individual levels. At the
upper level, there is formal rationality which is based upon the calculation of
means and procedures. Alongside this, substantive rationality exists which is
principally the evaluated value of results. By comparison, formal rationality
dominates the substantive and its advance has led to the replacement of
value-based action by instrumental individual-based action and magical
beliefs have been seriously undermined. Adapting Weber's rationalization
thesis, Murphy relates the development of formal rationalization to the displacement of collectivist by individualist exclusionary criteria. Basing exclusion on individual achievement was seen to rationalize the process compared
with the increasingly discredited collectivist criteria. Murphy argues that
processes of exclusion changed to connect into processes of rationalization
and legitimize intergenerational inequalities. People were now selected
according to skills and attributes, with exclusion depersonalized and objectified, and not social factors like gender, race and religion.

The process of formal rationalization of closure and domination can,
Murphy suggests, be observed in state apparatus like legal, educational
and military spheres. This formal rationalization has enabled states to
justify and legitimate internal domination through monopolization of
exclusion at local, national and, in some instances, international levels.

The principal rationalized rules of monopolization and exclusion in the pursuit of mastery of nature and other people are based upon private property in the market and rules of bureaucracy. However,

> the rational pursuit of mastery and control is ... an elusive process in which rationality, elimination of contradiction, control and predictability paradoxically result in irrationality, contradiction, unpredictability, and lack of control. This could be called the 'uncertainty principle' of formal rationalisation.
>
> (Murphy 1988: 251)

In other words, claims for the legitimation of the system are based upon superior performance, but if this should be considered inferior then closure processes could be threatened. Additionally, the linkage between individual progression with performance can also cause tension and conflict if the contradiction with reality is noticed.

Summary: adapting closure

Despite claiming that 'closure theory brings about the social determination of exclusion and its social consequences', Murphy (1988: 47) concentrates upon economic criteria with other forms deemed secondary. Groups may be excluded according to social formations and react to the same social situations. Ultimately though Murphy is arguing that their exclusion is based upon the distribution of resources and subsequent reactions will always be motivated towards improving their share of resources. By suggesting that private ownership is the principal[1] rule of closure for both social class and status groups under contemporary conditions, Murphy overlooks the dispersal of power to include non property owners. In this he continues the Weberian tendency to neglect the role of religion as a contemporary source of identification and exclusion. For example, both environmentalist and Islamic movements propose alternative 'world images' that include economic matters, but as part of an overall package that also accords priority to political, cultural and social change. Within Muslim societies and communities, social class loyalties are often not instrumental within contemporary political divisions. MacDonald (1985: 541), despite concentrating upon occupational patterns, provides a useful definition that extends the applicability of the concept beyond materialism. For him, 'the essence of closure is the definition of membership at a particular point in time, and the setting of criteria for those who may join subsequently'. These rules of closure are not inevitably designed to protect or usurp material interests but can be based upon social, political or cultural criteria. Equally, as Brown (2000) identifies, closure theory has not placed enough attention on the social and economic consequences of exclusion nor upon the experiences of individuals and social groups. Brown (ibid: 639) also draws attention to the impact of globalization (of positional competition) upon the need to extend a conceptual framework between and within societies. Finally, with the partial exception of Murphy (1988), there is inadequate attention placed on the interrelationships between excluders and excluded and, in particular, the processes and experiences that result in individuals experiencing exclusion in isolation or becoming part of a group challenging the dominant discourse.

The evolution of the concept of social closure can therefore make a useful contribution to the study of the dynamics of conflict and, in particular the interwoven relationships between domination and usurpation. Within militant Islam, it is argued that these processes are informed through socialization in conditions that contribute to the 'uncertainty principle' which both undermines the dominant secularism and legitimizes Islamic usurpatory challenges.

Closure within Muslim societies

Across Muslim societies, the struggle for control is not restricted to the ownership of the means of production. Conflict is about the very essence of the state and society and is a struggle over the public and private spheres. For militant Muslims, this conflict can be traced to the *Qu'ran* and *hadiths* and the early period when Islamic communal and status groups were both prominent and dominant. To understand the origins of the different perspectives and rules of closure within and against militant Islam, it is important to outline briefly changes that have occurred throughout the formation of modern states and subsequent processes of modernization and internationalization.

Within Islam, demarcations between and within theological interpretations are drawn between Good and Evil, what is permitted and forbidden. For militants, the distinction is extended beyond private behaviour to incorporate cultural, economic and political behaviour. Status is attributed according to these parameters. Codes of closure result that seek to eradicate deviations from the word of Allah, exclude those who fail to attain the required standards of piety and purpose and accept people who emphasize ascetic discipline and theological purity. In this sense, militant Muslims seek to impose a particularly prescriptive style of life that both includes and isolates and was prominent, they believe, during the successful origins of the religion. The period when the implementation of these rules of closure was undermined is the source of considerable debate within militancy. And outside militancy, as Turner (1993: 51) observed, 'most scholars have recognised that the *Shari'a* was an ideal law which allowed a gap to emerge between ideal and practice'. Militants argue otherwise. Habeck (2006) suggests there are three main arguments, although it can be argued that these are ideal types that are not mutually exclusive and militants draw upon different aspects within the arguments. For some militants, the problem can be traced to the establishment of a hereditary Abbasid monarchy following the 'Golden Age' of Muhammed, the four righteous *Caliphs* and arguably their charismatic authority. The Abbasids introduced an unlawful system of government, creating their own rules rather than those implementing God-given laws.

The second period Habeck (2006) identifies is the abolition of the Ottoman *caliphate*[2] by the Turkish leader Mustafa Kemal Atatürk. The *caliphate* was considered to be the only universal authority for Islam, although it was not widely respected and at the time its dissolution did not cause widespread consternation (Toprak 1981; Vertigans 2003). Many militants since, including both Qutb and bin Laden, have drawn reference to the event, arguing that the role of the *caliph* was central to Islam. They argue that without the *caliphate* providing the source of unification and leadership, the religion became seriously weakened.

Finally, there is a popular perception that the loss of Muslim dignity and honour was the outcome of a deliberate attempt by 'unbelievers'. Falsehood and unbelief (*kufr*) has always existed. Since the time of Muhammad, the struggle with the *kufr* has concentrated upon Jews and Christians who have rejected the Truth. The crusades and colonization of Muslim regions and contemporary processes of Westernization, including the pervasive penetration by the media, are considered to be part of the attempt to undermine and ultimately eradicate Islam. And crucially American reactions and actions post September 2001, including the war in Afghanistan, invasion of Iraq and ongoing aggressive rhetoric against Iran and Syria, are viewed through this framework of understanding against a historical backdrop of crusades, colonialism and the establishment of Israel on Islamic territory. Marranci (2006) explains how the West is thought to be spreading *jahiliyya* (ignorance) weakening collective Islamic identity and which in turn contributes to feelings of anti-Semitism and anti-Westernism discussed below. In other words, the problems that Muslims encounter in Muslim societies are due to external enemies and, for those living in the West, the foes are internal.

Secular rules of closure

Although there is clear disagreement within militancy about the historical origins of Islam's decline, there is common agreement that the formation of modern Muslim nation-states, and in particular, processes of secularization, has undermined Islamic institutions. Theological influence was formally excluded based upon criteria established by governments causing, it is believed, immense damage to faith and the *umma* generally. Islam in the post-independence era, and even before in the case of Egypt (Gershoni and Jankowski 1987), was devalued, for a variety of reasons. In particular, Islam was considered to be an obstacle to modernization, capitalist development and industrialization. The universalism of religion meant that it was viewed as being unhelpful in strengthening the specificity of the particular nationalism being developed. Across Muslim societies, administrative and legal systems were introduced based upon Western processes of rationalization and domination. Islam was excluded through formal rationalization, secular-derived rules of closure and the emergence of associative relationships. Religion became concentrated within the sphere of individual commitment. Therefore, the extent to which individual Islamic values impinged on behaviour and contradicted the secular nature of the state became a potential source of exclusion. Governments placed Islam under specific departments and were considered to be irreligious. Through processes of rationalization, attempts were made to transform what was frequently anti-colonial nationalism that had absorbed Islamic influences into the basis for modern nation-states. Shaped to a large extent by the restrictions they were facing within the world system, these newly formed nations were heavily influenced by the previously dominant colonial principles, practices and methods, with many experiencing a history of tension between secular and religious identities. Despite the longevity of secularization, to varying degrees these attempts have failed and arguably were rarely implemented in the Western manner. Lapidus (2002) explores the changes instigated by the Dutch and British in Southeast Asia which resulted in conflict between supporters and opponents of secularization. Nor were these tensions restricted to Muslim areas. Chatterjee (1993) points out that India under Nehru's government sought to shift Hindu consciousness to rationality and reason. Religious institutions continued to provide spiritual and social services including education and cultural activities in regions beyond the modernizing core. Yet, conversely, the surge of militancy appears to have gained momentum at a time when secularization is less oppressive and Islam has been encouraged to enhance religiosity and address social and cultural concerns. For example, when Malaysia faced growing Muslim political and student activism, the government co-opted the activists during the 1980s through the positive encouragement of Islamic institutions and greater participation within politics and state bureaucracy (Rubenstein 2002) and by implication the exclusion of Chinese and Hindu nationals.

However, this encouragement of religion has also had an undesired political impact across the different nations. Three very different examples Turkey, Pakistan and Saudi Arabia are illustrative of government attempts to implement rules of closure while seeking to utilize Islam for their own ends. Arguably the latter aim has hindered, even prevented, the former.

Following the end of the Ottoman Empire, the most notable processes of secularization were initiated by Atatürk after the formation of the Turkish nation-state in 1923. These processes followed more tentative attempts at reform undertaken by the Ottomans as they sought in vain to protect their diminishing empire. After the formation of the Turkish republic, formal laws adapting German, Italian and Swiss codes were introduced, designed to ensure consistency and stability on which to develop the nation-state and to protect the rights of individuals. As part of the management of change, the sultanate and *caliphate* were abolished and the state controlled Islamic institutions, leaders and activities. New forms of associational relations were introduced which sought to expand citizenship and remove forms of discrimination.[3] Yet, despite the apparent openness of these relations, outsiders were excluded, and communal affinities associated with religion were isolated. Change was extended to the type of clothes people wore providing an easy method of establishing habits of 'taste'. New ways of domination and emphasis on a new Turkish pre-Islamic 'nationalism', banning of religious sects, *tarikats*, and Westernization that included the adaptation of a Latin-styled alphabet, meant that a distinct divide emerged between the ruling elite and the majority of the population who were excluded from power relations. Large sections were neither able to communicate with the elite nor to engage in the new dialogue as the republicans sought to create modern citizens (Berkes 1964; Lewis 1974; Vertigans 2003). Within industrial urban regions, the rationalist reforms transformed local communities and ways of thinking, imposing their own 'styles of life' and appearance. But as Karpat (1959: 271) remarked, 'villages and small towns ... continued to preserve their basic Islamic customs and traditions, and the cultural goals of secularism were only partly fulfilled'. Therefore, distinct 'styles of life' remained. With the introduction of democracy after the Second World War, rival parties were able to connect with and inflame religious sentiments amongst the excluded who had not been integrated into the modern nation-state. Islam became an electoral tool for attracting political support. The use of religion was not, however, restricted to electioneering. A range of governments throughout the history of the Republic, harking back even to the early period of Atatürk, have sought to utilize Islam to justify actions, legitimize policies and safeguard support. And religious supporters have been installed within important state institutions as part of the system of patronage employed within Turkey. The penetration by different ideological supporters and their vested interests, of course, conflicts with the Weberian hallmark of bureaucracy and the dominance of impersonal rules. In other words, the secular attempts at social closure have only been partially successful, partly because the nation-state continues to rely on religion for a range of functions. This is highlighted by Turkey being ruled by the democratically elected Justice Development Party, a mildly Islamic party whose actions are causing increasing consternation to the secular military and intelligentsia. The inner contradictions within Turkey are magnified within less secular nation-states, particularly in their approaches to education.

Both Saudi Arabia and Pakistan sought to incorporate religion within their political arrangements from the onset of the newly formed nation-states. Saudi Arabia was created in 1932 based upon its self-declared role of custodian of the holy places. By basing legitimacy on central components of Islam, the Saudi monarchy has created two central problems for development options, and ultimately its survival. First, the focus upon a transnational role and the significance of Islam beyond the country has resulted in Saudi citizens attaching primary allegiance to the religion and not to the nation-state. Devji (2005: 67) notes that conceptually this approach 'subordinates his country and its sovereignty to an Islamic universalism over which he [the King] has little if any control'. Saudi nationalism is consequently underdeveloped when compared with neighbouring states. And second, the emphasis upon the Islamic *umma* and widespread Wahhabi teachings across state institutions and civil society highlights, to the informed, the contradictions of the nation-state discourse at national and transnational levels. Namely, internationally Saudi Arabia as a geographical entity is an obstacle in the implementation of the *umma*. And nationally, the nation-state has failed to impose the *shari'ah* in a manner that is acceptable to most militants. Secular processes remain prominent and more radical forms of Islam are largely excluded across the political, legal and public educational institutions. In other words, the Saudi government is promoting values and principles that undermine its close relationships with Western nation-states and multinational companies and ultimately its own existence. Therefore, the Saudi government is contributing to the formation and reinforcement of the rules of closure that are being used against it.[4]

Pakistan, formed in 1948, lacked Saudi Arabia's association with the history of Islam. The traumatic period prior to the partition of India and birth of Pakistan resulted in heightened religious consciousness and subsequently antagonism amongst Muslims and Hindus. With the Muslim population also divided by experiences, linguistics and cultural distinctions, Islam became the common source of collective identity to unite the populace and to provide the basis for national sovereignty. The *shari'ah* was to be the template for individual and collective behaviour. Since then the balance between secular and religious influences has varied, depending largely on the nature of governments. However, the concessions granted and explicit programmes of Islamification introduced during the period of control by General Zia ul-Haq (1977–88) reinforced the relationship between Islam and the nation-state and again contributed to rules of closure that challenged its own processes of exclusion.[5]

The role of education within Muslim societies

Within the overwhelming majority of newly created Muslim nation-states, education was integral to the formation of new national consciousness. The widespread introduction also had another consequence, namely that new forms of derivative and contingent codes of exclusion were implemented

which placed emphasis upon credentialism and the internalization of secular methods and values. Qualifications and other depersonalized characteristics became a standard way of establishing entry to organizations.
Individualist criteria therefore became more prominent and other, more
'traditional', collectivist allegiances associated with lineage and ethnic
group diminished in importance, although in many instances familial and
political ties retained some significance. As Parkin (1982) points out in his
critique of Weber, these rules for closure are grounded in state policies.
Crucially individuals for whom Islam provided a specific style of life, and
who were part of a status group or communal relationship under Weber's
classification, were increasingly isolated from political influence, as secular values, institutions and ideologues became dominant. Governments
sought to implement secular criteria that needed to be internalized with
particular levels of competence achieved and measured through qualifications. These systems of learning would deliver graduates capable of undertaking the required roles that would enable the nation-state to develop. And
at the level of the hidden curriculum, they would contribute to the development of modern, rational identities. The internalization of these forms of
knowledge became central to individual progression. McCrone (1998: 47)
adds that the main purpose of schooling was to 'imbue pupils with the new
patriotism. ... This can be seen in the mobilisation of "national" history,
geography and the "national curriculum".' However, in many Muslim societies this outcome has been far from universal. The continuing, arguably
increasing, influence of religion can be noticed within a range of national
school curricula. Unsurprisingly, Islam is prominent in schools across
countries like Iran, Pakistan and Saudi Arabia, and Judaism can be widely
observed within Israel. But in societies that are generally considered to be
secular, like India, Indonesia and Turkey, government commitment to religious teaching, and its broader appeal, has grown. Smith (2003) identified
that within these settings, religion is used to help define and underpin ideas
and policies and reinforce national loyalties. In some respects, the intentions, if not necessarily the outcomes, connect with Gellner's (1983) view
that cultural homogenization occurs as schools are introduced across territories teaching the dominant language and emphasizing national loyalties.

The impact of educational schemes in Muslim societies is mixed.
Education is paradoxically instrumental both in the formation of secular
and Islamic nationalism. This is at least partly because the purely secular
curricula associated with leaders like Atatürk were rarely implemented.
Instead, governments sought to utilize religion within education as a
means of addressing concerns over *anomie,* to offset perceived threats
from other ideologies and to gain political support (Ahmad 1977; Heper
1985; Vertigans 2003). Despite their rhetoric, the secularists continued to
rely on Islam for a variety of functions within their respective nation-
states. In Turkey, schools and universities were key components of a

modernization scheme designed to 'Turkicize' the people, their language and their culture (Kazamias 1966: 148) as a 'vehicle for national integration, economic regeneration and modernization' (Williamson 1987: 11). Certainly there has been a tremendous increase in the number of places at learning institutions. However, since the 1970s, for the pragmatic reasons explained above, there has also been an even greater rise in numbers of religious schools and the prominence of Islam within national syllabi. Other countries also sought to implement secular education but gradually became infiltrated by a religious curriculum. And similar to happenings across West Africa from the 1970s and from 1990 in Indonesia, governments declared religion to be an integral part of national identity and enhanced processes of Islamification (Lapidus 2002). But as Boukhars (2005) comments with regard to Mauritania, these policies contribute to a strong impetus for the growth of religious and political activism that governments struggle to control.

When nationalism decreased in popularity within Muslim nation-states, religious influence was utilized across social relationships to provide legitimacy for the government, which led to the greater and unchallenged penetration of militancy within schools. ICG (2004a) argues that the strict guidelines issued by the Salafi movement and emphasis upon a supra-national community offer migrants, both within Muslim countries and to the West, a framework for behaviour and help to provide security and a sense of purpose and collective identity that contributes towards greater empathy for Muslims in other troubled parts of the world. Certainly the nature of Islam embedded within state institutions is not acceptable to militants nor is the religious component within school curricula sufficiently rigorous or radical. However, the enhanced learning opportunities and religious curricula have enabled more Islamic views to develop and more militant Muslims to attain the credentials required to succeed under rational criteria. The lack of subsequent opportunities or their denial due to a social characteristic, namely the individual's religious interpretation, often highlights the inconsistencies and contradictions within rationalization principles and further delegitimizes the associated adapted secular processes. Conversely, militants who attain influential positions following graduation can utilize these posts to work towards enhancing radical discourse.

In Egypt and across the Middle East, the Muslim Brotherhood, Jamaat-e-Islami in South Asia and the more extreme Jemaah Islamiyah across Southeast Asia have sought to use education as a means of recruitment and of transforming individual conduct and social activism. In evening and Friday classes, clubs and summer camps, communal activities like prayer and fasting are practised, enforcing collective consciousness through common activities. *Da'wa* is propagated and the purity of devout Muslims and corruption of 'others' stressed. Education is therefore viewed by militants as 'a means for purifying faith, but also as a lever for activism in the service of Islam and the community' (Hatina 2006: 195). The violet off-shoots of the Muslim Brotherhood and arguably Jamaat-e-Islami and even Jemaah Islamiyah are the consequence of these rules of exclusion being applied in circumstances that can be seen to legitimize their imposition towards an alternative society that is more implicit within the peaceful discourse of much taught militancy. In other words, to bring about funda-mental change requires more than education, a strategy of violence must be implemented alongside proselytising and indeed for some militants, *jihad* as a method of *da'wa* must be given precedence (Hatina 2006).

Attempts to utilize Islam, and in particular, government efforts to incor-porate religion and leaders who have sought to promote their own reli-giosity, contribute to different types of problems. For example, Sadat's self-proclaimed image as the 'pious president' and his programme of greater incorporation of Islamic scholars and institutions within govern-ment did not ultimately diminish militant criticism, indeed the false hopes he created contributed to widespread dissent and disillusionment. As a leading Egyptian militant informed Gerges (2006), Sadat's most unfor-givable sin had been when he reneged on the promise to install the *shar-i'ah*. But conversely, the same respondent stated,

> thanks to Sadat, a new healthy Islamic generation was born unfet-tered and unscarred by persecution and torture like the previous gen-eration in the 1950s and 1960s. My generation had no complexes and no nightmares and we paved the way for all subsequent Islamic and jihadist waves in the Muslim world, not just Egypt.
>
> (Quoted in Gerges 2006: 47)

This point also hints at the contradictory impact that state repression has had in both preventing terrorism and mobilizing militant opposition. In other words, 'successful' counter-terrorism can ultimately be self-defeating. For example, Blom (2007: 74) explores the conflict in Kashmir and suggests that 'the growing efficiency of the Indian counter-insurrec-tion (which made imprisonment or death an increasingly likely end) was gradually driving the Jihadists to establish an ideological framework in which "martyrdom" was no longer simply an element of combat rhetoric, but its motivating force'. In Central Asia, the suppression of dissent, democracy and radical Islam that was prominent during Soviet domi-nance[6] has been resumed within the post-1991 republics. Multiple arrests of suspected militants have led to thousands of innocent Muslims being imprisoned (Rashid 2002). And, as with many other countries that employed similar tactics, many of these 'moderate' Muslims become radi-calized within prison through intermingling with militants and their anger and resentment at the government's treatment.[7] Hafez (2003) has suggested that the denial of political inclusion more generally is an important factor within radicalization. Shifting from political participation to exclusion within Algeria and Egypt contributed to the rise of violent militancy and gave militants' actions legitimacy. Similarly, the denial of credible opposition in Kashmir allied to multiple human rights violations have aroused considerable anger and resentment in conditions with severely limited opportunities for peaceful political protest. Finally, in the Philippines, MILF's predecessors, the Moro National Liberation Front, grew markedly in popularity as a consequence of the imposition of martial law in 1972, which led to political organizations being banned, alleged members being summarily executed, mass arrests, collective punishments on associated communities, torture and aerial bombardments. McKenna's (1998: 183) research identified that 'virtually all of [the fighters] reported that they had joined the rebellion to defend themselves and their families against the Philippine government'. Across these settings, and Chechnya and Tajikistan, Hafez (2003: 103) argues that 'in the context of institutional exclusion, rebellion became a legitimate strategy for countering repressive state policies.'

Consequently, government actions have strengthened processes of 'counter-terrorism' while simultaneously weakening secular codes of closure which have contributed to greater opportunities for enhanced religiosity and the learning of opposing rules through Islamist teachers or institutions that challenge those of the nation-state. Yet, many well-qualified Muslims have been denied employment opportunities due to their collective religious beliefs. Such denial highlights inconsistencies and contradictions within the rationalization principles. Associational relations are shown to be closed according to discursive allegiance and the related secular processes were further delegitimized.

Exclusion beyond

In Chapter 3, feelings of collective identities that revolved around territorial, ethnic and religious loyalties were outlined for Muslims living in the West. For many migrants, allegiances are further complicated by experiences of racism and forms of covert discrimination that impose barriers to integration and strengthen existing social and cultural networks. The rise of Islamophobia has resulted in many Muslims uniting around that which leads to their exclusion, namely their religion which becomes the basis for communal and status groups. Today, Muslims are living in the West where both they, and often their parents and even grandparents, were born. Yet, the experiences of many Muslims have resulted in their exclusion from economic, cultural or political spheres. These experiences contribute to opposition to tenets of Westernization. Related open, associative relations are considered to have failed to deliver or are viewed as inconsistent, flawed or closed through discrimination. Applying Weber (1978), the Western authorities could be considered to have cloaked themselves with the myths of their legitimations but increasingly groups refuse to endorse or accept their legitimacy. Instead, these Muslims demand the imposition of many of their specific ways of life associated with the *shari'ah* like alcohol ban, gender segregation and the *nijab*. Gender relations are particularly contentious, especially within the West. Wearers of the *nijab* and closely defined gender behaviour are considered to embody the patriarchy within militancy. And certainly gender is the source of status for men and exclusion from economic, political, social and cultural spheres which is enforced upon many women. However, this is not felt universally because other women consciously prefer this form of relationship.[8] For example, Pels' (2000) study identified that the majority of Muslim women that he interviewed rejected Western-style gender relations and preferred their central positions within the family. Similarly, Marranci (2006) discusses the concerns that Muslim females have over the 'freedoms' within the West and the need to dress in 'Islamic' attire to reinforce their religious identities and as a safeguard against temptation.[9] Rather than being forced to conform to Islamic interpretations, Marranci discovered that some women were responsible for encouraging religious commitment amongst male family members. And while male status is partly determined by female family members' behaviour, women's status is influenced by male activities. However it should be stressed that the appearance and style of life of many other Muslim women is imposed within communal and/or familiar relations.

Consequently, the reasons for females' associations with more traditional and radical forms of Islam are varied. What is however clear is that gender relations and other lifestyle choices practised by militants are resulting in them becoming increasingly segregated in the West into what Weber (1978: 933–4) described as a 'closed caste' in a diaspora based upon repulsion and disdain that excludes exogenous marriage and social intercourse.

Militant codes of exclusion and usurpation

Reaction to the exclusion of radical interpretations, from within both Muslim majority societies and minority communities, increasingly utilizes the concept of *tawhid*, oneness of ideas and behaviour. In other words, there is a stress on uniformity in thought and practice amongst believers that is contradicted by the multitude of Islamic beliefs and behaviour across the world. However, there are commonalities and militants have transformed the concept. For them, unlike the overwhelming majority of believers, *tawhid* has been politicized, justifying a range of control mechanisms and acts of violence. Shared structural experiences, including economic factors

alongside political, legal, social and cultural, are contributing to the formation of rival switchmen, world images and codes of closure. The rules are
based upon Islamic interpretations that are expected to be rigorously followed. In the Weberian sense, the emphasis upon lifestyles provides a
moral framework and the basis for positive group status that distinguishes
these Muslims from 'inferior' people with different beliefs and behaviours.
In a similar yet 'reverse' manner to that identified within the changes
imposed by Atatürk, specific styles of dress become symbolic of the militants' status. Taheri (1987) discusses Hizbollah's Sheikh Ragheb Harb's
comment that the individual should lose their identity within the community with no moment or act left to the individual's initiative. Imposing oneness has often become the responsibility of state or self-declared guardians
of morality who patrol areas, enforcing behaviour and appearance boundaries and punishing difference. Attacks on buildings associated with alcohol,
dancing, prostitution, cinemas, girls' education, mixed gender restaurants
and men and women who are 'un-Islamic' in appearance and strong opposition[10] to the *Sufi* veneration of saints and pilgrimages to the tombs of holy
men have been noted across Muslim societies, ranging from North Africa
to North Caucasus and Southeast Asia. Similarities within oneness are thus
given their distinction through clarifying both strengths and weaknesses
that result in inclusion and exclusion. Consequently within militancy some
of the regional variations, particularly with regard to local cultic practices,
are being eradicated, which strengthens the sense of similarity between
militant groups.

Problems within Muslim societies and communities in the West are
associated with processes and factors like modernization, globalization,
unrepresentative governments, weak civil societies, powerful military and
corrupt leaders, experienced or witnessed at local, national or international levels. And these problems contribute to what Murphy (1988)
described as the 'uncertainty principle' and perceptions that processes of
rationalization have caused irrationality, confusion and contradiction. In
these environments, a collective ethnic consciousness that may have
existed during anti-colonial movements has frequently not been transformed sufficiently into a social national consciousness. By comparison,
Islamic interpretations remained throughout processes of modernization,
deeply ingrained within social processes and traditions, retaining the
potential for radical mobilization if secularization should be seen to have
failed. And the nation-states' formal processes are failing to deliver promises of superior performance and related rules of closure are delegitimized. For Muslims, the poor performance can extend beyond market
economics to cause tension across all aspects of society where Islam has
not been applied.

Within militancy, the concept of *takfir* is central to exclusion and
usurpatory processes, meaning, for perceived misdemeanours, 'one who

is, or claims to be, a Muslim is declared to be impure: by *takfir* he is excommunicated in the eyes of the Community of Faithful' (Kepel 2004a: 31). For many militant Muslims, this means that the person is no longer defended by Islamic law and they can be condemned to death. Approaches to *takfir* can be divided into three ideal types. One form is isolationism such as that advocated by the Egyptian group Takfir wal-Hegira based upon *hegira*, fleeing to the mountains from the unbearable *jahiliyya* society. To remove themselves from the corruption and immorality, the group stated they were driven to 'go into the desert and live among the beasts in order to protest the purity of our faith' (quoted in Taheri 1987: 19).

Second, struggles against the 'near enemy', local impiety and rulers who are excommunicated have happened across Muslim societies like Indonesia, Saudi Arabia and Egypt. Government codes of exclusion are considered secular, inappropriate and to have failed. Militant groups have formed with contradictory 'world images' and opposing switchmen. During the Algerian civil war in the 1990s, the GIA expanded its use beyond the 'impious state' to include society. 'In the districts it controlled, it imposed a "re-Islamisation" of society and punished with death civilians who defied its injunctions such as women who refused to wear the *hijab*, hairdressers who ignored orders to close their shops and newsagents who continued to sell the national newspapers' (ICG 2004b: 13). After the further radicalization and fragmentation within the GIA, between 1996 and 1998, militants employed an extreme conception of *takfir* against all those who refused to support them, irrespective of the individuals' religiosity, and thousands of people were massacred.

Finally, there are the transnational approaches associated with al-Qa'ida which rally against the seizure and maintenance of power by Western-influenced governments and global impurity. Responses include the targeting of non-Muslim infidels and non-militant Muslims who are considered to be apostates. Within this politicized context, *jihad* is central in challenging *takfir*. Groups have argued that this is the only appropriate course of action because violence is the only language the West understands.[11] Comparisons are drawn between the similarities of the pride, arrogance, greed and thievery of the Bush administration and Muslim military regimes and kingdoms.[12] Contrary to popular perceptions that the United States' military presence indicated strength, for al-Zawahiri (2001), their actions showed weakness. America will, he argues, be overstretched, overreliant on repression to maintain control that will result in a popular backlash, isolating the Americans and their puppet regimes and contributing to eruptions against occupation.

To try and ensure control over issuing the sentence of *takfir*, only the *ulemas* have been authorized to make such pronouncements and they have done so with great caution, usually as a last resort. Even Wahhabis who have a reputation for readily dismissing non-Wahhabi Muslims as *takfir*, tend, Steinberg (2006) suggests, to be circumspect about excommunication. Certainly, the rigidity and separation espoused by Ibn Abd al-Wahhab were lessened with the formation of the Saudi nation-state, although *Shi'ites* have continued to be considered to be apostates and rejectionists (Solomon 2006). Today, however, many Muslims are disillusioned with the religious establishment,[16] and their role in providing theological legitimacy[17] for unpopular regimes has meant that there is scope for unqualified group leaders to make these accusations in seeking to eliminate the threat of disbelief and prevent its spread. For Qutb,[17] the loss of faith was so extensive that Muslims were living in a state of ignorance or even pre-paganism. Consequently, believers should not cooperate with those involved in the society and should instead seek to impose the *shari'ah*.

The role of nation-states in developing militant Islamic codes of closure

By adapting classical religious concepts, militant Muslims are seeking to legitimize their processes of exclusion and methods of usurpation. Rules of exclusion are applied against Muslims and other religious denominations in a usurpatory manner that helps to strengthen militant status. However, there is not an inevitable collision between militants and other denominations. For example, groups like Hamas (1988) state that it is possible for Muslims, Jews and Christians to coexist peacefully within the Middle East providing the other religions acknowledge the sovereignty of Islam in the region. And it is possible to observe pragmatic relationships that do not revolve explicitly around religion, between Hizbollah and Christian groups in Lebanon and within Islam, Hamas and Islamic Jihad undertaking operations with the more secular al-Aqsa Brigades and Popular Front for the Liberation of Palestine. But generally, emphasizing religion within national or transnational parameters excludes people belonging to other denominations or weaker interpretations. People, communities and nation-states associated with Christianity and Judaism in particular are ostracized through processes also associated with anti-Westernism and anti-Semitism. In conducive conditions, these rules transcend passive forms of exclusion into violence and ultimately closure through death. Processes of dual closure can be found between secularists and militant Muslims using a mixture of discourse and methods to isolate and exclude. Muslim nation-states are further contributing unintentionally towards these processes.

In Saudi Arabia, the balancing act between the Kingdom's self-declared role as defender of the faith and close Western ally is notable in the seemingly contradictory approach to anti-Westernism. While opposition to other Islamic allegiances has lessened, partly through the networks established across Muslim societies and through migration into the country, Steinberg (2006) argues that they have been replaced by varying degrees[16] of anti-Western attitudes, with xenophobia prominent in Arabian regions. Within the Najdi region, anti-Americanism is extended to incorporate the Saudi royal family because of their close relations with the United States and the considered role of the latter in protecting the former. Across the country, the West generally, and America in particular, is considered ethically and morally weak. Religious institutions are prominent within anti-Western sentiments, for example, the most widely read scholars of the twentieth century, especially Abd al-Aziz Ibn Baz (d. 1999) and Muhammed Ibn Uthaimin (d. 2000) made numerous anti-Western judicial rulings. In the edicts, drawing upon a Qu'ranic verse, Muslims are told not to travel to non-Muslim countries, not to make friends with, or trust, infidels. As Steinberg (2006: 82) comments, 'the anti-Western stance adopted by the country's leading scholars is problematic because they control the religious sector of the Saudi educational system and have considerable influence on the non-religious branch'. However, the support that the religious scholars provide to the Saudi government's pro-Western foreign policy contradicts their internal policy and has contributed to them reinforcing anti-Westernism without addressing the lack of endorsement of their own legitimacy and tarnished status. Periodic attempts are made to curtail the influence of the Wahhabi scholars on education and public discourse but these have proved only partially successful and are quickly overridden. Internal dynamics facing the Saudi regime have contributed to support being provided in exporting Wahhabi-based education and other institutions across the Middle East, South and Southeast Asia, North Caucasus, Europe and West Africa both to enhance Saudi influence and counteract the threat of Iranian influence. At one level, this expansion of Wahhabism and related learning institutions has caused conflict within other Muslim societies and communities. Rigorous, collectivist interpretations of the Wahhabis as a style of life frequently challenges the indigenous *Sufi* and *marabout* strands that incorporate the veneration of saints, pilgrimages to local tombs and mysticism, and were attributed by Weber (1965) to be an enemy of asceticism. The reverse of this approach is that it also extends the dilemma that Saudi Arabia faces internally, namely the paradox on which it is based and the standards it promotes but cannot meet. These incompatibilities become visible to a wider audience and further undermine the regime's rationale and legitimacy for global leadership.

Feelings of anti-Westernization are considered by Western political leaders to be a consequence of ignorance or manipulation by opposing demagogues. The Iranian description of America as the 'Great Satan' exemplifies the perception of militants to the United States. Certainly there are common elements within extreme criticism of American actions and policies. For example, Abdallah (2003) details American attacks and sanctions in Muslim countries and support both for Israel and unpopular 'Muslim' governments like in Egypt, Pakistan and Saudi Arabia. However, anti-Americanism is neither a recent nor a generic response, but is often a reaction to the direct impact of American measures upon a country following the enhanced role of the United States after the Second World War. For example, impressions in Iran were heavily influenced by the involvement of the United States in returning the Shah to power in 1953 and maintaining his position. Taheri (1987) highlights how many of the Iranian militants who first propagated anti-Americanism, and Lebanese Hizbollah commanders, had spent time in the United States working or studying. And leading 'students' involved in the US diplomat hostage crisis in 1979 were graduates from American universities. Today, Muslims are living in the West where both they, and often their parents and even grandparents, were born. Yet, many are opposed to similar tenets of Westernization and demand the imposition of many of their interpretations of the *shari'ah* like Islamic education, alcohol bans and gender segregation. In Muslim societies these anti-sentiments are often not inevitable and are also associated with government manipulation. Using the example of Sudan, Hofheinz (2006: 61) points out that government outbursts of anti-Americanism followed American actions and statements that were considered to be against Sudan or the Sudanese people. This anti-Americanism is rooted 'in a broad scepticism toward U.S. political and economic intentions in the region, fuelled by experience as well as differing ideologies, both secular and Islamist'. In Indonesia, feelings against the United States rose dramatically during the Asian economic crisis during the 1990s and the IMF-imposed policy which increased dependence on Western economic institutions (Ufen 2006). Similarly in Malaysia, Mahathir Mohamad, the leader between 1981 and 2003, regularly denounced Western actions and policies, which enhanced his popularity amongst Muslims in the country and beyond, and this became particularly pronounced during the 1990s financial crisis. Reetz (2006) points out with respect to Pakistan that the prevalence of radical forms of anti-Americanism fluctuates according to domestic politics and international relations, especially involving India. The extent that anti-Americanism rose after September 2001 was, Reetz suggests, largely due to the commitment of the Pakistani government to the anti-terror coalition.

Conversely, many Muslim governments with close relationships with the United States seek to overcome the common perceptions of themselves as American satellites or stooges and are complicit within processes of anti-Americanism specifically, and anti-Westernism generally. Contradictory policies are followed that seek to restrain militant anti-Western rhetoric and actions while simultaneously tolerating, if not encouraging, anti-Americanism within the media and public demonstrations. As Abdallah (2006: 46) comments with respect to Egypt, 'the paradox of Mubarak's regime is that of an era in which Egyptian–American relations were consolidated at economic and military levels although political discourse and media exposure became more anti-American'. Again, it is important to stress the continuing admiration of many Muslims for American values and culture and a separation of feelings for the government and its people. As Steinberg (2006) noted with respect to Saudi Arabians, extensive criticism of the policies and actions of the United States is often accompanied by the embrace of American technology, cultural icons and consumerism. Even in Iran, where the 'Great Satan' has been officially lambasted for nearly 30 years, there was popular support for the reformist President Khatami's ultimately doomed attempt at rapprochement with the United States, and American goods continue to grow in popularity (Buchta 2006).

For other militant groups, people holding different religious beliefs become legitimate targets based upon their faith. The Coptic minority of Egypt constitute around ten per cent of the total population. They trace their roots to the ancient Egyptians and consider themselves to be custodians of this civilization. Although relationships with moderate Muslims remain secure, historical considerations and a perception of disproportionate economic prosperity and influence create tremendous consternation amongst militants. The Copts have been attacked frequently, most notably during the early 1980s (Kepel 2005). With the recent turmoil in Somalia, the enactment of a constitution that recognizes only Islam as the national religion has contributed to ingrained anti-Christian feelings. Terdman (2006) argues that these feelings stem from colonialism and the banning of Christian literature during Said Barre's rule during the 1970s and 1980s, with over 500 Christians killed since 1995. Similarly, in countries where Muslims are the minority, Islam has become a mobilizing discourse within nationalist struggles and the source of legitimacy in attacking representatives of the dominant 'other'. For example, in Nigeria, the establishment of a Universal Primary Education in the 1970s was considered by many Muslims to be part of an attempt to enhance Christianity at the expense of Islam. In the northern states where Muslims are concentrated, there were concerted efforts to strengthen Islamic institutions and behaviour and a concomitant rise in the politicization of religion. During the 1980s, the tensions spilled over and violence between Muslims and Christians became a regular occurrence. As Lapidus (2002) observes, while the fighting has reduced, the tensions remain and indeed have been exacerbated by the implementation of the *shari'ah* in the north.

Exclusion within

Within all the major religions, there are prominent fractures that frequently result in violence. Differing interpretations of doctrine and behaviour can result in violent clashes and forms of terrorism. Van der Veer (1994) outlines one of the most notable disputes during the 1980s that arose amongst Sikhs associated with religious conformity and nationalism. The conflict attained international significance when Jarnail Singh Bhindranwale and his followers took control of the Golden Temple until they were killed by the Indian army. Prior to this, the group had also been responsible for killing 'heretic' Sikhs who did not belong to the same brotherhood, as part of attempts at homogenization and purification. Divisions within Islam are most notable around the *Sunni/Shi'ite* fracture currently contributing to the sectarian violence in Iraq. These differences are embedded within the application of codes of exclusion within and between religious denominations and groups. For example, in Pakistan, groups like Sipah-e-Sahaba and Jaish-e-Muhammad are vehemently anti-*Shi'ite* and have been responsible for brutal massacres. It is important to stress that this is not universal.[17] However, rigid rules of closure are also noticeable within the binary classifications *Dar al-Islam* and *Dar al-harb* or the House of Islam and the House of War. The former refers to those territories governed by the *shari'ah* whilst the latter is the remaining territory that is controlled by non-Islamic rule and is thus *jahiliyya*. This highly contested usage of *jahiliyya* differs from the traditional approach and is another innovation associated with Qutb and his adaptation of Syed Abu A 'La Mawdudi (Zimmerman 2004). Calvert (2004) points out that use of the term shifted from a temporal meaning that distinguished Islam from the pre-Islamic epoch to the application against forces that prevented the implementation of the *shari'ah* throughout history. These forces were deemed especially prominent by Qutb during his lifetime, with particular reference to the Nasserist state. Developing this point, Qutb argued that 'any society that is not Muslim is *jahiliyya*' (quoted in Kepel 2005: 46). And most militants agree that there are no territories governed according to (their interpretations of) the *shari'ah*, with Islam inadequately implemented across societies and within individual habits of taste. Consequently, as Habeck (2006) observes, they focus upon achieving this and create a separation between supporters of true Islam and *kufr* which includes other Muslims. Religion is firmly intertwined with politics. Any individual or institution can now be declared *takfir*. Muslims, even Islamists, are subjected to attack if they criticise the *jihadis*. For example, on the al-Tajdeed militant Web site, Amir Abd al-Mun'im confronts those 'in the movements that call themselves Islamic … that desire to profit from Islam yet do not wish to make sacrifices on Islam's behalf', before denouncing those Muslims who have criticized the *mujahideen* that includes bin Laden, al-Zawahiri and Zawqawi.[18] Yet, within al-Qa'ida there has been a tendency to focus on the death of Jews and Crusaders while the killing of other Muslims has been opposed. This can be traced to the influence of Azzam and, although al-Zawahiri in particular considered his definition of *jihad* to be too defensive and reactive, al-Zawahiri has retained a perception of the need for sectarian restraint, famously reprimanding Zarqawi in Iraq for the extensive killing of *Shi'ites* (Brisard 2005; Gerges 2005). And support for the *Shi'ite* Hizbollah during the 2006 conflict with Israel, despite opposition from some groups, was noticeable across Muslim communities, both *Sunni* and *Shi'ite*. Similarly, Hizbollah has historically had close relations with Sunni Hamas and Islamic Jihad from the neighbouring Palestinian territories.

By comparison, Zarqawi extended the term unbeliever to also include *Shi'ites, Sunni* Kurds and other Muslims associated with the American 'collaborators' or who did not adhere to his Salafi perceptions (Brisard 2005). The targeting of local Muslims, both *Sunni* and *Shi'ite* can also be noticed in attacks on Muslims during localized conflicts in places like Algeria, Saudi Arabia, Turkey, Morocco and Indonesia. It has become clear, as Khosrokhavar (2005) identifies in the case of Sheikh Omar Abdel Rahman,[19] that the graduated scale of judging leaders between just Muslim ruler and unjust has been eliminated for many militants. The latter would be based upon ignorance and idolatry and, whereas previously it was up to Allah to pass judgement on the unjust, it was, Rahman argued, the duty of Muslims to fight it. Gerges (2005) discusses Osama Rushdi, a former member of the Shura Council of the militant *al-Jama'a al-Islamiyah* and the role he ascribes to Dr Abdel Aziz bin Abel Salam, founder member of Tanzim al-Jihad. Salam, it is argued, introduced what Gerges (2005: 97) describes as 'a blanket takfeeri judgment' that applied to all those Muslims who did not join in the battle against 'apostate' rulers and who were as a consequence 'impious'. This extensive use of *takfir* was to supply the justification for massacres by the GIA in Algeria. Similarly, Devji (2005) has pointed out how the language and tactics of *jihad* have been used against *Shi'ites*. He argues that previously anti-*Shi'ite* attacks were confined to particular persons, places or events and that indiscriminate violence is a new phenomenon. And this is happening at a time when, Devji believes, the *Sunni* militants are adopting more *Shi'ite* terms and practices. In some respects, it is this similarity and competition over ideas and behaviour that is motivating the violence. *Shi'ite* groups like the Nizari and Ismailis whose beliefs and practices are widely considered to be heretic by *Sunnis* have not yet experienced targeted campaigns of sectarian violence. Similarly, other religious groups like Hindus, Sikhs, Zoroastrians and Christians are rarely attacked. At a broader level, Devji observes that al-Qa'ida have tended to concentrate upon other monotheist religions with polytheistic religions in South and Southeast Asia neglected or associated with the Jews-Crusader alliance. In other words, groups within militant Islam tend to target religions with which it has most in common.

Conclusion

Weber's social closure provides an insight into the historical and contemporary processes behind the exclusion of militancy and the establishment of usurpatory militant codes of closure. Following the formation of independent Muslim nation-states in the aftermath of the Ottoman Empire and Western colonialism, an array of different ideological stances, structures and levels of secularization were introduced to enable modernization. Processes of rationalization were implemented to help develop the nation-state based around associative relations and individualist criteria. However, increasingly, the secular codes of exclusion were compromised and governments sought to utilize religion within cultural and social realms. The unintended consequence of this has been the reinvigoration of Islamic influence in challenging political discourse that establishes different rules of closure that are more absolute and opposed to the nation-states. Many problems remain within these nations and communities and national consciousness has frequently failed to attract widespread endorsement. Instead, across Muslim societies and communities in the West, there has been a growth of collective consciousness and common identity of interests. Self-conscious religious groups and institutions have utilized traditions, community relations, common feelings and patterns of behaviour across socio-economic groups. Education has contributed to credentialism and both national and Islamic consciousness. These sources of identification cross-cut economics to incorporate political and cultural consciousness which can result in formal rationalization being undermined. If peoples' experiences suggest governments' failure to deliver promises and inconsistencies within credentialism, then the dominant codes of closure are undermined and vulnerable to challenge.

Today, more Muslims are willing to adopt 'world images' that form the basis for exclusionary codes that challenge those of the dominant nation-state and associated (*Sunni*) religious leaders. They contribute to the reinforcement of 'otherness' amongst people belonging to different faiths. These militant Muslims object to the monopolization of closure according to secular nation-state criteria. And despite a weakening in the rigidity of secularization, they demand the implementation of fundamentally opposing values and ways of regulation. The expected evolution of codes of closure from social to individualist criterion has been reversed. Rules have shifted from credentialism to religious denomination and within this code, Islamic interpretation and practice that form the criteria for membership and associated status. Formation of these boundaries results in rigid codes of exclusion of 'pariah' groups and the strengthening of exclusivity within, resulting in further distanciation. A dynamic conflict emerges over the processes of domination and the nature of society. For transnationalists associated with al-Qa'ida, non-Muslims and Muslims who do not share the same beliefs and commitment are excluded and frequently excommunicated, to be punished by the ultimate form of closure, death.

5 Challenging the risk society

Contextualizing the impact of 'Islamic' terrorism

Donncha Marron

Introduction

In this chapter and the next, the impact of 'Islamic' terrorism upon the West is explored. It is argued that the threat of terrorism has become inflated because of a combination of political and populace reactions, existing perceptions of risks and feelings of vulnerability and fear. Chapter 6 explores the potential consequences of these shifting emotions and restraints that are resulting in the reduction of freedoms in the name of freedom with only limited opposition. First, it is important to establish the extent to which risk has become an embedded concept within Western societies before determining how acts of terror, and the threat of attack, connect into these broader perceptions. The purpose of this chapter, then, is to identify and analyse how militant Islam and acts of 'terrorism', specifically in the West, have become understood under the rubric of risk. Further, it seeks to explore the relationship between risk and uncertainty and between risk, as a specifically negative event, and the generation of fear. As Manning (2006) identifies, risk lies somewhere between what is 'factually known' and what is 'completely unknowable' and so, as Frank Knight (1971) famously pointed out, it is as much a product of our ignorance as of our knowledge. Lying somewhere within this domain of uncertainty, risk needs to be understood not simply through the language of control but through the idiom of critique, dissidence and counter-accusation (Sparks 2001). Risk condenses a sense of an amorphous and abstract future and transforms it into something which must be accounted for in the present within systems of human decision-making. In fact, Luhmann (1993) suggests that modern society will only take danger seriously when it is couched in terms of risk. In this, the unknowability and relative uncertainty of risk generate possibilities for authorities and different social groups to advocate or contest the importance of possible future events and current social organization within specific relations of power.

Drawing from significant schools of social theory, this chapter assumes a three-pronged approach to the analysis of risk within the context of militant Islamic actions. A 'risk society' perspective sees the threat of terrorism as a real risk, a more-or-less true ontological category of the world set loose by the specific contemporary character of social organization, and which has specific and identifiable consequences for social life. In contrast, a social constructionist position would lay emphasis on how risk is a product of a particular way of thinking about the world. Yet, this label is somewhat misleading. For social constructionists, risks like terrorism do exist in reality and so maintain an ontological substance. What is argued, however, is that such risks are given form, shape and effective consequence by the structure and culture of subgroups, powerful interests and wider society. Finally, a governmentality perspective addresses how risk is constituted within particular relations of power and knowledge. In this approach, then, the risks of Islamic militancy assume no ontological reality and so are not held to exist 'out there'. Rather, risk exists as a way of imagining and calculating certain contingent events within the systematic management of individuals and populations. However, just because risks are constituted through the duality of power/knowledge, it does not imply that they do not have real effects; on the contrary, their production engenders very real consequences for those whose actions are imagined as risks.

Risk, terrorism and the coming of 'reflexive modernization'

In any sociological attempt to address the question of risk, the work and profound influence of Ulrich Beck cannot be ignored. Although anthropologist Mary Douglas was an early progenitor on the cultural construction and social mediation of risk, it was Beck who brought risk to the forefront of sociological thinking. He did this by positioning it as a central concept for attempting to understand the apparently novel, dynamic and unstable features of Western societies as the end of the twentieth century approached. What others had tried to articulate in adjectives such as post-industrial and post-modern, Beck understood differently. As he describes it, Beck (1992, 1995, 1999) sees a 'risk society' as a characteristic, emergent feature of a new period of 'second modernity', with risk the conceptual fulcrum for explaining the waning of one kind of society and the emergence of another. In this sense, risk is significant both in terms of its increased scope and scale but also as a new modality of understanding and awareness. However, this transformation results not from the failure or obsolescence of industrial modernity but its very achievements; in essence, its authority and expertise, its productivity and success in meeting the material needs and desires of mass society in the West.

At its heart, the risk society thesis posits that risks really are increasing – the world is a more dangerous place to live in. 'Manufactured uncertainties' of human decision-making – global warming from industrial carbon emissions, accidental radioactive release from nuclear installations and the destruction of the very genomic structure of life through biotechnological research – pose new threats to the well-being and lives of millions. They also present new challenges to humankind's ability to calculate and to act upon the future as risk. At the same time, these risks are being interpreted through a new risk consciousness that Beck identifies as part of a wider process of 'reflexive modernization' – individuals are increasingly sensitive to the risks that they face while a disaster-trumpeting mass media constantly seeks to entrench this awareness, keeping us up to date, for example, on the latest figures for anticipated global temperature increases. At the same time, new activist social movements spring up to agitate against GM crops or for the fate of the arctic polar bear. Yet new knowledge brings no safety or security. On the contrary, as Luhmann (1993: 28) puts it, 'the more we know, the better we know what we do not know'; scientific expert contradicts scientific expert on the seriousness and likely impacts of a multitude of risks while the risks themselves appear beyond the scope of knowability. Beck's conceptualization of contemporary risk, in a sense, actually changes the meaning of risk to one denoting more danger and inelucidable uncertainty than one based upon ideas of calculability, control and management implied by probability theory – what might be called 'speculative risk' (Furedi 2007b: 64) or the 'precautionary paradigm' (Ewald 2002).

Gerda Reith (2004) has termed Beck a 'neo-realist' in his elucidation of this risk society; despite teasing out the ways in which risks are elevated for attention under reflexive modernization, they are nonetheless held to be objectively real and compelling. Whereas industrial society had been able to contain the negative side effects of human decision-making within the institutional frameworks of insurance and monetary compensation, the potentially catastrophic nature of the new risks, their disregard of spatial borders and predictable time horizons, exceeds the limits of calculability and thus insurability. Like a caricature of Marx's belief that the bourgeoisie become their own gravediggers within the dialectics of capitalism, Beck too sees an endogenous social transformation beckoning. In pressing forward its attempts to dominate nature, it is industrial modernity, not merely capitalism, which overreaches itself and sets in motion the uncertainty of new catastrophic risks whose potential and realized effects ultimately serve to dissolve the institutional and organizational edifice of industrial society and herald the arrival of a new risk society.

More recently, Beck (2002a, 2002b, 2003) has attempted to parlay this theme of risk into the development of what he calls 'cosmopolitanism'. Keen to address the pervasive influence of globalization and the effects of other risks beyond the ecological, he defines the development of cosmopolitan society as one where a process of greater global interdependency comes to undermine the classical sovereignty of the nation-state. Where the conventional nation-state coalesces a sense of identity through a process of constituting an 'other' (Chapter 3; Elias 1991, 2000; Saïd 1995), Beck's cosmopolitan alternative is an embrace of the 'other', not just competing national identities but the otherness of the 'future' and of 'nature' itself. In this more positive vision that contrasts heavily with the endemic pessimism of a 'neo-feudalist' risk society, Beck sees the cosmopolitan state as being based on a permanent inclusiveness built around the recognition of shared principles, norms and laws, an embrace of the possibility of multiple, entangled paths to modernity and a frictionless interplay at the level of the global and the local. It is not that the nation-state disappears; rather it becomes progressively globalized from both without and within, globalized through its very fabric as a state founded on the 'otherness of the other' (Beck 2002b: 50).

Within this framework, Beck is sceptical of multiculturalism with its presupposition of historically bounded essentialist identities as well as the effects of nationalism which asserts 'his own' against the 'foreign' (Beck 2002a: 38). He sees these as regressive forms of identity at odds with the openness and dynamism of the cosmopolitan impulse (cf. Gilroy 2002; Young 1999). In this, the likes of Islamic identity politics represent the antithesis of cosmopolitanism in its assertion of a distinctive oppression and historical condition that defines and binds the members of this global group and closes them to the recognition of a shared global destiny. Yet, the response of supposedly liberal nations to the problem of militant Islam is also problematized by Beck as an anticosmopolitan impulse. In what he terms 'democratic authoritarianism', the nation-state attempts to combat its fading authority through a ramping up of its capacity for technological surveillance and the enactment of punitive legislation – two fields through which that state, under a liberal facade, has attempted to combat the spectre of a 'new' global terrorism. However, according to Beck, this response can only strengthen and reinforce what it attempts to subdue.

In Beck's world risk society, the new adjective of 'world' emphasizing the geographically unbounded nature of the risks that beset a collective humanity, he stresses not only ecological but also global financial risks and the 'transnational threats of substate perpetrators and networks' (Beck 2003: 259). Of course, these risks impact more heavily, and are more keenly felt, upon the global periphery where poverty exacerbates financial crises and weak states are unable to suppress the depredations of terror attacks. Yet, for Beck, the principle stands that risks do not respect borders – as 11 September 2001 so graphically demonstrated – and remain intractable to nationally focussed solutions. However, Beck's new attention to the novel risk of terrorism also suggests his recognition of differences in the quality of the threats that face a world risk society (Beck 2002b: 43–4). While ecological risks slowly but inexorably rebound upon social structures from the 'outside', the risk of financial crises emanate suddenly and unexpectedly from within the 'expert systems' of global capitalism. Yet, terrorist risks are again further distinct from both of these. What distinguishes terrorism is that it is not an accidental outcome of decisions involved in the production of goods within expert systems but one willed by human agency. Further, where production and distribution invoke trust in abstract systems, terrorism invokes suspicion and, in consequence, heightened cycles of mistrust and an unfurling of ever-greater perceptions of risk. Beck seems to suggest that terrorism is also distinctive to the extent that it obliterates the perception of risk as an individualized threat that can be insured against; as such, it elevates into view the ways in which risks are systemic, inhering in the interrelations between individuals rather than as an external threat that burdens the individual alone. To use C. Wright Mills' (1959) terminology, the risk of terrorism reveals itself more readily as a 'public issue' than other risks. In this, though, Beck sidesteps the role of individual trust in the 'abstract systems' of national intelligence services and governmental strategies designed to prevent the occurrence of terrorist acts, responses which we will examine later on in this chapter. It seems, too, that Beck is not altogether clear as to why terrorism should appear as more of a public issue than any other kind of risk.

A line of distinction is drawn by Beck in terms of how quickly the 'new terrorism' became recognized by Western state authorities. Whereas he argues that ecological and financial risks remain underacknowledged by elites, the 11 September attacks '*instantly* established themselves as new global players competing with nations, the economy and civil society in the eyes of the world' (Beck 2002b: 45). Here Beck seems clearly to locate the effectiveness of terrorism less in the durable reality of the threat it poses than in the subjective understandings and perceptions of Western publics – although, as risks, they remain comparable as fallout of modernity. In this then, a further distinction can be drawn between 'new' terrorism and environmental or financial risks, in how the image of the former has become radically simplified by national governments who have taken a lead in defining the nature of the threat faced (Beck 2002b: 45). Whereas the latter risks have brought about the fragmentation of expertise and belief in the authority of science, governments have succeeded, in Beck's view, in coalescing a view of terrorism that excludes the contesting definitions of experts and political groups.

In identifying the risk of terrorism, it is its qualitative novelty that is important – a novelty implied by the nature of contemporary modernity within which it and all other risks arise and confront the conditions that give birth to them. In this sense, the risk of terrorism is both reactionary and 'progressive'. Militant Islam rails against the decadence and degradation of the West behind the cloak of religion. Yet, as Chapter 2 highlights, it utilizes the Internet to transmit its ideology and can even speak, in perversely liberal tones, of the environmental destruction wrought by Western industrialization. Although projecting a superficial similarity with an older tradition of nationalist, anticolonial movements, the planning and execution of terror attacks both inhabit and embody the process of globalization through their fluid transnationalism, their distanciation of time and space, and their contestation of the state's monopoly of violence without the laying of a claim to a state-based alternative. In this respect, for all intents and purposes, they are no different to Greenpeace and other subpolitical movements thrown up by and seeking to contest modernity's progress; they are, as Beck (2003: 260) catchily frames it, the 'NGOs of violence'.

In calling attention to 'terrorist dangers caused by transnational terror networks', Beck (2003: 257) makes the claim that such a risk is a product of the infrastructure of globalization as much as the regressive intentions of its perpetrators. It is late modernity itself that is throwing up a self-confrontation to its own project, a project that begins to work against itself from within. In this sense, it is instructive that Beck prefers the description 'network' to describe contemporary terrorist formations precisely because the term, as noun and verb, is so frequently used to capture the essence of today's liquid, globalized world – in education, business, culture and communications. In a simple example, Mythen and Walklate (2006a) draw attention to the way that the Madrid train bombings were remotely activated using Spain's mobile phone network, the mobile phone perhaps being the paragon of fluid interconnectedness that characterizes contemporary society 'on the move'. In such a fashion, it appears almost as if the very tools of modernity are being turned, guerrilla fashion, against itself (Bauman 2006: 108; Sassen 2002: 235). This connects with the arguments of other authors like Urry (2002) that locate the planning and delivery of terrorism in global 'complex flows' and 'networked networks' in a manner which almost appears to present militant Islamists as arch proponents of post-Fordism and flexible accumulation. The same can be observed in the manner that they are understood to be able to manipulate adeptly the Internet and other communications technologies for organizational and propaganda purposes (Anderson 2003). Along these same lines, Lyon (2006) identifies how globalization unleashes the free flow not only of goods, persons and data but also of practices, identities and conflicts, while Jock Young (2007) argues that globalization puts individuals into greater contact with one another, thus heightening feelings of relative deprivation on the part of subordinate groups who turn to terrorism to right their feelings of powerlessness and injustice.

Perhaps, though, we might heed the observations of Bauman (1992, 1998) on the dangers and risks given attention by Western elites. It may be the case that such talk of global, amorphous networks of terrorism fluidly but purposively seeping into the interstices of globalization provides a negative image, an inverse projection of elite fears whose interests are bound up in the advance of neo-liberalization and who benefit from the growth and expansion of 'disorganized' capital. Historically, Bauman attests, such fears represent an inner ambivalence that elites feel towards the social formations that they have engineered or set loose, a concern for their order, function and the purpose of modernity itself – fears that must be manifested as an external threat in order for a positive vision of progress to be channelled. It is, perhaps, within this projected space that varieties of contemporary 'Islamic' terrorist are now held to stand.

Within a global risk society, a mix of risks exhibiting intended and unintended harm must imply that these risks cannot remain aloof from one another. In this, Beck's imagination draws from a wider set of anxieties on the possibility of terrorists possessing and deploying weapons of mass destruction. However, Beck goes beyond more conventional concerns of 'rogue states' harbouring and arming terror networks or such state-created weapons finding its way into their possession. For Beck, the transformation in the quality of risk is a more fundamental opening of a 'Pandora's Box' (Beck 2003: 260). New weapons stemming from developments in gene manipulation, communications and artificial intelligence are enhancing the possibilities of an individualization of war. Now destructive potential is dependent less on massive state-funded infrastructures than on an autonomously dynamic knowledge that eludes the grasp of state monopoly and can presumably find its way into the possession of terror networks willing to make the necessary investment or recruit the necessary asset. So, terror groups may intentionally infect information and computer technology systems with viruses that cripple global financial markets or target specific ethnic groups with a genetically manipulated agent designed to target only those of a certain genetic profile.[1] As Beck pithily notes, Western populations bred on a diet of disaster movies propagated by Hollywood now become agents of their own terror – busily imagining horrific scenarios that the terrorists might be concocting (Beck 2002b: 46; see also Bourke 2005: 357–91; Furedi 2007b)

It is more difficult, however, to see how Beck's new terrorism qualifies as a risk in the same manner as ecological destruction and nuclear catastrophe. Terrorist attacks may be temporally and geographically unbounded and so qualify for the term 'risk' as he categorizes it; yet individual terror acts themselves are relatively bounded. In this, they are not necessarily different from the reproduction of a rate of normal accidents across a population that institutions such as insurance have systematically embraced since the eighteenth century. In consequence, it seems as if Beck must draw upon the nightmarish science fiction of 'genetic bombs' and such like to invest the necessary degree of harm required of his risks. Yet Beck's catastrophic fantasizing about intersecting risks seems to outstrip the mundane reality of how they might work in practice. It has been argued that biological and radiological weapons remain relatively ineffective for inflicting civilian casualties and it is more likely that their potential lies in the terror that they impart rather than the death they would inflict if used (Cooper 2006; Durodié 2004b; Furedi 2007b). Therefore, it remains something of an open question in Beck's work as to the degree to which the risks of terrorism lie within the independent reality of the threat presented, or in the self-perception, self-organization and self-understanding of Western society itself.

In describing this 'miasmic' formation of unbounded risks in this period of modernity (Reith 2004), Beck prefers to overlook the interconnections between Islamic terrorism and much more mundane events and situations understood to be risks, particularly by liberal commentators. For example, the hijacking of aircraft and the attempted car bombing of airport terminals represent an attack on consumers of mass air travel, problematized by Green activists as the fastest growing contributor to carbon emissions and the 'risk' of environmental change. Sites such as pubs and nightclubs, similarly threatened by attack, are also understood to be sites of risk in other senses – of binge drinking, violence, unprotected sex, drink spiking and date rape. Similarly, alleged planned attacks on sports stadia like Manchester United's Old Trafford are themselves represented as sites of everyday risk; of football hooliganism, racist chanting and abuse, and the unhealthy consumption of pork pies and burgers. On one level, this might be explained as a coincidence, particularly given the ubiquity of a risk discourse that can now be applied to virtually any social practice, with risk serving as a framework and discourse for amorally moralizing upon the individual choices and behaviours of others (Fitzpatrick 2000; Hunt 2003). However, as Brendan O'Neill (2006) has provocatively suggested, perhaps these particular targets are selected by middle-class, Western-educated Islamic militants partially because they are drawing from and reproducing, consciously or unconsciously, a wider cultural distaste for the consumption practices of the masses (cf. Bourdieu 1984). Indeed, as argued in Chapter 1, Western varieties of militant Islam are in many ways parasitical, drawing their themes and justification less from religious scriptures than from the secular Western culture from which their members are drawn.

Despite considering the subjective understanding and definition of the risks that a second modernity both bequeaths and faces, Beck's analysis ultimately rests on the objective reality of risk. In the last instance, it is this reality that blindly propels forward a new kind of social organization. Contained within this process, negative global risks demand new positive forms of globalized response that usher in a new type of cosmopolitan society on the coat tails of disaster. The terrorist risk now confronting Western nations invokes a response whereby, for Beck, the traditional nation-state, in the interests of preserving its very sovereignty, must sacrifice its increasingly suspect inter-directed autonomy for an outer-directed multilateralism. It is not globalization *itself* which is objected to or which is called into question but the *type* of globalization that has emerged to date – specifically a neo-liberal globalization that repudiates political influence in favour of free market flows and the unhindered accumulation of profit. In this, then, 'new' forms of Islamic terrorism contain the kernel of a valuable political opportunity. In the face of this world risk, the authoritarian state attempts to retreat behind its national borders and clamp down on civil freedoms and liberties; yet, rather than retarding the pervasiveness of globalization, the action and reaction of both can only impel it hopelessly further. This will be discussed in more detail in Chapter 6. Like the risk society, the cosmopolitan society is not an engineered utopia but one predicated on crisis – an interwoven, triumviral crisis of control, of nature and of politics (Beck 2002a: 26). Incubating within the very process of neo-liberalism and globalization, cosmopolitanism emerges as the irresistible side effect of neo-liberalism's inability to contain its own negative side effects. There are, however, negative connotations to this positive interpretation of global events, as Beck appears to have reversed the Enlightenment dream of social change through human rationality. Now, progressive change is a painful, undirected and unanticipated process through which humanity has to respond; ironically, the more reflexive that humanity becomes, the more it is seemingly unable to act its own right. Within this sociological framework of understanding, human progress becomes, at best, an unintentional side effect of wider, uncertain social processes that are not amenable to intervention or control.

Risk and the construction of fear

Ulrich Beck's approach to understanding the significance of the contemporary risk of terrorism might be defined as neo-realist; in other words, he recognizes the ways in which both risks and the conceptualization of risk emerge within the context of second modernity. Nevertheless, his analysis rests ultimately on the objective existence of an unbounded set of risks and the failure of the political and economic institutions of 'first modernity' to contain them. However, this raises the question of the degree to which a supposedly novel risk like contemporary terrorism can be accorded such ontological significance. Sociologists and anthropologists, as is their province, have tended to address the issue of how risks are more or less socially constructed, how risks are less the literal manifestation of economic and social transformations than a symbolic representation of a contingent future historically created through particular forms of social organization. A simple observation of this fact is that today risk is understood in overwhelmingly negative terms as the probability of harm – yet risk had more neutral, even positive, connotations in the past when 'to risk' implied the likelihood of benefit or gain (Furedi 2002a; Luhmann 1993). This then opens the question of how and why society has come to understand risk in specifically negative terms, terms that appear to be intrinsically bound up in questions of fear and dread. More generally, it also raises the question of how the growth of risk thinking resonates with the cultural and social formation of Western societies.

One of the earliest and most influential analyses of risk from a cultural theory perspective has been that of Mary Douglas (Dake 1992; Douglas 1985, 1990; Douglas and Wildavsky 1982; Hacking 2003; Wildavsky and Dake 1990). Douglas, juxtaposing contemporary Western society with small-scale, non-Western societies, identifies a genealogy between the concept of sin and risk from pre-industrial to industrial society. She suggests that both have symbolic, forensic functions in allocating responsibility for dangers and reaffirming the structure of the social grouping, community or society within which they are produced. However, where sin posits the threat of an individual to a community, connecting taboo acts to real dangers threatening the community, contemporary individualized society and its associated deployment of risk represents a reversal of this polarity in marking out the dangers the individual faces from society. As such, 'the slope is tilted in the reverse direction, away from protecting the community and in favour of protecting the individual' (Douglas 1990: 7). What makes risk attractive as a conceptual category and creates an elective affinity between risk and modernity is its apparent dissolution of morality and how, through its seeming objectivity and appeal to scientific definition, calculable risk elides questions of meaning and political contestation. However, the impetus of Douglas's work has been to disassemble this ideology of risk and reveal its political construction. Risks are not understood or acted upon in a consistent way by different types and groups of individuals. For Douglas, this reveals not the failure of cognition or knowledge but the individual's political affiliation, their connection to the social structure and the manner and degree to which this is internalized. As Sparks (2001: 163) comments, Douglas's conceptualization of risk is about getting outside the individual and attempting to denaturalize the naturalness of our own understanding of, and responses to, uncertain events. To put it in symbolic interactionist terms, the self comprehends risk under the rubric of a range of 'generalized others'.

This, however, does not imply a radical constructionism or relativization. Douglas (1990: 8) is adamant that risks, as contingent events with negative consequences, do exist and are therefore not simply a product of institutional or social labelling. In fact, Ewald (1993: 227) further subverts this dualism of the 'real' and the 'socially constructed' by arguing that risk is 'entirely real', giving 'effective – quantifiable – presence to that which is nevertheless only probable'. In other words, risk transforms amorphous future events into tangible factors that must be accounted for in the present. In our case here, the social construction of risk does not deny that there are young militant Islamists who may well attack western targets with a greater or lesser degree of severity at some future point in time and that some degree of likelihood can be apprehended, through the accumulation of intelligence and knowledge of their activities. However, at the same time, risk is not only connected to questions of knowledge but to relations of power. As Luhmann (1993: 29) and Ewald (1993: 224–5) attest, as well as Douglas, risk, risk acceptability and perceived control are always dependent on a given political context. Therefore, for the individual, the flow of data about a whole constellation of risks is filtered through a culturally biased mind. The socialized individual selects risks for consideration and attention to the extent that they are understood to impact upon their world perspective; their set of cultural, social and political allegiances; their fears of being held accountable; and their desires to hold others accountable. To put it crudely, we tend to choose fears and select risks in order to support our way of life.

Therefore, a culturalist perspective rejects distinctions between subjective fear of risk and its objective measurement. On the contrary, what is of interest is how certain perceived risks, like crime and terrorism, become a metaphor for the experience of social change under late modernity as exemplified by the decline of the welfare state, the growth of neo-liberalism and processes of individualization that increasingly renders individuals responsible and culpable for their individual fates (Bauman 2006; Ellin 2001; Glassner 1999; Holloway and Jefferson 1997; Sparks *et al.* 2001). In essence, the disorder and uncertainty of crime and terrorist risks capture the embedded concerns that people have in the pursuit of their everyday lives and provide a channel through which some kind of sense of order can be projected and acted upon.

The concept of fear appears to enjoy an intertwined fate with that of risk. If risk represents a conceptualization of future events in terms of individual or social harm, then it might appear to be a corollary that risk represents a particularly feared and fearful outcome. In a recent popular account of the role of fear, Barry Glassner (1999) argues for the existence of a contemporary 'culture of fear'. However, as he sees it, it is a hegemonic culture that elevates fears of only certain things, fears which are in the interests of capitalism and ruling elites to promote – for example, child abduction, sexual abuse and school shooting rampages. The central thrust of Glassner's argument is that society, specifically the United States, is unable to grasp with fundamental sources of inequality in power and resources. Accordingly, anxieties and feelings of trepidation become played out for the benefit of elites through these metaphorical safety valves that detract attention away from more entrenched political and social issues. In many way, his analysis resembles classic moral panic theory and how societal dislocations and transformations are simplified through short-lived and disproportionate bursts of concern for the activities of fabricated 'folk devils' which may very well include the figure of the terrorist (Cohen 2002; Ungar 2001). For Glassner then, certain more pervasive harms that cannot be so easily attached to a stigmatized group become repressed, for example, fears about poverty, gun ownership and murders, and road traffic accidents. Yet, Glassner falls precisely into the trap of understanding risk as an objective category, independent of belief and political mediation – a trap that cultural theory should be seeking to de-reify (Haggerty 2003: 197). In fact, using Douglas's perspective, we can, in turn, see Glassner's worldview determining his selection of risks for attention: as an American liberal academic, he himself minimizes certain risks and selects others for attention – poverty, inequality and gun ownership – that reflect back his own ostensible political concerns, worldview and cultural biases.

In Frank Furedi's conceptualization of a 'culture of fear' (2002a) and the related interplay of a 'politics of fear' (2005a), he has sought to tease out the fundamentally intertwined nature of fear and risk. Like Douglas, or even Beck for that matter, Furedi's social constructionist approach does not constitute a denial of the ontological category of risk. However this approach differs in that he is somewhat less interested in unpicking cultural variances in the reading of risk between different groups. Instead he exposes how the general political and economic climate of Western nations, more generally, is fostering both a heightened concern with risks and an endemic fearfulness on the part of both elites and individuals.

In analysing the growth of concern with new forms of Islamic terrorism and distinguishing his approach from 'traditionalist' accounts, Furedi (2005b: 308) explicitly denies the necessary relativism of a social constructionist approach. In fact, Furedi appears to parallel Beck's sociological interpretation as to the rise of contemporary forms of terrorism. For example, Furedi understands its conceptualization as a historically unique phenomenon stemming from the intensification of globalization and the erosion of the pre-eminent role of the nation-state. He pinpoints its peculiar blend of modernism (especially in the deployment of technology) and antimodernism. Like Beck, he seeks to locate its rise sociologically in the pervasiveness of individualization in late modernity and the collapse of social institutions and their all-embracing moral frameworks. He also notes how recent terrorist attacks have given rise to the playing out of fearful fantasies and reflexivity whereby potential attackers feed upon and reinforce wider feelings of anxiety and concern (Furedi 2007b: 52)

Where Furedi's (2002a) understanding of risk, including terrorism, diverges from Beck's is in his particular concern with how it has become such an important epistemological category for understanding the world and how it has acquired such a fluid applicability. Specifically, he notes how it can be applied to encompass such diverse areas as terrorism, food, mobile phones, child safety and medicine. Accordingly, he explicitly rejects explanations for the rise of risk that blame an overweening modernity – the enhanced dangers unleashed by scientific development and the growth of human knowledge – and instead points the finger of blame at a timorous modernity and its preoccupation with harm reduction and risk calculation. In other words, it is not modernity in a new reflexive stage that spurs the production of risk but an excessive reflection by contemporary culture and elite groups upon negative consequences that has brought about the ubiquity of a risk discourse. Although risk has historically been part of the project of modernity in terms of 'taming chance' (cf. Hacking 1990), making it calculable and thus knowable within the calculus of probability, the conceptualization of risk today radically repudiates the capacity of accumulated scientific knowledge to systematically understand, intervene within and control both the natural and social worlds. In doing so, it leans ever more heavily on the fantastical, the irreversibility of potential threats and the speculative imagination of worst case scenarios. In Furedi's (2007b) view, then, there is a cultural transformation away from 'probabilistic' to 'possibilistic' thinking, or what John Adams (2003: 91) identifies as the realm of 'virtual risk'.

While individualization and the collapse of encompassing moral systems are partial explanations for this state of affairs, Furedi (1992) is no conservative. He seeks a more fundamental explanation in the decline of politics and political contestation, a post-modern loss of belief in the unique meaning and capacity of the human subject, and the dismantling of the last vestiges of Enlightenment belief and historical progress (see also Heartfield 2002; Malik 1996, 2001). Therefore, it is not the risks themselves that are important but what risk indicates about the kind of society and elites that put such store in conceptualizing social events, and thus inherently humanly made phenomena, as objectified risks. Thus, for Furedi, preoccupation with risk denotes a profound fear of the future and of change and connotes a diminished belief in human endeavour. In this sense, the risk of terrorism is but a subset of a wider cultural understanding that society, or more properly humanity, faces catastrophic threats to its existence, be it the H1N1 bird flu virus or the fundamental climatic changes being wrought by global warming.

Looking at the radical retraction of the insurance industry in the wake of 11 September 2001, Furedi (2002b) suggests that the relative decline in insurance provision for terrorism was less as a result of a calculative assessment of potential profits and losses, and reflected more the degree to which a dispassionate risk assessment has become swayed by a wider 'culture of fear'. Within such an environment, he argues, every commercial activity, from opening mail to the location of corporate headquarters, is anxiously assessed through the rubric of terrorism risk analysis to the extent that this concern detracts from business confidence and commercial efficiency. Thus, risk management rather than profitability becomes the keystone and an autonomous dynamic is set in motion where fear and risk feed back on to one another and become constantly amplified (ibid: 15). Claims for the uninsurability of disaster then, terrorist or otherwise, speak more to the pessimistic nature of contemporary society and its sense of disbelief that it can contain the threats and risks that increasingly appear to remain outside the scope of human control. 'Once the threat of terrorism is perceived according to the possibilistic paradigm, real live terrorists do not have to do very much to achieve their objectives. Societies that are wedded to fantasizing about worst cases soon learn to live them' (Furedi 2007b: 73).

Bill Durodié (2004a: 15) has adopted a similar culturalist perspective by arguing that terror attacks tell us more about ourselves than they do the intentions of terrorists. Although terrorism has an objective reality, how such attacks impact upon Western societies is filtered through social and cultural factors that dampen or amplify responses to the potentiality and reality of the risk. In this, Durodié delves into the question of social capital as conceptualized by Robert Putnam (2001) and argues that the risk of terrorism is refracted through a society's level of social cohesiveness as manifested by such indices as voter participation, participation in voluntary associations and everyday trust. Mirroring Durkheim's (1982) account of the functions of crime, Durodié (2004a: 15) turns the question of terrorism around by asking whether disasters such as terrorism might not function as a means of affirming 'core social bonds' and increasing social capital, even as its economic equivalent is destroyed. On the contrary, identified declines in social capital amplify a sense of risk and vulnerability – as the anomic individual is cut adrift, capricious fears and fantasies about terrorism remain outside the regulative scope of the collective. As the state is increasingly distanced from the individual, it attempts to give succour to its legitimacy through acting as a risk manager for an increasingly vulnerable, risk conscious public. Despite his polemic tone, Durodié is not necessarily averse to responsible risk management. Nevertheless, he contests the increasing preoccupation with risk as it exists at the very heart of political discourse where it increases suspicion, promotes individual vulnerability and thus exacerbates the very declines in social capital that gave rise to it in the first place.

In directly assessing this 'culture of fear' thesis, Durodié along with Edgar Jones *et al.* (2006) have sought to compare levels of public anxiety and morale in the current British antiterrorist campaign with the civilian experience of the Blitz during the Second World War. Looking at ranges of measures including morale, panic and incidences of psychiatric disorder, they argue that the harm or fearfulness attached to attacks on civilians is a product not only of the seriousness of the risk but the degree to which individuals are 'actively engaged in their own protection' in order to foster a capacity for resilience (ibid: 69). The political significance of risk therefore embodies more than just harm or probability of an event; it also encompasses the social organization within which those subjected to the risk are embedded and how authorities seek to actively engage the public through purposive practices of risk communication, response and minimization. Through a strong resilience capability, individuals are hardened to risk and better able to adjust to new risk situations, are more focussed and prepared to meet both its contingency and reality. Resilience inures the public with a mentality that mitigates against individual and collective panic and the consequential breakdown of the dense web of social interdependency. This use of the term 'resilience' can be contrasted with other approaches where it is applied to the construction of a defensive architecture, crisis planning, contingency management and other measures designed to mitigate the impact of any potential terrorist attack (Coaffee 2006). Of course, this form of resilience, if it becomes overarching, is precisely the manifestation of a fearful culture that Furedi sees as being the problem. On the contrary, resilience, in the former sense, mediates the degree to which risk undermines individual and collective ontological security in everyday life (cf. Giddens 1990, 1991). For Jones *et al.* (2006), this factor of resilience was much stronger during the terror raids of the Blitz compared with the terror attacks of the present day where they argue that the public are inculcated by governing authorities into a much more passive role of vigilance and conceived of as objects of both state protection and professional therapeutic intervention (see also Furedi

2004). In consequence, despite the contemporary cultural emphasis placed upon 'accountability' and 'transparency' through mechanisms of audit and control (cf. Power 1999), they argue that the public is increasingly cynical of the state's position in relation to terrorism risk.

Yet there are notable problems with this 'culture of fear' thesis (see Tudor 2003). The embrace of a cultural explanation is rather reductionist and, to a certain extent, elides wider transformations in the field of the economy, the social and everyday life. It also appears as quite a totalizing framework wherein culture is formed through its particular relationship to the sphere of politics, and so ignores the cultural variability that pertains to specific risks, and the ways that these may be adopted, amplified or de-amplified in particular ways. Despite discussing fear – a fundamentally embodied emotion experienced by individuals – Furedi glosses over the individual within his analysis in terms of how people actually experience the sensation and feeling of fear (cf. Bourke 2005: 73–6). Elsewhere, in his critique of the state in terms of how it infantilizes the individual and invokes negative images of the masses, he correctly pinpoints how this has been a historic strategy for the elite to define themselves and justify their position (Furedi 1992: 197). However his analysis implies a tendency for the mass to panic as somehow being propelled by media reporting and expert intervention. In this sense, his politico-cultural view fails to bring out how individuals might resist, or at least question, projected messages of fear and risk. Perhaps, like Beck, a totalized perspective on risk loses sight of its particularities where risks are taken to be symptoms of 'something else' rather than specific objects of analysis within themselves.

With respect to fear, the question arises as to what extent the promotion and 'politics' of fear suit the interests of the state and other authorities. Robin (2004) and Mythen and Walklate (2006b) have argued that fear can be accumulated as a form of political capital on the part of state authorities and specifically point to the growth of a 'new terrorism' discourse that attempts to both direct and harness fear towards a diversity of governmental ends – from attempts to gain support and justify military intervention in Iraq to wider policies of pumped up security measures and the deployment of surveillance technologies – grouped under the rubric of an unclearly delineated 'war on terror'. In particular, the latter authors point to the deliberate elevation of public insecurity through the identification by political leaders and the mass media of an amorphous threatening terroristic 'other' bolstered by a network of aberrant nation-states and a perpetual sequence of close-calls and near-miss terror atrocities that keep precaution and insecurity at the forefront of individual awareness. Fear, or more specifically fear of an 'evil other', is certainly a motivating emotion that allows a society to coalesce firmly against a threat to national security (Stern 2003b). However, as Robin (2004) identifies, such fear is always and everywhere political, mediated by the interests of elite groups and deployed in such a fashion so as to reinforce the interests of power.

Similarly, Burkitt (2005) – putting it in governmentalist terms – argues that emotions, including fear, provide an opportunity for authorities to govern the population through setting out the terrain for a specific field of actions. For example, a range of emotions including fear and anxiety, but also hope, were harnessed in justifying military operations against Iraq. However, as he asserts, it remains an unpredictable strategy to govern through emotion as state exhortations meet popular indifference or emotions are channelled in popular protests against governmental aims.

Fear may indeed possess this cynical purpose and function, but we should heed Furedi's (2007b: 162–8) warning that it is not merely the tool of an all-powerful elite. Looking beyond notions of a culture of fear, or how fear is directed or used by government, David Altheide (2002, 2003, 2006) has attempted to articulate the process through which fear is gener-ated within the fabric of social life – as a media scholar, giving explicit recognition to the crucial role of the mass media within this process. Accordingly, 'the terms crime, victim, and fear are joined with news reports about terrorism to construct public discourse that reflects symbolic relationships about order, danger, and threat that may be exploited by political decision makers' (Altheide 2006: 422). In this sense, fear has become a dominant perspective in social life but, in contrast to the past, it represents not a fear of tangible things or events within themselves but a specific kind of discourse that engages individual identity and participa-tion within social life. The irony, of course, as Altheide recognizes, is that 'post-industrial citizens' have never been safer or more removed from danger – and it is precisely this removal from bodily threats that infuses contemporary consciousness with such a potent fearfulness (Campbell 1987; Elias 2000).

For Altheide, as for Furedi, it is fear that has become the critical site of collective consciousness in a secular, affluent age characterized by public suspicion of institutions and a pervasive individualization and social frag-mentation. However, adopting a symbolic interactionist perspective, Altheide stresses how fear, of crime since the 1960s but now increasingly of terrorism, created and filtered through mass media forms and popular culture, emerges as a key basis for the formation of identity and social engagement within Western societies. On the one hand, fear is scripted through news narratives and the establishment of a 'problem frame' through which media reports are directed, both nurturing and relying upon audience familiarity with the script of a gun-shooting in an American classroom or a terror attack in the making thwarted by authorities near the final stage of its reckoning. Fear is also consumerized and rendered as entertainment, as Hollywood blockbusters and critically acclaimed HBO series interweave audience familiarity with crime and terrorism stories to sell fictionalized versions of these phenomena, and news reports are fol-lowed by advertisements for products that help individuals feel safer against whatever fear they are being encouraged to feel. Finally, Altheide agrees that fear is useful for the state which relies upon the deployment of a 'politics of fear' in order to direct, encourage and govern the public towards the achievement of certain goals to which elites lay claim.

Terrorism, governmentality and the constitution of risk

Within this chapter so far, we have analysed neo-realist and social constructionist accounts of risk and its manifestation within the phenomenon of a 'new terrorism'. Where the former lays emphasis on the reality of risk but articulates the cultural and social fabric within which this risk becomes meaningful and an impetus to action, the latter gives primary emphasis to the social, cultural and historical context through which a modality or modalities of risk are constituted, and risks like terrorism become 'selected' by different groups for attention. Cutting across these poles of risk is a third, highly influential perspective on risk that can be traced back to a famous essay by Foucault (1991) on the concept of governmentality and how the emergence of bio-politics and liberalism were predicated on a new reflexive questioning of what it meant to govern. Stemming from this brief work, numerous writers have attempted to demonstrate how risk exists as a key concept for articulating and understanding shifting rationalities of government, particularly in terms of the rise of 'neo-liberal' or 'advanced' liberal government (Dean 1999; Ewald 1990; O'Malley 1996, 2004; Rose 1999). Rather than risks representing an effect or a crude 'construction' of society, governmentalists emphasize the way that events are constituted by experts as risks and become embedded within certain governmental practices organized for the management of populations (Mythen and Walklate 2006a: 385). 'Through these never-ceasing efforts, risk is problematised, rendered calculable and governable. So too, through these efforts, particular social groups or populations are identified as "at risk" or "high risk", requiring particular forms of knowledges and interventions' (Lupton 1999: 87).

In such diverse fields as crime control (Feely and Simon 1992), welfare insurance (Ewald 1986), organizational management (Power 2004) and consumer credit (Marron 2007), authors have attempted to demonstrate how centres of authority adopt a discourse of risk and attempt to deploy risk as a technology, or an 'art of combinations', in order to govern both individuals and populations toward certain ends. It is the utility and malleability of risk, the ease with which in contemporary society it is transmissible across fields as an effacious technology for the government of individuals and populations that opens it up, within specific contexts, as the discourse and technology of institutions *par excellence* (Reddy 1996). This leads us back to Douglas's attestation that risk's claims to objectivity and rational science and its eradication of an overt moralism (in contrast with, for example, sin) conditions its current ubiquity within governmental practices – with terror prevention being no exception. As the following authors have noted, risk has proven, or has been claimed as, a key technology within which the perceived uncertainty and dangerousness of terrorism has been imagined and acted upon. These include: urban design and the target hardening of risky buildings (Coaffee 2003, 2006); the curtailing of flows of undesirably risky bodies (Levi and Wall 2004); international money flows and the constriction of modes of financing deemed at risk of supporting terrorism (Amoore and de Goede 2005); and mass information campaigns that sensitize the public to terror attack risks (Mythen and Walklate, 2006b).

The paradigmatic case of governmental risk technology is that of insurance. Since the nineteenth century, the growth of insurance has been embedded within the development of new welfarist rationalities of government that have sought to alleviate the externalities of industrial life and the threat of class conflict through the principle of collective distribution (Castel 1991; Ewald 1991; O'Malley 2004). In effect, the organization of 'social' forms of insurance has allowed the individual burden of random threats like unemployment, illness and workplace accident to be calculably absorbed across a whole population. With the authoritative or cooperate application of a statistical framework and the accumulation of data on the empirical recurrence of specified accidents and harms within a population, insurance transforms incalculable uncertainty into calculable risk. In doing so, it allows a capital fund to be predictably and efficiently accumulated and apportioned to financially compensate the individual for the costs of these random harms.

In contrast to the realist and constructivist accounts that we examined earlier, it is argued that there is no intrinsic risk attached to particular events. As Knight (1971) specifies, the concept of probability is an empirical generalization with reference to a group and is not comprehensible independently of this context – thus risk does not exist in 'reality' nor does it exist outside of the collectivity to which it refers (Dean 1999: 131; Ewald 1990: 142; Garland 2003: 56). Risk is thus a particular means of ordering reality as it is seen to take place at the level of the population – it seeks to manage events affecting a group of individuals as a whole so as to order those events in a specific, calculable way in relation to the future. From such a perspective, then, the conception of a potential terrorist attack as a risk comes into being within particular discourses and practices. Effectively, the idea of an attempted terrorist atrocity is not a risk in and of itself; it becomes one within the context of attempts by authorities to govern a particular space or field with respect to the future.

However, there is no fixed or universal way that risk becomes deployed or understood within relations of governance. In addition to insurance risk, that is, concern for the probabilistic distribution of harms across a population, Dean (1999) also identifies two other categories: *epidemiological risk*, the identification and management of health outcomes within population; and *case management risk*, characterized by qualitative identification and intervention in relation to 'dangerous' individuals within a social body. Therefore, risk can only be understood within the particular practices and relations of power that constitute it and give it meaning. In fact, O'Malley (2004, 2006) pushes this further by arguing that social embeddedness and moral context make superficially similar technologies of risk significantly different in operation and in terms of what they imply for the individual so subjected. In this sense, then, the technology of risk becomes manifest in a whole continuum of different practices, where it is constituted with its own unique characteristics and attributes depending on the institutional, social and historical context of its use. For him, there is no 'reality' to risk, nor even a definitive range of features through which we can distinguish 'calculable' risk from 'incalculable' uncertainty; on the contrary, uncertainty and risk are fluctuating modes and practices through which the real is imagined and made amenable to governmental intervention.

The question of insurance is particularly apposite in relation to terrorism. As for all kinds of insurance, terrorism coverage represents an organizational attempt to govern the uncertainties and costs of a potential terrorist attack on a specific target through a marketized distribution of capital, providing a calculative mechanism to monetarily distribute and compensate the insuree for the potential costs borne. One of the key elements of Beck's original risk society thesis was that the sheer unbounded nature of contemporary risks makes them increasingly uninsurable in a world risk society. In relation to the risk of terrorism, insurance became a high profile issue after 11 September 2001 when public institutions and commercial enterprises found it increasingly difficult, if not impossible, to receive economically viable insurance coverage for terrorism risk. For Beck, the risk of what he sees as a 'new' terrorism – as with ecological and financial market risks – is unbounded and so becomes fundamentally incalculable, and it is this sheer incalculability that undermines the possibilities of governing terrorism as a problem through such traditional, institutional risk-distributing practices as insurance.

Within the United States, the attacks of 11 September 2001 produced an unprecedentedly costly exposure of $55 billion and quickly led to the acute retraction of insurance coverage for terrorism across broad swathes of the institutional landscape in America and beyond. As Ericson and Doyle (2004) relate, this catastrophic event ushered in not only an actuarial re-evaluation of the risk of terrorism but a profound new sense of uncertainty as to how the insurance industry conceptualized this new kind of terrorism as a risk. In this, a precautionary approach came to the fore, provoked by a sense of magnified uncertainty on the part of insurers as to their capacity to know, to make predictable, and thus governable, a terrorist attack. Paralleling Beck's notion of the unboundedness of contemporary risks, insurers conceived that terrorism could not be localized, that the element of intentionality would disrupt people's sense of ontological security, that correlation and reinforcement effects of an attack would

exacerbate cost outlays, while notions of profitable risk (high rise buildings and affluent middle-class employees) became radically inverted
(ibid.: 145–7).

These authors, though, are critical of what they see as Beck's simplistic assessment that insurance breaks down in a risk society or requires
propping up by the state in order to survive. In fact, in the aftermath of the
events of 11 September 2001, the principle of risk distribution did work in
the face of an (effectively) unimagined catastrophe, while elements of the
institutional and legal environment, including multi-year contracts and
state compulsion, prevented insurance companies from retracting so easily from the market. Authors like Furedi (2002b) are critical of insurance
companies whom he accuses of allowing a culture of fear to interfere with
the rational weighing up of costs and revenues and who were irrationally
propelled to withdraw from market coverage. On the contrary, Ericson and
Doyle (2004: 148) present the case that insurers 'thrive on conditions of
extreme uncertainty'. Such profoundly new environmental uncertainties,
as they see it, not only provoked tentativeness but also profit-extracting
tactics in a hardening market and the production of new, albeit more speculative, modelling techniques to tame chance (ibid.: 149–52). Pushing
beyond the boundaries of actuarial risk, Bougen (2003) has explored how
the very technology of actuarial risk itself has been reconstituted through
new hybrid forms of insurance and capital investment. In effect, this new
combination allows potential terrorist harms to be governed in ways based
not only on the principles of actuarial probability but on speculative capital investment (see also O'Malley 2003: 277). What is occurring, then, is
not the unravelling of insurance under new conditions of uncertainty but
its reconfiguration. This involves, on the one hand, a more risk-averse,
precautionary approach to the framing of uncertainty. Yet, it also involves
a disassembling of actuarial risk technologies in relation to the question of
terrorism and their reconstitution in ways that actively seek to incorporate
or embrace its uncertainty as a source of profitability (Baker 2002;
O'Malley 2004).

Of course, actuarial risk represents only one form of risk technology
through which the uncertainty and harm of terrorism is governed. Another
type can be discerned through the deployment of surveillance and associated practices of profiling, or what David Lyon (2003) calls 'social sorting'. Like insurance, risk profiling in its broadest sense is concerned with
the calculation of individuals as risks within the context of a population.
However, instead of being concerned with the distribution of harms, risk
profiling is developed for the identification and pre-emptive neutralization
of dangerous individuals. Essentially this occurs as accumulated data on a
population is mined for characteristics and attributes in an attempt to link
these to potential terrorist activity – either through a systematization of
'expert' knowledge or a quantitative empirical derivation from past events.
Authorities hope, with the use of risk profiling, to anticipate, prevent or

ameliorate the effects of a low probability but high impact event like a terrorist attack (Manning 2006: 457). Although the deployment of risk represents an apparently coherent organizational response, nevertheless, how individuals are constituted as risks is ultimately dependent upon how the risk profiling model is constructed. Key dimensions include whether the model is based on subjective expertise or objective historical data, the degree of formalization applied to it and the specific organizational and cultural setting within which it functions.

In discussing the increasing ubiquity of electronic surveillance, Lyon (1994, 2001, 2003, 2006) notes not only its expansion but its increased tendencies towards integration and automation as well as its greater dispersion within the interstices of everyday life. Here it links up to wider organizational objectives of control, profit and rationalization. In this sense, 'social sorting' is significant as it leads to the formulation of abstract coded categories through which individual subjects are allocated and acted upon within and through surveillance data flows (see also Adey 2004; Castel 1991: 248; Gandy 2003; Levi and Wall 2004: 197–8). The intensification of surveillance and the growth of risk profiling tends to be understood within the conditions of late modernity, of disembedded institutions and international flows, as individuals come to be governed as clusters of attributes in motion within the flux of a population. It is in this sense that Deleuze identifies how such control technologies attempt to manage individuals as 'dividuals', combined and recombining data elements, rather than autonomous, coherent and grounded subjects (Deleuze 1992; see also Castel 1991; Ewald 1990; Rose 1999).

In relation to the risk of terrorism, airport and passenger screening represents a specific site within which threats or harms are framed within a calculable rubric of risk. O'Malley (2006), addressing airport security in Canada, claims to identify a shift from an homogenous rule-based security to one based on risk-based selection. This shift, however, does not represent so much a disjuncture as a 'formalization' and 'intensification' of already-existing security practices (ibid.: 414; Lyon 2006). Interestingly, Curry (2004) puts practices of airport screening in a longer historical context and suggests that increased anxiety surrounding aircraft safety is traceable to the growth of mass air travel, its growing anonymization, and the loss of social distinction inhering to it. He sees the emergence within the United States of national risk profiling systems like the Computer Assisted Passenger Prescreening System (CAPPS) and its stillborn successor CAPPS II, which links air passenger name records to government information databases to create risk indices of passengers, as an attempt to reimpose a sense of understanding, familiarity and grounded narrative upon the abstracted circulation of 'risky' travellers. In this sense, for Curry, the use of risk is not merely concerned with the quantitative assessment of threat but represents an attempt to impose a certain symbolic representation of what constitutes that threat. Ultimately, it might be argued that in order to function, risk does not so much override trust as fundamentally depend upon it.

Despite pretensions to scientific accuracy and objectivity, risk technologies constitute individuals or events as risk rather than knowing them as such. In this sense, the use of management tools like risk profiling represents an attempt by organizations to impose certainty where certainty does not, and cannot, exist (Ericson 2006; Zedner 2006). Of course, this is exactly the point made by Beck and others – that knowledge in a 'risk society' is characterized precisely by a radical contingency and uncertainty (see also Reddy 1996). In consequence, as a statement of numerical probability, risk can only ever offer a statement of possibility in any given case, and so any decision justified on the basis of risk is prone to a rate of 'normal accidents' which may call into question the reliability of the system, especially for a public that may increasingly demand the impossible of absolute safety (Ewald 1993, 2002; Sunstein 2005). On the other hand, an excessive rate of 'false positives' may put an excessive strain upon organizational time and resources to the extent that the costs of using risk ultimately exceed the benefits (Ericson 2006: 348; Levi and Wall 2004). However, it is not only that risk overlays uncertainty; as risk is constituted within particular relations of power, its constitution is inherently political and its use inevitably reflects the interests of those in power. In a Weberian sense, the use of risk management may come to reflect internal organizational interests or be brandished as a response to demands for accountability rather than embodying the substantive goal of pinpointing suspect or 'risky' individuals (Manning 2006; Rothstein *et al.* 2006). Of course, such is the hold that risk management has upon the bureaucratic imagination in its search for technological fixes to complex issues, failure may ironically impel a 'spiralling' of risk management, an endless search for new, more developed, more all-embracing systems of control. Zedner (2006: 431–2), too, questions how the erosion of public privacy and the denial of certain freedoms to suspect individuals may constitute a sacrifice of individual welfare for the benefit of collective security. As an alternative to the self-delusionary rationalizing excesses of risk profiling, she proposes an alternative 'deliberative' model that embraces uncertainty by revealing the political claims that risk represses, and the psychological and cultural variables that shape risk acceptability on the part of individuals at different times and within different contexts.

Conclusion

The purpose of this chapter has been to examine how the West has understood the phenomenon of militant Islam and the threat of Islamic terrorist attack, and how risk is a potent concept for framing a sociological interpretation of this understanding. Despite its relative novelty of interest for the social sciences, risk has a long genealogy stretching back to the eighteenth century and the development of modernity. In this particular sense, risk alludes to the implicit or explicit probability of a certain harmful future state, one stemming from human choice and decision-making. What risk does, as Ewald (1993) and Luhmann (1993) explain, is draw an abstract sense of the future, with all its uncertainty and hazy contingency, and concretizes it in the reality of the 'present' as something that must be dealt with and accounted for. What is novel, however, is the increasingly more numerous areas of social life that are interpreted through this prism of risk, and within which terrorism itself has been drawn. Yet, it is not simply its quantitative significance, but also the qualitative shift in how risk is approached and understood that is relevant for our understanding here. Risk is increasingly being framed in a precautionary manner, used to articulate contingencies in a way that is not only negative, but catastrophic. In the past, where risk was used to assess the likelihood of certain harms and then weighed up against the likely benefits of certain choices, now risk becomes something to be repressed or avoided at all costs, regardless of what it is attached to.

In applying the question of risk to militant Islam and the deliberate recourse to attacks on Western targets, three theoretical perspectives on risk have been drawn upon. The theoretically pre-eminent one, of course, is the 'risk society' thesis. This understands risks as having a real tangible basis and of being of a qualitatively different order to those encountered in the past. As its progenitor Ulrich Beck understands it, such risks stem from a contemporary period of 'reflexive modernization' where the unavoidable side effects of a rampant global modernity come up against, and begin to challenge the limits of, the current institutional and international order. In the second perspective, contributions from cultural theory are located within a more general 'social constructionist' position. Social constructionists interpret risk understanding through the beliefs, norms and values of social groups, or of 'society', whereby cultural formation leads to the interpretation, elevation or dismissal of particular events as risks. A third perspective, that of governmentality, emphasizes how risk is constituted, as a discourse and a technology, through particular relations of knowledge and power. Risk, in this sense, becomes utilized within particular practices and programmes for the management of conduct of individuals and populations.

Despite the contrasts identified here, these three perspectives hardly remain aloof from one another: each is concerned with the phenomenon of uncertainty, with how future events are interpreted and understood within particular frameworks of thought, and with how these are bound to particular social contexts. Indeed, each perspective takes pains to challenge any conception that risk, as a way of framing events, has any independent objective basis, although Beck might sometimes be read in this way. All of the perspectives also allude to the growth of the precautionary paradigm whereby much risk assessment takes places with an overriding emphasis on worst-case scenarios and where lack of evidence of harm is not sufficient for certain modes of action to be deemed acceptable – in essence reversing the balance of proof test. Historically, this has been associated with the environmental movement and has been given institutional recognition through such environment frameworks as the Rio Declaration; yet today, the precautionary principle undergirds many areas of risk analysis, from child protection to the development of genetically modified organisms (Sunstein 2005). The risk of Islamic terrorism too has been incorporated into the precautionary paradigm in a rather extreme manner, not as one cautioning inaction but one that has spurred radical forms of action on the basis of overwhelming, threatening and catastrophic risk (Aradeau and van Munster 2005; Cooper 2006; Furedi 2007b; Mythen and Walklate 2006b). So, it was fear of 'unknown unknowns', risks that were apprehendable but not assessable, which led to such uncompromising initiatives as the invasion and occupation of Iraq, the curtailment of civil freedoms within the United States and United Kingdom, recourse to home detention and the extensive use of the shadowy practice of extraordinary rendition (discussed in more detail in Chapter 6). Each is or may be justified by Western governments, in the absence of 'actionable' evidence, on the basis of endeavouring to prevent the however slight or insignificant risk of catastrophe occurring, precisely the same precautionary attitude governing such areas as biotechnological development.

Such an understanding of risk bestows a new defensiveness, a permanent rearguard strategy of ducking and diving in the face of this new, unknowable but compelling reality of Islamic militancy and terrorism. Ironically, in the face of such a Damoclean sword dangling over the heads of Western populations, threatened individuals, states, institutions and private enterprises turn to risk-management strategies and technologies as the best response to tame this radical uncertainty and contingency. Yet, this is not the risk that locked individuals into a web of solidarity as in the heyday of welfarism, the defence of individual freedom through social insurance (Rose 1999: 78–83). On the contrary, shaped by the contours of neo-liberalism, it is one of individualized precaution where those that are risk-exposed are compelled by authorities to embrace the risk that appears before them. And so the targeted, from commercial businesses to state authorities to the private individual, must 'target harden', seek insurance where possible, and constantly assess and reassess the chances of attack and the scope of their 'resilience'. Diverse agencies and private authorities deploy risk as a resource to profile suspicious flows across their borders, blockading and neutralizing those exhibiting the most intolerable accretion of the wrong kinds of attributes flagged by their risk model. Whereas the prevention and distribution of risk papered over the cracks of capitalism's contradictions, presenting a progressive vision of a 'freedom from fear', the simultaneous individualization and globalization of risk represents just its inverse – a system sustained through and upon the perpetual generation of fear (Bauman 2006).

Why Western governments and authorities interpret the phenomenon of militant Islam via risk is interesting precisely because of what risk represents more widely. As Beck brings out most acutely, risk thinking today rescinds knowledge and refutes the possibility that the actions or strategy of foreign or domestic militant groups can be understood or grasped. In a sense, a curious parallel reveals itself between the newly renamed 'long war' and the open-ended, unbounded nature of risk as it is understood today. Political elites cling to the notion of freedom versus totalitarianism and label these opposing militant groups as evil, debased and aberrant. They are incomprehensible and so, through the deployment of such a moral rhetoric, are marked out as intrinsically and autonomously 'other'. In consequence, the social formation of these groups, the legacy of history, politics, racism and imperialism interweaving around their development, becomes repressed and hidden away from view. At the same time, once reified as being forever 'other', the discourse of risk becomes a central means for framing the problem; if they cannot be changed or transformed, then the risk that they represent can only be ever minimized or avoided, never quelled or eliminated. In Chapter 6, some of these issues are further developed when the interactions between acts of terror; associated threats, political, cultural, social and economic processes; and individual consciousness are explored.

6   Reacting to the militant risk

Decivilizing in the name of civilization?

Introduction

Within the West, notable shifts in political and civil societal consciousness can be noted. Freedoms that were previously considered to be synonymous with Western 'civilization' are disappearing into possible oblivion to be replaced by increasingly pervasive surveillance within a framework of repressive social control mechanisms to counter the challenge of militant Islam. These forms of psychological and legalistic constraints are part of a broader approach that also includes the militaristic strategies within the 'war on terror' that are being undertaken to defend Western peoples, their values, way of life and ultimately 'civilization'. Yet the paradox of using contradictory methods and practices in the name of civilization has attracted only limited concern across the West. Clearly events like the war in Iraq have aroused considerable levels of dissatisfaction and anger. By comparison, the insidious erosion of civil liberties and deteriorating community relations have attracted meagre opposition. Equally, in the aftermath of the September 2001 attacks on America, the death of thousands of Afghan civilians became a rarely read footnote to the 'war'. Why these acts, both military and legalistic, can be implemented with little popular protest requires examination if we are to begin to understand why 'civilized' peoples are allowing social, cultural and political precepts to be surreptitiously eradicated, in some instances seemingly unintentionally. By understanding why this is being allowed to happen, the tentative process of considering the consequences to the West can commence. This chapter is dedicated to exploring these issues, principally within the United States and, to a lesser extent, the United Kingdom.

Post-11 September 2001 reactions

Explanations concerning how America and the United Kingdom reacted to forms of terrorism after 11 September 2001 tend to be split into two camps. The first perspective, dominated by governing politicians and supported by mainstream media, portrays the 'counter-terrorism' that has emerged under the 'war on terror' umbrella as a necessary evil to fight inherent evil. Both the introduction of legal restraints and violence in the name of freedom are considered to be essential in order to safeguard what is under threat. By comparison, the opposing perspective argues that the September 2001 attacks have been manipulated by governments to enhance internal control, whilst the invasion of Iraq was driven by the political and economic interests of Western governments with vested interests in the manufacture of weapons and the plentiful supply of oil. Within this camp, there is a lack of dominant focus, with proponents split across an incompatible coalition that includes libertarians, neo-Nazis and militant Muslims. The aftermath of the 2003 invasion of Iraq and, in particular, the growing usage of Western body bags has contributed to levels of cynicism and support for the counter-argument to grow. To understand why this shift has occurred and why it has not necessarily translated into similar opposition to encroaching social controls, it is important to examine the immediate and longer term public and political responses to the September 2001 attacks. Consequently experiences and interpretations allied to social representations of acts of terrorism and subsequent events and political reactions are analysed to try to illuminate the ethical responses and non-responses or silences. It is argued that both terrorism and counter-terrorism have influenced people's moral boundaries, challenging their perceptions of safety, risk, control, public space, violence and the 'other'.

In the ensuing hours and days after the 2001 attacks on America, widespread feelings of loss, bereavement, anger and hatred were reported. Across the world, images permeated into social and individual consciousness whether in commiseration, commemoration, confusion, confrontation or celebration. The impact of the images and accompanying narrative were, like other media occasions, heavily dependent upon the social context in which the messages were received and the individual interpreters' habitus. Thus, it is reasonable to suppose that people in Rwanda's perceptions of the deaths of over 3000 people in acts of violence would be influenced by their own experiences and the widespread massacres that occurred during the 1990s. By comparison, the relative absence of violent death in the West, indeed the general seclusion of death from any cause, would be likely to contribute to greater feelings of shock, dismay and anger. The use of violence with such dramatic outcomes, injuries and deaths has been challenging to senses of social identity that were bound within perceptions of passive social controls and self-restraint. Violence as a form of collective corporal punishment that targets people based on the grounds that they are guilty of being Western is discordant with processes of justice that emerged within the Enlightenment.[1] To a certain extent the taming of public exhibitions of brutal violence and the shift from expressive to instrumental forms (Elias 1978, 2000) is also challenged. And as the following sections will argue, the processes through which the consequences of the attacks became collective, part of national mythology, grounded within the 'war on terror' discourse resulted in a sense of violation of moral sociality that extended beyond physical damage and those directly involved to incorporate a way of life. In the same way, as Kleinman *et al.* (1997) note, historical memories of social suffering, like slavery, wars, genocide and imperialism continue to have resonance within nationalism or ethnic resistance. Similarly, greater cooperation and familiarity between the United States' and United Kingdom's politicians, peoples and places can be seen to have resulted in Brits empathizing with Americans in the aftermath of the attacks. By comparison, feelings within other nation-states were influenced by restricted personal awareness of America or their political views, dominated by the perceived dominance of American hegemony. However, such theoretical comparisons fail to explain why indigenous peoples allowed, and indeed often agree with, counter-terrorism that may undermine the basis of the nation-state. To achieve this, it is necessary to examine government reactions and interactions with public consciousness.

Images, narrative, symbols and emotions became embedded within mainstream American culture and were to be reproduced within novels, plays, cartoons, documentaries, music, television and cinema. Initially cultural representation, like political and social, was dominated by the 'war on terror' discourse (Croft 2006) with limited scope or demand for challenging narrative. Consequently in the aftermath of the attacks, sources of information and representation were dominated by the government. Across the broader American public, the attacks led to a huge surge in national sentiments. Chants of 'USA, USA' accompanied Presidential public addresses and sales of Stars and Stripes flags rose dramatically.[2] These nationalist sentiments were accompanied by an atmosphere in which criticism was condemned and levels of support evaluated. Universities and academics were monitored by organizations, like Campus Watch and the American Council of Trustees and Alumni, and listed if considered to be subversive or lacking in patriotism.[3] In this sense, from the Foucauldian perspective, the 'war on terror' and subsequent public exhibition of sovereign power became defended by disciplinary power that normalized everyday behaviour during an extraordinary period of recent history. Criticism or in some instances even raising queries were quickly denounced. Croft (2006: 188) refers to the Democrat Senate Leader, Thomas A. Daschle, asking in March 2002 for clarity about where the 'war on terror' was going. In response, the Republican Senate Minority Leader, Trent Lott declared, 'How dare Senator Daschle criticise President Bush while we are fighting our war on terrorism, especially when we have troops in the field? He should not be trying to divide our country while we are united'. The media were instrumental in seeking to maintain this sense of unity that hindered or sought to ostracize critical analysis. Gradually though it became apparent that a warning had been issued to the administration prior to the attacks and support became more conditional and opposition to government policy increased. Yet even here, as Croft (2006) explains, this 'alternative discourse' operated at the margins, appealing within arts, music and broader 'alternative' scenes and protest institutions. The extent that support remained steadfast can be noticed in nearly 70% of Americans who continued to believe that Saddam Hussein was linked to the September 2001 attacks, despite lacking any tangible evidence.[4] Gradually, however, as events in Iraq unfolded and success against the perceived main 'al-Qa'ida' perpetrators was limited, levels of disquiet, distrust and disenchantment with government policy became mainstream. Yet, it will be argued that this growing counter-discourse has not significantly altered government policy in either the United States or United Kingdom. And to understand this, a more detailed examination of the cultural, political, psychological and social impact of the attacks needs to be established.

Formalizing and normalizing the 'war on terror'

In the immediate aftermath of the attacks, confusion and uncertainty were prevalent. Senses of shock and disbelief were widely reported.[5] In this, and similar situations, Wilkinson's (2005:58) interpretations of Weber's analysis of peoples' exposure to painful irrational experiences can be applied. Namely, cultural perspectives of the everyday are unable to provide meaning for acute experiences of personal suffering and social injustice. In such extreme circumstances, individuals 'are made agonizingly aware of our inability to act effectively so as to overcome the apparent causes of our affliction or, indeed, that of others'. It will be argued that the lack of meaning helped to explain political and public reactions. For both Marx and Weber, 'there is the understanding that through the pain and in the face of the horror of human suffering, people are *compelled* to change the ways they think and act' (ibid.: 66). Americans, like other peoples facing a national crisis, relied upon political leaders and media sources to provide information and levels of explanation. In other words, common meaning was constructed out of the social experiences. Many people also went to places of worship and attendance at churches and religious practice generally increased.

It will be suggested that the political interpretation of events quickly became dominant because of the inability of the general population to understand and apply meaning to proceedings. This is not to support popular perceptions about public reactions to disasters that are dominated by the legacy of Gustave le Bon (1968 [1895]). Environmental disasters and terror attacks on crowds are both considered to be the cause of mass panics when generations of civilizing processes are quickly reversed and social consciousness is decimated. Within these settings, people selfishly strive to survive irrespective of the damage their activities may inflict upon other individuals with similar aims. Yet such impressions are contrary to studies of public reactions to disasters. In reality, public and emergency services are generally considered socially responsible and effective.[6] By comparison governments have been criticized for their restricted communications following terror attacks and other forms of disaster. Sheppard *et al.* (2006) report on the delay after planes hit the buildings on 11 September 2001 before Americans were formally assured that President Bush was safe and addressing the crisis. In subsequent days, little information was provided to advise citizens on their possible involvement, which contributed to the sense of uncertainty and reliance upon the government. As Croft (2006: 103) reports, on 11 September, 'there had been no understanding of what was occurring, whether in government, media, or public as the attacks were actually happening: there was no template that could be readily deployed. Meaning had to be ascribed; and that meaning was created over hours and days'.

Within a few days, government policy became clearer as the 'enemy' was identified and targeted and the significance of events established. Quickly the government and its cultural and religious allies achieved discursive dominance that established legitimate authority and compliance during this traumatic period. Numerous members of the administration drew comparison with other traumatic episodes in American history like Pearl Harbour (Bush), and previous widely despised enemies like fascism, Nazism and totalitarianism (Bush) and the date has been described as the end of the post-Cold War period (Powell, Rice), leading Deputy Secretary of Defense, Richard Armitage, to declare 'History starts today'.[7] Thus, for Vice President Cheney, '9/11 changed everything'[8] for America and the world, a prognosis shared by security analysts, politicians and other populations.[9] Within academic circles, there was also widespread agreement over the magnitude of the event. Miller (2002: 15) reflects the views of many, when suggesting that 'the terrorist attacks of September 11 will scythe through history, separating a naively complacent past from a frighteningly vulnerable future'. These views were widely held across the population. Gaddis (2004: 80) exemplifies this when stating that 'it was not just the Twin Towers that collapsed on that morning of September 11, 2001: so too did some of our most fundamental assumptions about international, national and personal security'.

Comparisons with the Cold War period became prominent, with the new threat considered more insidious, formidable, unpredictable, flexible and ultimately destructive. Facing a threat of this magnitude, various members of the administration stressed the essentialism of the military response. For example, Donald Rumsfeld stated that 'there is no choice but to fight that war with the kind of campaign that the President has put together'. Other nations had a stark choice, expounded by George Bush, to 'stand with the civilized world, or stand with the terrorists. And for those nations that stand with the terrorists, there will be a heavy price.'[10] To help address the confusion over why the attacks had taken place, or as President Bush rhetorically enquired 'Why do they hate us?', a list of key characteristics of American life were identified. That 'they hate our freedoms' became central to the emerging level of understanding, although there is little documented evidence in support of such a claim. The significance of hate quickly became established. McCauley (2002) reports on how the links between hate and terrorism were widely supported within the media with thousands of articles connecting both words in the subsequent months. These perceptions of the 'enemies' hatred' became integral to the resurgent nationalism and the integral role of the patriot. As Hedges (2003: 10) suggests, 'patriotism ... celebrates our goodness, our ideals, our mercy and bemoans the perfidiousness of those who hate us'. By frequently referring to attacks as against all America, and associated 'way of life',[11] the 'characteristics we most cherish – our freedom, our cities, our systems of movement, and modern life – are vulnerable to terrorism'.[12] Recovery, and the defence of the nation, became the responsibility of all Americans. In so doing the administration connected into nationalist sentiments that were further strengthened through the perceptions of the victims of 11 September being sacrifices for the nation.

The centrality of the patriot within the emergent discourse is demonstrated when new laws passed in the wake of 11 September were bound within the 'Patriot Act'. Attorney General John Ashcroft explained the intentions behind the plethora of laws that were introduced, for 'the death tolls are too high, the consequences too great. We must prevent first, prosecute second.'[13] Enhanced powers in the name of protection were allocated to the government with greater jurisdiction over civil liberties that enhanced powers of arrest, detention, deportation and surveillance across social spheres ranging from telephones, email, transport to employment. A new Department of Homeland Security was created with a budget of $19.5 billion in 2002, rising to $37.7 billion in 2003.[14] The administration also arranged clandestine deportations, 'torture taxis',[15] and suspended the Geneva Convention for those interned in Guantanamo Bay. And by distancing itself from civil liberties, the United States could be considered to have implicitly supported the tactics of allies across the Middle East, Central and South Asia within the 'war on terror', who suppressed national protests for localized issues in the name of the fight against international terrorism. Within the United States, opposition to the reduction of freedom in the name of freedom initially attracted little popular protest. Across the political spectrum there was an absence of blame and concomitant consensus on the 'war on terror'. When the Senate passed a resolution shortly after the attacks, which authorized the President to use force to retaliate, the voting was 98–0. In the House of Representatives, the vote was 420–1. The dissenter was Barbara Lee who expressed concern that the bill allocated too much of Congress' power to the President and she was concerned that the approved force could result in the situation deteriorating, stating 'as we act, let us not become the evil we deplore'.[16] Croft (2006: 109) concluded that 'Democrats and Republicans, therefore, shared the responsibility – though unequally – for the decisive intervention that occurred in the aftermath of the attacks. . . .' For Croft this led to an acceptance of the 'war on terror' discourse as a form of 'common sense'. With informal social control mechanisms regulating group discourse, to question the 'war' and applied methods was to challenge liberty and freedom. From the Durkheimian perspective, critical evaluation offended or attacked the collective conscience, defiling social norms and perceptions that were grounded in the belief that America was under threat and needed to be defended. And while political division became more prominent after 2001, general consensus remained about the necessity of the 'war on terror'. Consequently, the issue was prominent within the 2004 Presidential elections, yet there was little dissent about the significance of the threat or the need for stringent measures. The debate tended to revolve around who would be better at managing the 'war' rather than its necessity.

The extent to which the terror 'threat' has been manipulated by Western and Muslim governments is contentious. It is not the intention to determine that extent here. For the purposes of this chapter, a brief review of the counter-claims will suffice, partly because they help to illuminate the challenge to the dominant discourse. The primary aim for examining the material is to establish the consequences rather than the intent. American and British governments have argued vigorously that legislation and military interventions have been primarily motivated by the desire both to eradicate terrorism and protect their own citizens against determined and unpredictable terrorists who aim to cause mass destruction and casualties. Suspicion of government actions has probably been disproportionately noticeable within the United Kingdom. This could be partly because widespread displeasure and cynicism with the 'war' was prominent before the 2005 London bombings. The attacks in America created such a shock and aroused such unity that was only fractured when allegiances, collective effervescence and common sentiments were weakened through time and events. By comparison, although the London bombings were shocking, they were less of a shock, not least because the attacks had been forecast by the British government. And the lesser impact of these bombers in terms of the mode of attack, element of surprise, numbers killed and (non) visual events restricted the extent to which experiences could become dynamic forms of social consciousness and the sites attain totemic qualities. Consequently, the social outcomes of these attacks were restricted, unable to overcome the widespread negativities about the 'war'; indeed 7 July could be considered to vindicate the opinions of those who argued that the 'war on terror' was raising the threat to British lives. Criticism of the British government's policies and the 'politics of fear' has therefore been more widespread across the media, academia and wider population. This is not to overlook the growing criticism within America, where it is argued that the 2001 crisis provided the opportunity for the neo-cons to gain prominence. Zbigniew Brzezinski, former national security adviser to President Carter, raised similar issues with respect to a 'culture of fear'. He argues that the ambiguities of the 'war on terror' have enabled the US administration to spread fear which 'obscures reason, intensifies emotions and makes it easier for demagogic politicians to mobilize the public on behalf of the policies they want to pursue'.[17] The impact of fear is discussed in greater detail shortly. Lustick (2006) observes how Republican pollster and strategist Frank Luntz recommended a strategy that continuously appealed to the memory of 11 September.[18] And there appears to be grounds to suggest that there has been an overreaction to recent bombings. Mueller (2006) provides numerous examples including more Americans being killed in car crashes, drowning in toilets or bee stings than by international terrorism. Yet the attention to such 'killers' is scant. By comparison, billions have been spent on securitization and militarization, yet the outcomes in terms of prosecutions and proven failed attacks are minimal.

However, Furedi (2007b) points out, the political reactions to terrorism need to be considered as part of a broader 'culture of precaution' and broader concerns within a 'risk society' (discussed in Chapter 5). Thus, terrorism is another omnipresent risk alongside global warming, environmental disasters, nuclear meltdowns, cancers, heart disease, obesity and so on to be feared and wherever possible prevented. Advancements in technology, communications, chemistry, physics, economy and transportation are seen to increase the risk of terrorism while terrorists are more willing to take risks. Examined from this perspective, the 'successes' that characterize late modernity could be considered to be contributing to greater feelings of vulnerability and unpredictability. As Bauman (2002: xvi) states, 'risks and contradictions go on being socially produced' before going onto declare 'it is just the duty and the necessity to cope with them that is being individualized'. For many types of risk, most notably health related, the latter part of the statement is true. However, there are some ambiguities over the extent to which individuals are expected to manage the risk of terrorism which is explored later.

Similarly, the utilization of fear for political purposes is not unusual. Indeed, there are obvious security reasons why governments are selective with released information and 'facts'. And most important, for the development of this chapter's argument, irrespective of the purposes and transparency of government actions, American and British policies have both fuelled levels of fear and original sources of unity. They have also been countered by growing dissent and anger. Analysing the outcome led Brzezinski to comment, 'We are now divided, uncertain and potentially very susceptible to panic in the event of another terrorist act in the United States itself'.[19] As Furedi (2007b: 157) argues, 'there is little evidence to substantiate the claim that the politics of fear and the associated "terrorism industry"[20] has succeeded in promoting a mood of unity in face of an external enemy.' And rather than governments seeking to reassure populations that they have the problem under control, they have fuelled levels of fear and perceptions of the 'enemy's' potential by stating that attacks will be inevitable, will involve weapons of mass destruction (WMD) at some point[21] and the 'war' will be long.[22] In addition, not only will nation-states be involved in a 'long war' but the enemy's threat would be constant and all inclusive. According to the American Office of Homeland Security (2002: 1), the terrorists 'can strike at any place, at any time, and with virtually any weapon'. Unsurprisingly, these reactions are being utilized by the militants. Furedi (2007b) comments on how bin Laden has a grasp of the 'rules of fear' that prevail in Western societies and attunes his statements to these anxieties through popular culture and media. Consequently, without a 'robust system of meaning, the threats have been far more effective in producing fears than in encouraging the emergence of new solidarities. Sadly, shared meaning for most people is confined to fear of being a target, rather than being inspired to stand up for a way of life' (Furedi 2007b: 98).

Clearly perceptions of security and interrelated feelings of threats[23] and fears are socially constructed. As such, they vary across time and place, heavily influenced by cultural mores, social consciousness and political discourse. And fears about terrorism connect into broader levels of uncertainty and insecurity. The debate about the political manipulation of fear also connects into the post-11 September analysis. Robin (2004) argues that political leaders and militants can define the public's object of fear that usually connects into a real threat. This allocates considerable power to the definers who are able to identify the threat, its origins, sources and methods for eradication, although without necessarily being deterministic. Members of the public may fear the identified threat differently. Political control of fear will establish the extent to which it will be prominent across society and the response will be heavily influenced by the definers' ideological persuasion and strategic purpose. Thus, 'political leaders view danger through a prism of ideas, which shapes whether they see a particular danger as threatening or not, and a lens of political opportunity, which shapes whether they see that danger as helpful or not' (ibid.: 16).

Feelings of vulnerability are therefore at least reinforced by the government sponsored perception that anyone and anywhere is a potential target, no one can be safe and no place totally secure. As the Office of Homeland Security (2002: vii) stated, 'Our society presents an almost infinite array of potential targets that can be attacked through a variety of methods'. Fears are further inflamed by officials stressing the unpredictability of the terrorists. Contemporary feelings of vulnerability connect into the broader debate about risk society outlined in Chapter 5.

The threat of terrorism can therefore be incorporated within a general framework of risk analysis. It is another uncertainty, another uncontrollable that is beyond the individual's control, further reinforcing senses of powerlessness. The technologies, freedoms, transportation and communications that are the bedrock of contemporary Western societies also benefit terrorism. And this is one of the ironies of the American and British emphasis upon terrorism threatening the 'way of life' because it is Western ways of life that are providing the targets and the means of attacking those targets. Western governments therefore face the dilemma of protecting their values and practices against people who are utilizing the opportunities that these offer. Consequently, this mythological way of life is under threat from both terrorists and from Western governments.

Roots of contemporary (counter) terrorism discourse

The 9/11 Commission Report stated that the 'most important failure' of the US government was 'one of imagination'. Furedi (2007b) argues that on the contrary, American society, particularly the mass media, is embedded with images of conflict and terrorism. And over recent generations, there has been fertile imagination of a terror threat emphasized when a large majority of Americans considered terrorism to be their number one concern between 1980 and 1985. Yet acts of terrorism were responsible for 17 deaths during this period compared with 25,000 people who were murdered. And government agencies have since fuelled fears of 'imaginative' threats with their emphasis upon the all-pervasive and omnipresent terror threat.

History and subsequent cultural and political developments are also important when seeking to understand recent behaviour. Today's norms and values can be traced to the legacy of (White) Christians embedded within American representations and arguably have influenced the relatively high rates of religiosity within the country. Religious values like other forms of social explanation will therefore be influential for interpreting terror attacks and seeking to attain meaning even within secular institutions. Hedges (2003: 146) has suggested that following events like the Gulf War and 2001 attacks,

> the enterprise of the state became imbued with a religious aura. . . . And because we in modern society have walked away from institutions that stand outside the state to find moral guidance and spiritual direction, we turn to the state in times of war. The state and the institutions of the state become, for many, the center of worship in wartime. To expose the holes in the myth is to court excommunication.

Contrary, however, to Hedges' implicit remark that Americans do not attain moral guidance from religious institutions, millions continue to do so. But many of these believers of a transcendental unitary god face a dilemma. As Weber (1965) observed, believers have to reconcile the all-powerful God with imperfections like inequality and injustice. In the aftermath of terror attacks, people seek to make sense of the attacks which challenge both secular and theological meanings. This may partly explain the tendency for 'Islamic' terrorists to be dismissed with rhetoric that fails to engage with rational explanation. Instead, as the 'axis of evil' emphasis showed, there has been an utilization of the neo-cons religious sentiments and an irreversible battle between 'good' and 'evil'. For example, Bush (2002a) interconnects the good and the evil when stating that 'the prayers of this nation are a part of the good that has come from the evil of September the 11th, more good than we could ever have predicted.'

'Scapegoating', which became noticeable immediately after the 2001 attacks, also has historical precedents. In the Second World War nearly 100,000 Japanese Americans were interned after Japan attacked Pearl Harbour in 1941, which Kaplan (2006) notes aroused little popular protest. However, the use of fear can be traced throughout modern American history. Robin (2004: 14) suggests that 'from the Alien and Sedition Acts of the late 1790s to the repression of abolitionists in the early nineteenth century to the various red scares of the twentieth, the United States has hardly been immune to the use of fear as a form of intimidation'. To this list, the civil fears of nuclear attack, WMDs, 1970s terrorism and global warming could be added.

Consequently, the history of the United States is embedded with images of religion and national superiority, inflated fears of challenges from an 'other' to that superiority and a willingness to suspend universal human rights in a manner that is particularly damaging to the potential 'others' who may be part of the supposed challenge.

Collective conscience and unity in times of crisis

Following terror attacks, a greater sense of togetherness is reported or as Durodié (2004a) suggested, in Chapter 5, social bonds are reaffirmed and social capital increased. Individuals possess a shared sense of violation, moral indignation and frequently consider the acts to be against national values and symbols and the collective 'we'. Blom *et al.* (2007: 16–17) develop these points when suggesting that 'the effect of suicide bombings and to a lesser extent hostage-taking, is . . . to create a "community of insecurity"'. However, the extent to which insecurity permeates or dominates the community is heavily dependent upon the collective identities and personal habitus which the acts impact upon. This impact also has to be countered by studies that indicate that disasters, including terror attacks, tend to result in huge increases in social solidarity.[24]

The sense of 'symbolic community'[25] that formed from witnessing the events, generally on television, became a social force to encourage and recreate. When examining responses to the attacks, Durkheim's (1984 [1893]) common or collective conscience can help to illuminate the shared beliefs, practices and effervescence that emerged in the immediate aftermath. Such beliefs become spread throughout society, providing definitions and meaning to experiences and actions. The extent to which both the beliefs and practices were shared, and the impact upon individual consciousness, depended upon characteristics of the volume, intensity, determinateness and content. Of particular relevance here is the pervasiveness and intrusiveness of the common beliefs and practices across society and the degree both to which individuals were attached to common beliefs and the impact upon their values and behaviour. When attachments were strong, there would be greater commitment to prevailing collective beliefs and similarities between individuals. For Durkheim the most obvious example of the collective conscience could be noted in the form of legal rules that formalized common behavioural codes and specified sanctions. Rule breakers were established as deviants. However, in the context of contemporary United States and United Kingdom, the specification of legislation that informs common conscience and results in differentials between social groups and geographical regions within and between countries infers that the 'suspects' are beyond the consensus, outsiders to the 'we-image'.

But as the preceding discussion suggests, how people interpret and react differs. At one level, there is greater consensus and sharing of experiences, fear and vulnerability. But despite providing feelings of communal belonging and greater unity, these social bondings do not address the broader concerns. For this, individuals and their 'communities of insecurity' seek guidance and the imposition of power from government and related agencies. Yet as Furedi (2007b) points out, this does not inevitably mean that individuals will adhere to government interpretations of the threat. At this point Furedi's analysis appears somewhat confusing. In essence, he is arguing that individuals adopt moods of fatalism as a consequence of living within a free-floating culture of fear immersed with government-induced feelings of vulnerability. This then results in people becoming cynical about government versions of events. However, only a minority of the people within the survey supported this claim and expressed the view that the threat of terrorism was inflated. Nor is it clear why individuals continue to feel vulnerable despite many believing that the threat of terrorism is exaggerated.[26]

The appeal to collective consciousness and the common threat to social identities is, as Robin (2004) notes, most prominent during wartime. And he argues, without generic moral and political principles, it is only fear that can unify the people during crises. Fletcher (1997), when discussing the work of Norbert Elias, suggests that at these times, the 'we-I' balance swings more towards the former. At this stage, the group becomes the primary focus of loyalty and people will acquiesce to the need to protect and maintain the broader entity, generally the nation-state.

The role of remembrance

Integral to the formation of the collective national conscience have been the processes through which the attacks have been subsequently observed. Remembrance of the dead happened almost instantaneously, embedded within narrative and images that emerged, reinforced through local and national vigils, advertisement hoardings marketing a particular idea like 'Remember 9–11' and 'United We Stand' (Croft 2006), regular commemorations across economic, social, cultural and political spheres and media portrayals of the attacks and acts of heroism. Commemoration has taken different forms, generating a remembrance economy with a range of memorabilia produced for a market that seems a hybrid of the 'celebration' of martyrdom in the Palestinian territories and tourist gift shops outside the Tower of London.[27] At times this has become veneration of the dead which has continued with a series of commemorations signifying dates and connections with issues of national and local importance. Comparisons can be drawn with Ramphele's (1997:110) study of political widowhood in South Africa. In South Africa, the label 'political widow' carried with it public ownership of the labelled who was also a valuable resource for the organization to whom her husband was affiliated. And 'she embodies the social memory that has to be cultivated and kept alive to further the goals of the struggle, and hopefully to also act as a deterrent against further losses such as hers'. Similarly common memories surrounding the 11 September attacks and the roles of the victims' families and friends were instrumental in the public senses of grief and recovery and the need to prevent similar episodes of loss. Ground Zero, the site of the Twin 'Freedom' Towers, remains a national focal point. In some respects the site has been attributed with totemic qualities, personifying and representing American experiences and feelings of the attacks. Arguably the site is a source of shared social consciousness that revolves around a negative event rather than a positive embodiment of the collective. And this ritualization of grief through actions, memorials and media coverage of the shock, devastation and associated sacrifice and heroism strengthens senses of loyalty and nationalist commitment. It is argued that these shared experiences contribute to emotions being coordinated or shaped.

The impact of this extended form of mourning connects into Durkheim's (1996 [1912]) study of religious life. For Durkhein, the 'communion of mourning' neutralizes and becalms feelings of bereavement and distress. These processes also provide a form of 'moral communion' that affirms people with a clearer sense of collective loyalty and concern. Therefore, the collective effervescence that is generated provides intense relationships by which the community recovers from the loss of a valued member or particular tragedy. However, compassion can also have a dark side that is explored by Arendt (1963: 86–7). She also observed a potent force of 'human solidarization' but argued that these feelings could be subjected to political exploitation by leaders who override ordered processes of 'persuasion, negotiation and compromise'. Bauman (1989) also suggests that social solidarities can be constructed for different purposes including inclusive and exclusive. When moral capacities are shaped by the state then solidarities can result, other factors depending, in xenophobia and, as Bauman illustrates, ultimately in the holocaust. 'The commitment of people to ideals of community and in particular to certain sets of values and collective identity can become restrictive, resulting in pressure to keep the intended flock in the fold ... the craved-for cosiness of belonging is offered as a price of unfreedom' (Bauman 1995: 277).

But while terror acts in the West have been followed by well-publicized forms of commiseration, the killing of civilians by the American-led coalition in the 'war on terror' has been notable for its lack of compassion.

Deaths of the (non) others

We do not acknowledge the destruction of beings outside our moral community as suffering; we detach ourselves from their pain as if it were an incomprehensible behaviour encountered on some Swiftian island. Within a moral community, we employ names like *martyr* or *hero* and inscribe the suffering of our own people within narratives of hallowed sacrifice and epic achievement.

(Morris 1997: 40)

How the 'war on terror' has been interpreted is clearly heavily influenced by the international, national and localized contexts and time in which events are relayed and which can modify the effects. Across the West, people struggle to understand social actions, confronted by public death and suffering that is frequently and graphically depicted across the mass media but in reality has gradually become privatized or considered to be an aberration within modernity (Ariès 1974; Bauman 1992; Prior 1989). Uncertainty about public deaths, and the nature of those deaths, can therefore further confuse.[28] Following attacks both in the United States and within subsequent conflicts as part of counter-terrorism, the veneration of the American dead has continued. The 11th of September remains engrained within popular culture and the frequent deaths within the military are sustained as a major news item. By comparison, reactions to the deaths of non-Western civilians are rather different. Acts of national American aggression are sanitized, with the killing of enemies rarely questioned and innocent civilians ignored or briefly depersonalized as 'collateral damage', inevitable casualties of war. As Hedges (2003: 13) suggests,

While we venerate and mourn our own dead we are curiously indifferent about those that we kill. Thus killing is done in our name, concerns us little, while those who kill our own are seen as ... lacking our own humanity and goodness. Our dead. Their dead. They are not the same.

The dehumanization of enemies is a regular feature within war and needs to be considered as part of a process of moral disengagement that also includes the death of civilians. Studies of processes within terror groups can help illuminate actions and rationale across the spectrum of political violence. Bandura (1998) outlines a number of tactics that are applied by terror groups.

It can be argued that warring parties and governments have also tended to utilize similar practices to terror groups to justify the death and devastation caused by their actions. Moral justification categorizes the 'other' as evil or identifies a reason why the attacks were legitimate. For example, Muhammed Siddique Khan, the cell leader of the 7 July London bombers, referred to commuters being targets because they had either supported the government or had not taken the opportunity to vote against it. Stories emphasizing the 'evil' of the enemy are commonplace. German soldiers were widely considered to have bayoneted babies in the First World War while Iraqis in the 1991 Gulf War were believed to have thrown babies out of Kuwaiti hospital windows. There was no substantive evidence for either claim. Displacement is also used to blame others and can be a sign that many terrorists have become separated from grounded reality. Other tactics of disengagement are to minimize or ignore suffering from actions and to dehumanize victims who are described as animals or objects, epitomized by the West German terror group, the Red Army Faction's depiction of capitalists and security personnel as 'pigs' (Vertigans 2008). A mixture of these processes can be found within the (lack of) reactions to the Western military coalition's counter-terrorism based upon aggression/defence and in particular the destructive consequences. For example, Donald Rumsfeld (2001) sought to justify the killing of civilians by the American military by arguing that, 'We did not start this war. So understand, responsibility for every single casualty in this war, whether they're innocent Afghans or innocent Americans, rests at the feet of the al-Qaeda and the Taliban'. Attempts to depict the 'other' as evil or mentally insane can also be considered to be a method of justifying actions but also suggest a failure to identify, and thus address, underlying social factors behind radicalization. Portrayals in a speech in 2002 by George Bush were interpreted by David Frum[29] to suggest that 'Bush was identifying Osama bin Laden and his gang as literally satanic'. George Bush (2002b) extended the association of the 'other' with dehumanized characteristics into insanity when stating to the United Nations General Assembly in 2002 that 'our greatest fear is that terrorists will find a shortcut for their mad ambitions when an outlaw regime supplies them with the technologies to kill on a massive scale'.

The outcome of the Western-led attacks and their accompanying justification is represented across the media. In the age of 'infotainment' the regularity and persistence of media news coverage and competition for viewers and readers have led some to argue that people are becoming increasingly apathetic to human suffering because of their overfamiliarity and confusion over multiple environmental disasters, famines, civil wars and genocide. Ignatieff (1998: 24) argues that while there has been an 'internationalization of conscience' by which people feel they have a moral responsibility to alleviate the suffering of strangers in a strange land, this does not translate into humanitarian actions. Instead, viewers have become morally confused and develop a form of 'shallow misanthropy', overwhelmed by the range and magnitude of human suffering that they consider renders them powerless.

Consequently, while enhanced media coverage has contributed to greater awareness of international despair and devastation, it also 'encourages a retreat from the attempt to understand' (ibid.: 24). Conversely, more knowledge could be considered to result in less understanding.

Kleinman and Kleinman (1997) have argued similar points. What they describe as the mediatization of violence and suffering has resulted in human misery becoming normalized and voyeuristic experiences changing from moral responsibility to consumption of images. And as Beattie *et al.* (1999) and Philo *et al.* (1999) have shown, media representations of disaster, war, famine and disease are superficial, lacking detailed information that would contribute towards ethical engagement, enhanced understanding of the complexities behind the images and a resultant greater empathy. Faced with portrayals of extensive suffering and a sense of moral fatigue, futility or disinterest, the contemporary consumer can resolve their ambiguity or angst by switching channels, turning to another page or logging onto a different Web site. For Bauman (1998: 80) this is part of a wider trend of 'adiaphorization'. By this, he is referring to the moral indifference and ambiguities of individuals to overexposed levels of violence and suffering with boundaries between representation and reality blurred.

Differences between media providers are also noticeable. Comparing the coverage of al-Jazeera and Fox News quickly identifies that the former are much more likely to transmit images of civilian casualties and fatalities than the latter where the human cost of US actions is hidden. For example, American coverage of the invasion of Iraq concentrated upon real and graphic animation of military actions. These portrayals connected into concerns about the infotainment of the news, with the 'war' depicted as a spectacle, entertainment or game reinforced by the 'expert' commentary by former (military) players on strategy, goals, actions, offensive tactics, results and so on. Viewers connected into these anaesthetized impressions of dramatic explosions in multi-colour caused by technologically 'smart' weapons with no evidence of casualties from the safety of homes, thousands of miles from the conflict.

By comparison, satellite stations like al-Jazeera have challenged the Western dominance of interpreting events. The rise of such media outlets and the explosion of blogging have, as Kaplan (2006) notes, made it much more difficult for governments and consensual media operators to manage news stories. However, attempts to partially portray events continue. Kaplan (2006: 5) suggests that in the aftermath of the 2001 attacks,

> There appears to have been a conscious moratorium on reporting news that did not fit with the American self-perception of victimization and its sense of righteous indignation. There was from the beginning a conscious decision in the mainstream media – born as much of the bitter experience of Vietnam as of the post-9/11 surge of patriotism – not to show suffering other than that of the Americans themselves.

This resulted in a lack of human casualties being shown, and if there were any then these tended to be explained in the context of the suffering caused within America on 11 September. And during conflict, reporters have tended to be established within US combat units, thus ensuring that only the American perspective is shown. Yet, despite the connection between government and media narratives, the perception of the 'war on terror' was ultimately to be challenged not only by the civil conflict within Iraq but by the actions of the American military. Previously the abuse of human rights at Guantanamo Bay and the Abu Ghraib prison in Iraq and the use of 'torture taxis' may never have reached public consciousness. However, in the age of bloggers, mobile phone and digital cameras and competitive media rivals identifying and investigating unusual behaviour, stories or sightings, these images and narratives could no longer be suppressed and the associated images have become some of the best known of the 'war'.

Decivilizing on behalf of civilization

> The United States makes no distinction between those who commit acts of terror and those who support and harbour them because they are equally as guilty of murder. Any government that chooses to be an ally of terror has also chosen to be an enemy of civilization. And the civilized world must hold those regimes to account.
>
> (Bush 2005)

In this statement Bush seeks to connect into broader levels of 'self consciousness of the West' (Elias [1939]) drawing Western perspectives into the 'war' and, by implication, the defence of associated morality, values and behaviour; a tactic that was certainly fruitful in mobilising and maintaining the consensus. International tensions and intra-state reactions contributed to the formation of outsiders, although the lack of clarity of the nature of the 'enemy' contributed to an extension of the parameters and the national 'we-ideals'. In the aftermath, people of apparent Middle Eastern appearance were categorized by many Americans to be outside the 'we-ideals' and as such were a possible threat, exemplified by physical violence against people who 'appeared' Muslims and the broader rise in Islamophobia.

Collective constraints within norms and values associated with the 'war on terror' discourse enabled legislation to be passed that adversely impacted against an internal minority and external populations for the 'greater good'. And in terms of impact, there are clear demarcations between experiences. Residents of White middle-class housing zones will often only experience any inconvenience in transit through airports. By comparison, residents of overwhelmingly Muslim communities encounter enhanced police surveillance and are much more likely to be questioned under the anti-terror legislation. In other words, the legislation is largely being applied against people who belong to one religious group, namely

Muslims. The consideration of certain groups of people as being outside the jurisdiction of human rights legislation[30] is, Arendt (1973) suggests, the first step in treating them as superfluous. Government actions both internally and internationally could be argued to be a form of expediency that can be justified by the longer term benefits for the majority. Lord Cromer's (1913) statement when explaining the problems caused by legal reforms introduced in Egypt under British rule, that 'civilisation must, unfortunately, have its victims', continues to apply.

Croft (2006: 285) suggests that government policy has been to establish that 'the enemies in the "war on terror" are so appalling that it has been "common sense" to change the rules of war and detention' and 'constructing an ultimate enemy contains the seeds of dehumanisation'. 'In the "war on terror", the terrorists are all the ultimate enemies: they are barbarians, who seek to destroy civilisation itself. And so all means of defeating that enemy are in some ways legitimised' (Croft 2006: 283).

The legal restraints can be considered to be fundamentally in opposition to the very values that are being promoted and defended within the 'war', namely freedom, justice and democracy. Cromer's expediency approach becomes of even greater anxiety when interconnected with rising levels of fear and vulnerability. Elias (1996: 358–9) has argued that, for the established elite, an inflated fear of the 'other' and associated military and discursive contradictions increases,

> the more they develop the sense that they are fighting for their own supremacy with their backs against the wall, the more savage for the most part does their behaviour become and the more acute the danger that they will disregard and destroy the civilised standards on which they pride themselves. . . . With their backs against the wall, the champions [of civilization] easily become the greatest destroyers of civilization.

Consequently, while the overinflated fear of the 'other' may be part of an approach for manipulating the masses, it is also contributing to a greater sense of challenge to the long-established Western and in particular American hegemony. In other words, the attacks contradicted America's post-Cold War 'we-image' of global dominance attributed to their political, economic and cultural superiority. The events of 11 September shattered these illusions and suggested a large fracture between 'we-image' and reality. Facing this deficit contributed to inflated feelings of insecurity and vulnerability and the perceived need to suspend or subjugate standards of conduct in order to safeguard those very principles on which the perceived superiority was based.

Clearly the changes that have been implemented across the United Kingdom and United States are almost incomparable to the 'decivilizing spurt' (Elias 1996: 1) that was experienced in Germany that enabled millions of Jews to be massacred. Nor is such a spurt being predicted in the short term across the West, not least because the 'path towards barbarity and dehumanization always take a considerable time to unfold in relatively civilized societies' (Elias 1988: 197). However, this does not mean that encroaching state constraints and enhanced surveillance should not be viewed with concern. Broader feelings of fear, vulnerability and uncertainty across Western societies interact with governments' approaches which include a reduction in mutual identification between constituent groups and also nation-states, different cultural expectations about minorities and concomitant expectations of change that are contributing to a fragmentation of social interconnections.[31] And although these processes and emotions do not necessarily equate to a 'de-civilising sport', their extensive nature suggests it is possible to apply Burkitt (1996) and van Krieken's (1999) analysis of Western 'civilising' processes which can simultaneously incorporate both 'civilising' and 'decivilising' trends. These problems will become compounded if the wider changes occurring within Western societies including uncertainties, moral fatigue, ambiguity and distance contribute to weaker consciousness which would make individuals more fearful of 'outsiders' and even less likely to defend universal rights if they are introduced to safeguard the majority against the minority.

Formal and informal processes of rationalization

Despite the unintentional outcome of policies and actions identified in the preceding sections, it is important to establish that these were introduced within a framework of rationalization. Within the War on Terror there are clear signs of rationalization being introduced within the American reaction and formation of the 'war' discourse. Processes were implemented that were designed to ensure internal control and eradicate an 'enemy' through planning and procedure.

The social construction of compassion from the senses of despair, anger and suffering often succeeds terror attacks. Political leaders and cultural institutions are fundamentally important at this juncture. Following the 11 September attacks, the American administration, media[32] and religious leaders formed a consensual coalition that provided feelings of leadership, legitimacy and moral authority based upon historical charisma and rational principles of law, although those laws had to be changed to reallocate the exercise of power. By a combination of laws, personalities and historical interconnections, the coalition, taking the lead from the political administration, collectively strived to unite Americans in the face of attack and in turn to secure broad support to 'react'. In this, the American example exemplifies shifting normative standards of state violence and internal social controls. As Dunning *et al.* (1988) have noted, perceptions of what is considered to be 'legitimate' violence vary between societies and over time within societies.

During periods of emergency in the West, special powers are awarded to governments with little opposition. Since 2001 these powers have become enshrined within legislation with nations deemed perpetually under threat. Thus, on 14 September 2001, the US Congress granted the President the right to 'use all necessary and appropriate force against those nations, organisations, or persons he determines planned, authorized, committed, or aided the terrorist attacks'. Elshtain (2003) drew upon the Augustinian just war notion to describe the military reaction and connected into the political sentiments of the time. She argued that the grievous extent of the attacks demanded a forceful response which would reaffirm the value of civil peace and the basic rules of international society. Comparisons with wartime experiences can help to illuminate some of the reactions to terror attacks. These factors may also help explain why the American administration controversially titled the counter-terrorism strategy the 'war on terror'. Stress on the 'war on terror' or 'long war' and emphasis on the justness of defensive attack has created different tensions and allegiances than would have formed had the approach been described as 'counter-terrorism' and military actions as 'invasions.' However, by attributing greater powers to the President, existing formal laws and procedures were replaced by rapidly evolving ideas and opinions that were more grounded in personal, religious and political discourse and interests.

In times of war, as Bourne (1991 [1918]) noted, the government attains power and significance that was not possible during peace. Political constraints and critical challenges that are an integral component of democracy are subsumed by feelings of patriotism and the unquestioned necessity for uniformity of opinion and obedience. In such contexts, loyalty or 'war orthodoxy' becomes the primary determinant of social consciousness. Distinctions between society and individual diminish with social and cultural differences undermined in celebration of ideals, inherent superiority and collective uniformity. Conversely, differences with possible 'enemies within' and associated ethnic groups are extenuated (especially amongst those who are more 'patriotic' than the government). Such attitudes connect into shared memories of blood sacrifice within nations' mythology and common histories. For the individual, Hedges (2003: 3) suggests that,

> Even with its destruction and carnage it [war] allows us what we long for in life. It can give purpose, meaning, a reason for living. . . . And war is an enticing elixir. It gives us resolve, a cause. It allows us to be noble. And those who have the least meaning in their lives . . . are all susceptible to war's appeal.

The post-11 September emphasis on legal/militaristic rational responses connected into the normative shifts that people were undergoing as a consequence of the horrors they had witnessed and whose magnitude was continually being reinforced across cultural and political spheres. Peoples' realities could not adequately explain what had happened and the concomitant feeling of meaningless and social injustice at the collective punishment imposed upon Americans that lacked Enlightenment conditions for justice. Arguably such feelings were reinforced by the nature of the attacks which contravened pervasive health and safety regulations that citizens generally adhere to. Applying Elias (1978), peoples' feelings became expressed through the primacy attributed to the nation-state and the use of violence. Social allegiance to the nation-state over other loyalties such as cities, towns, villages and tribes is strongest when the group's survival is under threat, or their lives need to be defended or a united attack is required against another group. It could be argued that these features were prominent in the aftermath of 11 September and the support for retaliatory violence. And most Americans, and indeed most nationalities, knowledge about inter-state relations often restricted to acts of violence, famine and environmental disaster and develop few, if any, broader allegiances. By comparison, as Elias (1996) notes, individuals tend, and are encouraged, to develop strong beliefs in their own nation-state and are confident that it represents the high-est moral values, or at least the best available. And in doing so they con-nected into Weber's (1978) typology categorizing why people obey orders. In the aftermath of the 2001 attacks, the American people can be seen to have adopted the administration's 'war on terror' through a combination of a sense of duty and moral commitment, apathy or inability to identify other appropriate courses of action, fear of punishment (and in this example could be added social ostracism) and self-interest.

Emotional deskilling and diminished resilience

These political, cultural and social processes are happening at a time when the ability of Western societies to cope with crisis and related suffering seems contradictory. As Morris (1997: 27) notes there is 'an almost inter-minable discourse of complaint, lament, litigation, symptom-mongering, and public confession'. These persistent outbursts of emotion are also occurring alongside the 'silence of suffering' as most people are able to 'tune out unwelcome news'. At a pragmatic level, Bauman (2000) has pointed out that for people in the ambivalence of what he calls 'liquid modernity', flexibility is essential and knowledge and skills quickly become obsolete. And the awareness, techniques and technology required to undertake tasks that previously would have been the responsibility of the householder can now be resolved through purchasing a time-saving device or employing an 'expert' to quickly undertake an activity that would formerly have taken considerably longer. In these settings, people are becoming increasingly deskilled, reliant upon a multitude of services and professions. In a similar way it can be argued that people are less reliant upon social networks to resolve personal issues but instead rely upon impersonal paid assistance, which may partly explain the huge increase in therapists. Across the West, but particularly in America, there is greater reliance on these professionals to deal with vulnerability and private and public stresses, crises and disasters that would previously have been left to the individual and informal social recovery networks.

Increasingly there is an expectation that recovery will be required after events like relationship breakdowns and disasters. For example, three days after the 11 September attacks, CNN (Rowland 2001) was reporting that survivors develop symptoms associated with trauma in the aftermath. Quoting Dr Karen Sitterlee, a 'mental health expert', CNN reported that 'victims aren't the only ones who can suffer. Rescue workers, family members, co-workers, and even those who watched from a distance – including on television – are also at risk. . . . Because of the nature of terrorism and the unique features associated with terrorism, [it] really creates a much larger or greater group of victims.' Within social processes and activities that are enhancing feelings of helplessness and anxiety, what Furedi (2004, 2007a) describes as the 'therapy culture' has resulted in people being discouraged from coping without professional support. 'Help-seeking has been turned into a virtue' (Furedi 2007b: 174). Yet, Furedi (2007b) points out, this is a recent development. Physical destruction does not inevitably result in the destruction of social capital. Citing Dynes' (2003: 15) remark that 'social capital is the only form of capital which is renewed and enhanced quickly in emergency situations', Furedi (2007b) suggested that social capital can increase during times of crisis. Drawing upon examples from the Second World War and major flooding in the 1950s, he compares the circumstances whereby preceding communities would reorganize and adjust to threats to contemporary situations where the impact of disasters is indeterminate and the potential for long-term emotional damage considerable. 'In contrast to previous experiences the emphasis is not on returning to normal life but on providing support for people to cope with the new life ahead of them' (ibid.: 121). Historically, distress, disaster and death have been integral components of the life experience. Yet, the reduction or removal of individual capacities (and concomitant reliance on 'experts') has become a self-fulfilling prophecy. Namely, the view that individuals will suffer mental anguish because they are incapable of confronting shocking events and life experiences without professional assistance has become reality. Thus, Western societies have created conditions in which levels of resilience have diminished and there is both a deafening 'silence of suffering' and publicized expressions of emotion and professional coping mechanisms. Yet, in the immediate aftermath of terror attacks people directly involved were shown to cope effectively and responsibly.

War of ideas

Within the West generally, and the United States in particular, there has been confusion both about what is being fought for and who is being fought against. The confusion stems in part from naming the 'counter-terrorism' approach, the 'war on terror'. As the US senator, Rick Santorum, declared, this title is 'like saying World War II was a war on blitzkrieg'.[33] Describing the conflict as action against a tactic has, as Furedi (2007b) remarked, contributed to the enemy behind the tactic being ambiguous and exemplified the lack of lucidity within the American administration. Six years after the 'war' commenced, as Furedi (2007b) notes, beyond al-Qa'ida leaders there is no obvious enemy and thus no clear targets.

Equally though, as earlier chapters detailed, militant Islamists may be successful in encouraging people to adopt the lesser *jihad*. Yet, if militants beyond the 'hardcore' are examined, widespread and in-depth knowledge of the discourse is limited within the West. This is a combination both of the release of sparsely detailed political doctrine by groups relating to al-Qa'ida and activists' restricted knowledge of Islamic scripture. In other words, it is the failure and feelings of estrangement and disillusionment with the West which is proving to be instrumental in processes of Islamic radicalization, allied to perceptions of a glorious Muslim history which justified the reapplication of religion. How this could be achieved, what it would look like and what it would mean for the lifestyles of many supporters and possible activists' lifestyles remain fundamentally important issues. Yet, beyond the simplistic spectrum that incorporates idealization by the militants and stereotypes by the American administration, there is a lack of concerted attention placed upon the feasibility of the rival discourse.

In seeking to challenge militant Islam, Western values like freedom, justice and democracy have been promoted to attract support and undermine the appeal of the opposing discourse. However, this is problematic because these values and principles are also being utilized to highlight inconsistencies and contradictions which have seriously undermined Western ideals. And as Kaplan (2006) observes, events instigated after 11 September by the American administration, initially endorsed by a broad consensual spectrum, have led to a 'lack of certainty and confidence in America's own moral rectitude'.

There is also an implicit contradiction in that Western leaders are promoting ideals of the Enlightenment and the need for secular rationalization. Yet, within the American administration in particular, there has been a clear usage of religion, both in the promotion of common values and the manner in which the 'Islamic' terrorists and their alleged sponsors were denounced as 'evil'. Bush (2002a) reflected upon the role of religion when stating in 2002 that since the 2001 attacks, 'millions of Americans have been led to prayer. They have prayed for comfort in time of grief; for understanding in a time of anger; for protection in a time of uncertainty. Many, including me, have been on bended knee.' In this sense, the enemy are both explained and dismissed according to moralistic and relativistic mystical if not magical characteristics. The reliance on this form of 'explanation' does little to convince that the Western 'way of life' has indeed been mastered by knowledge and rational action. And if (Christian) religion is embedded within political decision-making, there is a real danger that people, groups and nations that do not share the beliefs will feel ostracized. As Bauman (1993) points out, moral phenomena are not governed by forms of instrumental rationality.

Conclusion

After the attacks on America in 2001, both time and space have been recreated to accommodate the magnitude of change, incorporating the populace in watershed moments. Across the nation, there was a search of meaning for actions that were beyond the comprehension of most who were unable to individually confront the new risk. The population were united in a 'community of insecurity' bound by the experiences and collective effervescence as the 'I-we' balance shifted towards the latter. The American administration connected into these sentiments and contributed to a further reinforcement of nationalism that has been regularly recreated through the processes of remembrance. By emphasizing the broad and insidious nature of the threat, the government, supported by the media and religious leaders, initially created perceptions of a nation under threat and a wartime mentality. In turn, this contributed to uncritical acceptance of the War on Terror and a general reluctance to comment in a manner that could undermine collective loyalties and the 'war effort'. Feelings of insecurity and uncertainty were further exacerbated by existing levels of risk, fear and vulnerability which have become further inflamed following the attacks and subsequent government policies and statements. People therefore accepted the 'war on terror' for a number of reasons including the wider cultural perceptions, historical legacy of fear and a willingness to obey the government at a time of crisis. And, despite growing levels of cynicism, it has been for these reasons that interconnect with pre-existing feelings of 'suffering fatigue', apathy and ignorance and lack of empathy that has resulted in the American population supporting either explicitly or implicitly the loss of civilian life and subsequent curtailment of internal human rights.

New laws introduced across the West in the wake of the 'new threat' are certainly based on the Weberian principles of legal legitimacy and universal application of codes. Rationalization was under attack and the reaction has been to reinforce aspects of rationality. Yet, despite the legalistic universalism, in reality the new powers are not being implemented across all communities and nation-states equally and are fuelling cycles of mistrust and contributing to processes of radicalization. In other words, short-term rationality has proved to be irrational if the longer term objectives are to secure 'civilization' as it was experienced before September 2001 and attain universal support for subsequent heavily promoted concepts such as 'freedom', 'pluralism', 'progress' and 'tolerance'. Understandably, security services and military forces calculate risk based upon existing knowledge and concentrate their resources on people and regions most likely to harbour terrorists. The application of this form of individual and community profiling can enhance levels of security but it can also isolate individuals and demarcate communities. Such profiling becomes particularly problematic when the levels of knowledge on which the risk calculations are based are incomplete or factually incorrect. Faced with incomplete databases, the developed profiles have incorporated people and communities who become, to paraphrase Lord Cromer, innocent victims of the battle to safeguard civilization.

7   Conclusion

Sociological characteristics, causes and consequences

In a number of ways this book has been designed to challenge normative standpoints. For example, contrary to popular opinion that depicts militant Islam as reactionary and antimodern, the religious interpretation is actually very much a product of our time. Yet conversely, as a discourse, it has existed in different forms during previous turbulent periods across local and global contexts. Two of the inspirational figures for contemporary doctrine, Qutb and Mawdudi, highlight this. During the mid parts of the twentieth century, before the obvious emergence of the contemporary militants, they were opposed to colonialism, imperialist controls, irreligious leaders, denial of liberty and argued for the need for modernity to be reinterpreted according to Islamic values and practices. On such issues, distinctions can be drawn with their ideological successors but, equally, common themes can be identified that help to explain their continuing resonance. Discursively, militant Islam, as it is recognized today, is a product of historical exegesis and events and contemporary adaptations that can vary according to location and experience. And just as characteristically, militancy today is a myriad of historical and contemporary Islamic doctrine interwoven with elements of Western political thought. The causes behind the phenomena are also diverse. It is therefore a mistake to overgeneralize through single causal factors because the diversity, both of discursive appeal and routes of radicalization, quickly disproves such an approach. This is not to state that popular explanations are invalid. On the contrary, economic exclusion, real and absolute poverty, threats from globalization, political suppression, cultural imperialism, alienation and anomie are all factors which can help to illuminate the contemporary nature of militancy, when established within a multilayered framework of explanation. This is what this book has set out to achieve.

By establishing social processes through which the above factors gain meaning and inform wider audiences, it is possible to grasp the significance of government policies and reactions which provide opportunities for militants to mobilize support and help legitimize their appeal and actions. Religious and secular forms of social identity revolve around allegiances that are based both upon characteristics that members share and features that 'others' possess. This is what helps to demarcate groups. What distinguishes 'us' from 'them' is often as important for social consciousness as what unites. Reciprocal processes of exclusion and usurpation help to establish these relationships. Secular governments have introduced policies that are designed to weaken, if not eliminate, militancy, and related individuals are denied participation – processes that are in contradiction of the 'achievement principle' and claims of meritocracy. Militant groups also form boundaries for inclusion and exclusion which provide the rationale for who is 'with us or against us'. In a manner similar to Western governments' definitions of who 'the terrorists' are, the rationale for exclusion drawn up by militant groups establishes who is a legitimate target for attack. And by focussing both upon specific commonalities and differences, individuals can feel affiliated with peoples whom they have never met whilst being able to attack others with whom they may have more in common. These feelings of inclusion and exclusion can help to contextualize and explain wars, acts of terrorism and counter-terrorism.

Just as it is important that religious groups are compared with secular institutions, it is also important that comparisons are undertaken with other movements. If analysis can be undertaken without being emotionally impaired by graphic outcomes of terror and the 'dark side'[1] associated with some interpretations of Islam, meaningful similarities with other forms of religious and secular discourse can be noted. Militancy is therefore not universally unique. Transnational militant groups share experiences, membership demographics, skills and methods with secular groups. And commonalities with other forms of social identities can also be noted. As an ideology of contestation, militant Islam appeals within global, national and regional settings. At a national level, militancy is integrated within struggles for independence and attempts to renegotiate the influence of religion within power structures. This is a form of Islam that is embedded within territorial boundaries, utilized discursively to transform political systems and civil societies, synthesizing images of a glorious past with contemporary sacrifices. In this regard, militant Islam can share similarities with other forms of national allegiances, for example, reference to a 'Golden Age', historical symbols and narrative interconnected to contemporary events and experiences. Perhaps surprisingly, similar reliance on modernist and primordialist characteristics found within secular nationalisms are also noticeable within transnational militant groups. There are, however, fundamental fractures within militancy, particularly over the extent that Islam can be applied within existing nation-state boundaries. In this regard, similarities can be drawn with debates within the communist movement about the feasibility of introducing communism within global capitalism or whether the international system had to change to enable localized discursive shifts to be implemented.

The extent to which American policies within the 'war on terror' were motivated by economic, political, religious or moral reasons has not been the focus of analysis of this book, which has been more interested in the explicit and implicit support for Western government reactions to the terror attacks and their consequences. In this regard, reactions within the West need to be considered alongside existing perceptions of risk and related feelings of fear and vulnerability. Popular views of uncontrollable risks have been strengthened with the initially unexpected nature of terrorism and then conversely by regular government predictions of the inevitability of future attacks. Equally, the ferocity of the West's counter-attack, particularly the United States, and the impact of the 'war on terror', was unexpected. In other words, neither the West nor the militant 'other' is totally in control of this asymmetrical conflict which further fuels perceptions of risk and uncertainty. The impact of the attacks therefore needs to be traced through multiple layers of social, cultural, political, economic, psychological and legal influences which dampen or augment the threat's potency. Within the West, and America in particular, the threat has become amplified through the uncertainties caused by the 2001 attacks and the immediate aftermath. These have connected with existing feelings of vulnerability and a belief generated by the government, media and religious supporters that a crisis of this magnitude invalidated previous ways of thinking and acting, and the administration, security forces and military needed fewer restrictions in order to counteract the threat. The resultant short-term rationality adopted by the American administration concentrated upon greater physical security and attack as the best form of defence. With hindsight, such an approach has been shown to be irrational over the longer term; the real threat has grown and fears have become further inflated. Ultimately, consideration of militancy and reactions depends upon perceptions of interactions between militant actions, political discourse of 'them' and 'us' and feelings associated with risk and vulnerability that are interpreted within social and individual consciousness. This will determine the extent the threat is challenged and challenges society and 'way of life'.

The way ahead?

Taken as a whole, this book raises a number of interwoven issues and dilemmas and calls for action including:

1   The more that is known, the harder it becomes to dismiss militancy and groups' appeal as irrational and antimodern. Considered, balanced and thorough academic and political analysis needs to be placed upon the appeal of militancy and the reasons for related

processes of radicalization. Without this, the phenomenon of militancy cannot be comprehensively understood nor the underlying causes addressed.

2   This leads into the second point, namely, aspects of militancy have appeal and interconnections with other forms of protest because they have validity. In other words, critical expositions of Western and Muslim governments and ways of life gain support because they accord with peoples' experiences. Equally, however, militant discourse should also be subjected to critical questioning. One of the difficulties that terror groups generally encounter is in translating acts of violence into a political platform. This can, however, also be an advantage, in that groups' political agendas lack the scrutiny of parties engaged within democratic processes. The ambiguous agendas of militants, particularly transnational groups, lack sustained examination, presumably on the grounds that Western commentators dismiss the likelihood of them ever being implemented. But demonstrating that the political manifestos are impractical or impossible or would be detrimental to the lifestyles or employment prospects of many existing and potential supporters would severely undermine the appeal of such groups. Let us not forget that many militants have the rather ambitious aim of establishing an Islamic government that extends from North Africa (and in some declarations Andalusia and Britain) across to Southeast Asia. How existing nation-states could be eradicated, unity created amongst tremendous differences in language, ethnicity, economic practices, infrastructures and religious interpretations and what the resultant Islamic state would look like are fundamentally important, and neglected, questions.

3   Clearer distinctions need to be drawn both between militants' and Islamic interpretations and within militancy. There is considerable outrage expressed by Muslims against terror attacks and the patriarchy and cultural restraints imposed within militant-dominated regions. Challenges within Islam therefore need to be acknowledged and relations strengthened with forms of civil Islam (Thornton 2005), people and groups who are unlikely to be universally supportive of Western behaviour. This will require Western governments to change their approach of concentrating upon building relations with compliant Muslims who lack popular support and credibility. Nor should religio-political parties be denied political participation. Contrary to the opinion of thinkers like Kepel (2004a), Islamic parties would be very successful within elections across Muslim societies. To deny such parties the opportunity disenfranchises large sections of the populace and prevents any other political discourse from attaining a popular mandate. It would also be hoped that should a political leader like the reformist and former Iranian President Mohammed Khatami gain power, then Western governments would have a broader inclusive

perspective than the one that contributed to the emergence of another nemesis, namely Khatami's successor, Mahmoud Ahmadinejad. Instead of the obstructive approach that was applied to Khatami's ultimately doomed reform programme and attempt at rapprochement, more constructive dialogue may be able to overcome ideological and personal disagreements.

4   Equally it is important to avoid categorizing all militants as potential targets within the 'war on terror' or by extending the threat to include indigenous nationalist protests. Such an approach implicitly permits governments' repression of popular protests and denial of human rights and ignores the injustices, inequalities and socio-economic conditions that are motivating militancy. Milton-Edwards (2005) observes that these tactics alienate and embattle large swathes of more moderate Muslims. And by being complicit in such actions, critical perspectives on the contradictions within Western policies are further strengthened. Such an approach can be further counterproductive. And as events in Egypt during the 1990s highlighted, the repression of the activities of country-specific Islamic movements can force activists to leave regions and change the nature of their targets to the 'far enemy' who are implicated in their localized defeat. Ultimately if the West wishes to re-establish its credentials for humanitarianism and the consistent application of principles, struggles for independence in the Palestinian territories, Chechnya and Kashmir need to be considered within a more balanced and receptive approach.

5   Within the West and across Muslim societies, many, but by no means all, Muslim leaderships have to be encouraged that are more inclusive and representative of broader interests, particularly younger generations who tend to lack political representation. Arrangements would need to be implemented incrementally alongside developments in civil societies and the promotion of gender, sexual, racial and religious equalities and in a manner that does not further destabilize nation-states and regions. Clearly this is a difficult balancing act and the numerous interests involved within current power structures are likely to hinder this.

6   If it is accepted that contemporary militant ideas and methods are very much a product of their time, then the utilization of the tools of late/post/liquid modernity creates a dilemma. Because transnational militant methods rely upon globalization and related communications, technology and transportation, nation-states and international organizations have to consider how to deny some people opportunities without disenfranchising the rest; an incredibly difficult requirement.

7   Actions of militancy and the counter-terrorism associated with the 'war on terror', increasingly referred to as the 'long war', are reinforcing divisions and processes of exclusion and usurpation. Within Western nation-states, restraints upon civil liberties are adversely impacting

upon Muslim communities, further reinforcing perceptions of injustice and persecution. This is fulfilling the militants' strategic aim, which suggests that, despite what conspiracy theorists may say, the counter-terrorism strategy is failing disastrously.

8   Consideration also needs to be given to the manner in which national sentiments are inculcated, especially during times of national crisis. Concern has quite rightly been raised about the blunt attempts of *madrassas* and media outlets to encourage militancy and the intensification of Islamic atmospheres within societies. These have contributed to normative standards of religiosity becoming more radical and the distance to militancy reduced. But more generally across Muslim and Western societies an omnipresent danger exists within a national or transnational 'we' and associated feelings of superiority. Such forms of collective consciousness divide 'we' from the 'other' and reinforce feelings of difference between the social groups. In other words, inter-woven processes of social closure can be traced both to national and transnational acts of terrorism, and counter-terrorism responses, that are further reinforcing those relations.

9   Based upon the preceding observations, it seems either naive, arrogant or foolhardy to idealize Western values as the solution to problems which they are implicated within. Support for the abandonment of elections in Algeria, the denial of human rights for Muslims in Guantanamo Bay, 'torture taxis', atrocities in Iraq, inconsistent approaches to emerging nuclear powers, post-invasion neglect in Afghanistan, and complicit support for authoritarian regimes mean that Western perceptions of justice, democracy and freedom are treated with considerable cynicism. As Burke (2006) documents, it is often the shattered hopes that the West promoted that are instrumental in radicalization. And if groups associated with al-Qa'ida are part of a wider inter-discursive and multi-issue protest, attempts to win 'hearts and minds' appear doomed to failure without fundamental national and international reforms that would be unpopular with millions of 'conforming' citizens. Consequently, Western governments may have to consider interpreting their own practices more realistically and developing more achieveable expectations. Alternatively, the extent to which Western governments, TNCs and peoples would be willing to change behaviour to accord with principles on which their modern nation-states are promoted seems slight.

10   In the neglected war of ideas, neither side is proving particularly adept at putting across their argument. For reasons identified above, the militants are overrelying on violent tactics and are failing to attract broader support. Both sides can easily identify problems with the other discourse (although as an earlier point indicated, greater critical scrutiny upon militancy and attempts at delegitimizing it are required)

yet struggle to evidence their own perceived superiority. Across the West, greater attention needs to be placed upon discourse being legitimized through Muslim experiences. Muslims in the West need more positive experiences. There are signs of hope. Kepel (2004b) discusses the political participation of younger generations and highlights the role of social mobility and economic and cultural entrepreneurs. However, discrimination and Islamophobia remain prominent and can easily be utilized by militants in support of anti-Western rhetoric. Greater mobility and accessibility are required both to undermine militant discourse and evidence Western values. At the same time, acts of brutality committed in the name of Islam, rapes in Algeria and Sudan, decapitations in Iraq and indiscriminate killings of Muslims and Western tourists across various locations have contributed to rising levels of repulsion, anger and condemnation[2] amongst people that the militants must attract if their struggles are to become mainstream (Burke 2006; Gerges 2005, 2006; Martinez 2007). It is only in places where the struggle is embedded within nationalist conflicts that militancy continues to attract broad support. And, in contexts where militant or more moderate groups have successfully implemented social welfare programmes to alleviate poverty and unemployment, and a lack of housing, health and educational facilities, their activities are embedded within communities. These *da'wa* groups seek to transform individual levels of consciousness and build upon social consciousness 'from below', contesting the transnational emphasis upon the vanguard and imposition of the *shari'ah* 'from above'. De Waal (2004) and de Waal and Salam (2004) suggest that what they call 'Islamism' in the Horn of Africa has proved successful at micro levels in providing 'little solutions', but when operating at a national level has generally failed. Conversely the lack of significant support allied to weakening levels of theological knowledge places even greater emphasis upon violence by relatively isolated transnational cells and the need for ever more gruesome acts to attract attention. Ultimately, like the 'war on terror', an overreliance on violence will prove self-defeating unless it is part of a more inclusive strategy.

11 Perhaps surprisingly, cultural aspects associated with the West, and America in particular, have retained their appeal in other parts of the world and provide a basis that could be advantageously utilized. For example, Faath and Mattes (2006) and Seeseman (2006) detail how aspects of American life are rejected as being too permissive or materialistic, yet music, fashion, movies, sports, food, drink and technology are popular, even in regions that are politically anti-American. This highlights distinctions that are being drawn between America as a political entity and cultural aspects.[3] Feelings about one sphere do not necessarily correlate with another. Similarly, studies have shown that Muslims also differentiate between the actions of the American government and

individual Americans and even have a manifest desire to live in the United States (Brown 2001; Tessler 2003). Seeking to utilize such attractions should, however, take into consideration the realization that levels of anti-Americanism are deep rooted across Muslim societies and beyond. Faath (2006) identifies the prominent rise of the United States in the post-Second World War period with the commencement of widespread anti feelings of the country. Since the 1950s, levels of anti-Americanism have grown, triggered by foreign policy, as the role of the country has become more noticeable – a development that many people consider to be detrimental to their prospects, region, nation or religion.

12   Finally, attention needs to be turned inwards. Reactions to militant Islam raise questions about what it means to be Western, what is worth defending, how much freedom people are willing to negotiate for greater security and to what extent will the Western 'way of life' dissipate as a consequence. In this regard, reference can be made to Freud's (1989 [1930]) perception that people are willing to sacrifice greater freedom and suppress the 'pleasure principle' for enhanced security and the 'reality principle'. In the 1990s, expectations were rather different, exemplified by Bauman's (1997: 3) statement that 'postmodern men and women exchanged a portion of their possibilities of security for a portion of happiness' and fewer constraints on freedom of choice and expression. Today it could be argued that this situation has been reversed with tremendous implications for contemporary 'ways of life'; yet such changes have aroused little protest to date. Seemingly, the bulk of Western populations are either ignorant of the implications, apathetic, experiencing suffering fatigue or accept loss of freedoms and the deaths of innocent foreign civilians as being necessary in order to safeguard 'civilization'. Instead, terrorism and associated fear and vulnerability within the broader 'risk society' have contributed to what Bauman (2004: 94) has referred to as the 'commodity of fear'. Certainly there has been a rise in demand for safeguards against terrorism but this has to be established alongside the potential damage that growing insecurities may have for the 'shopping experience'. Shopping environments are expected to be conducive to consumption,[4] yet the same arenas have been established by governments, security experts and academics as locations vulnerable to attack. In societies that revolve around consumption, such contradictory messages are likely to cause confusion and strengthen feelings of fear and vulnerability. And if societies are unable to guarantee both the reality and pleasure principles, namely security for citizens and protection for consumerism, then allied to the insidious erosion of the values being defended, Western governments may face a 'legitimation crisis' as a consequence of, and in reaction to, a small group of otherwise relatively insignificant individuals. Therefore, the biggest threat to 'our way of life' may not necessarily be from the people who want to blow 'us' up.

The role of sociology

The above list is daunting and may prove to be unachievable and/or undesirable. If many of these dilemmas are to be resolved, more detached research needs to be undertaken by sociologists, political scientists and psychologists. For sociologists, though not exclusively, there is a demand for greater examination of the social processes behind radicalization. Research questions to consider include which socializing agents are instrumental, which socio-economic conditions are conducive to their messages being internalized and which social processes and activities contribute to militant discourse being activated and in many instances people becoming de-activated?

In the aftermath of September 2001, there was an academic failure to provide what social ethicists describe as a 'hermeneutics of suspicion'. Academics, the media and political opponents within democratic societies should be a safeguard for the legitimate use of power. Yet in the months following the attacks, Durkheim's observation that, 'if a belief is unanimously shared by a people, then it is forbidden to touch it, that is to say, to deny or contest it' was particularly apt. In the period post-September 2001, the hostile suspicion of the small number of people who expressed their own interpretations, allied to the complicity of many of the above groups, contributed to those safeguards being weakened and individuals becoming ostracized. The uncritical acceptance of the 'war on terror' permitted actions to be undertaken and legislation to be implemented, the consequences of which are only now becoming truly apparent. It is therefore essential that academics are able to address the ambiguities they may feel over the use of political violence and utilize sociological ideas and methods to help illuminate the mistakes and the dangers of continuing with the same processes of exclusion and demarcation.

If greater understanding about militancy is attained then it has to be acknowledged that Muslims generally, and militants in particular, are also subject to many of the same social forces and pressures impinging on other groups. Thus, Muslims in the West possess multiple loyalties that can be compounded or complicated by what Bauman described as 'existential insecurity'. With competing religious and secular values, ethnic and national connections, people generally can encounter existential dilemmas within their everyday lives. For example, many Muslim women face contradictions between expectations of their role within societies and, if different, their family's country of origin and from peers, the media, educational and employment institutions and families. How they negotiate these competing expectations will depend upon their other loyalties and support networks. Why the overwhelming majority of Muslims are able to mediate these demands without recourse to militancy remains underexplored. Certainly much can be learnt from the release of security interviews with convicted militants and the greater opportunities available for academics to gain access to such individuals. Equally, however, reasons why people are not radicalized in similar circumstances and why some people are deradicalized (like Husain 2007) also require considerable examination.

The study of militant Islam needs to be reintegrated with research undertaken into other forms of religious and political movements. In this book, only limited comparisons have been undertaken with other religions and social movements, yet nonetheless important commonalities have been identified. To aid comparative analysis, social theorists, political sociologists and sociologists of religion need to set aside embellished differences and contribute their respective ideas and concepts towards a more holistic approach to militancy. In the process, levels of understanding about the social processes behind secular and religious radicalization and the broader appeal of such discourses or mobilising issues will be enhanced.

To conclude, sociology has neglected militant Islam yet hopefully this book has shown that the discipline can be considerably more engaged with the subject, providing comprehensive, detached insights into behaviour, processes and relationships that are instrumental within the appeal of militancy and Western reactions. The nature of contemporary militancy and resultant consequences suggests that greater sociological involvement is desperately required.

Notes

Introduction

1 For example, Croft (2006) notes how the Bush administration quickly categorized the 2002 Bali attack within the 'war on terror' discourse on the assumption that 'al-Qa'ida' was responsible. Yet, evidence to support such claims is often sparse.

2 There are some notable exceptions including Hassan (2002), Juergensmeyer (2003), Kurzman (1994, 1996, 2004), Sutton and Vertigans (2005, 2006), Turner (1994) and Vertigans (2003, 2007, 2008).

3 Obviously this is not to state that the author condones acts of terrorism either by non-state actors or governments.

4 Barkun (1997) suggests that many academics tend to be dismissive of movements whose beliefs and actions they find repugnant.

5 Important exceptions include studies of fundamentalism by Davison Hunter (1990), Keddie (1998), Marty and Appleby (1994), Munson (1995) and Bloom (2005), Juergensmeyer (2003a), Reuter (2004), Stern (2003a) and Vertigans' (2008) studies of religious groups that have used terrorism.

6 Exceptions include Beck (2002a, 2002b, 2003), Burkitt (2005), Furedi (2002b, 2005a, 2005b, 2007b), Halliday (2002), Levi and Wall (2004) and Lyon (2006).

7 Marty and Scott Appleby (1994) discuss the association of fundamentalism with American Protestantism. And as Hodgson (1974: 45) argues, academics have responsibility for 'selecting minimally misleading terms and for defining them precisely'.

8 Examples of political violence include physical attacks on individuals, guerrilla warfare, targeted assassinations and terrorism. This is generally undertaken to bring about fundamental change at both individual and societal levels.

9 In this sense, Juergensmeyer (2003a) and Milton-Edwards (2005) have identified how attaining feelings of empowerment is noticeable across 'fundamentalist' religious groups associated with Christianity, Hinduism and Judaism.

10 This is not to state that there is no variety across the Middle East. Within countries, tremendous vicissitudes can be noticed between 'orthodox' Sunnis and Sufis and between Sunnis and Shi'ites. Within denominations it is also possible to notice different practices according to interactions with existing cultures (Ahmed 1992).

1 The al-Qa'ida phenomenon and beyond: myths and realities

1 There are numerous texts discussing these issues including Armstrong (2000), Burke (2003, 2006), Gerges (2005, 2006), Hamas (1988), Kepel (2004a, 2004b, 2005) and Milton-Edwards (2005).

2 The four schools are Hanbali, Hanifi, Maliki and Shafi'i. Marranci (2006) provides illuminating examples of different interpretations in his research into militants based in Europe. Opinions ranged from the rejection of violence which is thought to be divisive to the *umma* and damaging to the image of Islam to the support for what is widely considered to be terrorism. A third, intermediate, category was also identified that accepts the need for violent *jihad* but believe that the current use is detrimental. Respondents suggested that this is happening at the wrong time because Muslims are not unified and thus are defenceless against the reaction by the West.

3 For example, Andalusia continues to be considered as part of a 'Muslim world.'

4 Examples of mainstream political parties include the Brotherhood in Egypt, Pakistani Jama'at-I Islami, Parti Islam SeMalaysia, the Justice Development Party in Turkey and Morocco and Tunisian Renaissance Party.

5 For example, Kepel (2004a, 2004b), Kramer (1998) and Roy (2004).

6 This form of *jihad* is controversially considered by many militants to be a sixth pillar alongside the universally agreed five pillars: to bear witness, to observe prayer, to give alms, to perform the pilgrimage, and to fast during the period of Ramadan.

7 Both Derbala and Ibrahim are discussed in Gerges (2005).

8 After taking control of the Golden Temple in 1984, the group members were killed following a controversial attack by the Indian army.

9 Ahmed (1992) and Milton-Edwards (2005) have outlined how Islam was transported through trade, commerce, politics, warfare and travel, and the extent to which it was accepted depended partly upon how the religion was integrated with existing practices. The pre-existing customs and relations shaped the form of Islamic beliefs and practices that help to explain the rich diversity, patterns of worship, appearances of believers across Muslim societies and the pre-eminence of Islam within individual identities and social relationships outside political realms.

10 Studies of terrorism are problematic because there is no definition that is universally acceptable. Definitions are rooted within the definers' values and the historical location and associated relations of domination and the power to define (Oliverio 1998). Despite these difficulties, it is important that some parameters are established to enable the application of the concept to a range of behaviour to be consistent and understandable. In this research, terrorism is defined as the targeted and intentional use of violence to intimidate and achieve political purposes.

11 Today, Hezbollah have become synonymous with political violence in Lebanon. But as Gerges (2006) observes they learnt from their Christian adversaries who were also partly responsible for embedding religious fundamentalism into the conflict.

12 Reported in Taheri (1987: 254).

13 Al-Maghili originated from North Africa in the fifteenth century and after locating to West Africa became renowned for his denunciation of corrupt leaders, un-Islamic practices and Jewish dominance of the economy. He sought to implement more rigorous Islamic traditions of leadership and scholarship.

14 The state was ultimately destroyed by British colonialists.

15 The self-declared Mahdi, of the Sudan, led an army that successfully defeated the British army under the banner of *jihad*. Mukhtar was the leader of the resistance movement against the Italian military and Ben Badis was a religious leader who sought to defend Islam against French colonialism in particular through reform Islam, purging *marabout* influence and embedding religious social institutions within Algerian communities.

16 It is estimated that *Shi'ites* constitute between 10 and 15 per cent of all Muslims (International Crisis Group [ICG] 2005).

17 ICG (2005) suggested that the lack of state patronage for the *Shi'ite ulema* and religious leadership role within their own communities resulted in clerical figures relying
on the support of the faithful, making them more responsive while acquiring the status
of authority that was autonomous from the state.

18 Blair (2003) at the United States Congress.

19 For example, Hassan (2001) and Reuter (2004).

20 For example, Bloom (2005), Davis (2003), Khosrokhavar (2005), Oliver and Steinberg
(2005) and Victor (2004).

21 Studies include Atran (2004), Berrebi (2003), Haddad (2004), Sutton and Vertigans
(2005) and Vertigans (2003).

22 Similarly, people involved with groups also appear to be pathologically normal or at
least not distinctively abnormal. For example, McCauley's (1991) research identified
no significant differences of diagnosable pathology for terrorists and non-terrorists
according to control groups.

23 Anwar is quoted in Abuza (2003: 16).

24 Islam remains heavily influential within Saudi Arabia and is strongly embedded within
social control mechanisms. However, it is the royal family who are in power and
ultimately control official Islam with religious institutions used to legitimize Saudi
policies and actions.

25 Concessions have been introduced for a number of reasons including attracting political support and/or to countering communism, opposing more militant Islamic schools
of thought or hostile nationalists, to engage traditional Muslims and to address concerns over alienation and *anomie*.

26 It should also be added that the Soviet Union's military power was also likely to be significant in the limited expression of radical Islam during this period: a point which
highlights that repression does not inevitably lead to a militant challenge.

27 In 2001, bin Laden declared, 'I say there is no doubt about it [that the theory is cor-
rect]; this is crystal clear and supported by the book and the sunna'.

28 Critical evaluation of the thesis can be found in Chiozza (2002), Fox (2001), Halliday
(2002), Russett *et al.* (2000), Sutton and Vertigans (2005) and Turner (2002, 2003).

29 The sociological concept of the unintentional consequences of intentional actions is
most commonly associated with Merton (1967) and Elias (1978, 1987). The concept
has been adapted for Huntington's thesis by Sutton and Vertigans (2005) and Vertigans
and Sutton (2006).

30 Merari is quoted in Reuter (2004: 109).

31 Reported in Admon (2007: 2).

32 Further details can be found in Bunt (2003), Khatib (2003) and Sakr (2001).

33 Butko (2004), Esposito (1999), Kepel (2004a) outline aspects of this explanation.

34 For further details, see Armstrong (2000), Davison Hunter (1990), Hadden and Shupe
(1989), Juergensmeyer (2003a), Keddie (1998), Marty and Scott Appleby (1994) and
Munson (1995).

35 The statements are included in bin Laden (1998a, 1998b, 2001a, 2001b, 2007) and
Lawrence (2005).

36 For further reading, see Burke (2003, 2006), Gerges (2005, 2006), Khosrokhavar (2005),
Oliver and Steinberg (2005), Reuter (2004) and Vertigans (2008).

37 These sentiments are found in many statements by leading al-Qa'ida figures including
al-Zawahiri (2001), bin Laden (1998a, 1998b, 2001a, 2001b, 2007) and associated militants like 7 and 21 July London bombers (BBC 2005b; Brady and Phillips 2005;
House of Common 2006).

2 Militant Islam in local, national and transnational networks

1 A recent exception is Cohen and Rai's (2000) collection, which includes two chapters on religious movements from the perspective of globalization theory.
2 Although Kurzman's (1994, 1996) work on Islamic social movements dates back over a decade. See also Moaddel (2001), Moaddel and Talattof (2002), Parsa (2000) and Voll (2001).
3 Examples specific to Islamic movements include Clark (2004), Wickham (2002) and Wiktorowicz (2004).
4 Representatives from these groups signed, with bin Laden (1998a), a statement announcing the formation of the World Islamic Front for Jihad against Crusaders and Jews, an umbrella organization linking radicals across the world.
5 Mohammed Atta and Ziad Jarrah, the two most influential pilots in the attacks on America in 2001, are good examples. Both were well educated and from middle-class backgrounds.
6 Al-Bahri is quoted in Middle East Media Research Institute (2004).
7 Disagreements exist about the legitimacy of suicide attacks in Islamic doctrine. Even radical groups disagree about the legitimacy of attacks by other groups. Hamas was extremely critical of the September 2001 acts, for instance (see Davis 2003; Reuter 2004; Wiktorowicz and Kaltner 2003).
8 bin Laden's austere lifestyle after the war continues to appeal as indicated by this former follower who informed Gerges (2005: 182) about his time at a camp in Afghanistan.
9 Burke (2006) details how bin Laden's attire and accoutrements connect with military symbols from the war against the Soviets and perceptions of a sheikh and associated characteristics of being wise, just and a leader of men. Finally, Burke draws attention to bin Laden's positioning in front of a cave because caves were important locations for the revelations to Muhammed and his escape from persecution.
10 The letter can be found at http:www.fbi.gov/pressrel/pressrel01/letter.htm.
11 Particular resentment is reserved for the United States and connects with broader sentiments of anti-Americanism that have arisen because of support for Israel, corrupt, brutal and/or inept Muslim rulers and the perceived pervasiveness of American led globalization and accompanying cultural imperialism (Faath 2006; Gerges 2006; Saikal 2003; Thornton 2005). Today, government policies are further complicated by extensive feelings of anti-Americanism within the populace.
12 See Richard Dawkins's (2001) inadequate response to al-Qa'ida's attacks on American targets in 2001.

3 Reinterpreting the *umma*: Islamic nationalism and transnationalism

1 For further details, see, for example, Hobsbawn (1990) and Horsman and Marshall (1994).
2 Durkheim is quoted in McCrone (1998: 18).
3 There are some who argue it emerged with the formation of nations in the fifteenth and sixteenth centuries (e.g. Dieckhoff and Jaffrelot 2005; Greenfeld 1992) while Gellner suggested the eighteenth.
4 Important exceptions include Chatterjee (1993), Jaffrelot (2002), Juergensmeyer (1993), Kinnvall (2002), Rieffer (2003), Smith (2003) and van der Veer (1994).

5 For example, Halliday (2000) examines the development of the nation and national identity in the Middle East.
6 Cited in Gerges (2006: 111).
7 Cited in Kepel (2005: 43).
8 Al-Zawahiri is reported in Ulph (2006b: 4).
9 Al-Aziz is reported in Lapidus (2002).
10 Ibid. p. 427.
11 Ibid. p. 819.
12 Quoted in Terdman (2005: 6).
13 Point raised by Pargeter (2006).
14 Quoted in McGregor (2006: 3).
15 For example, a declaration made by a Chechen group holding hostages in a Moscow cinema in 2002 stated 'Every nation has the right to self-determination, but Russia has taken that way from the Chechen people and today we want to take back that right granted to us – and to all other nations – by Allah the Most Gracious, the right to freedom and self-determination' (quoted in Larzillière 2007: 100).
16 Bin Laden is cited in Lawrence (2005:14).
17 Ibid. p. 74.
18 Ibid. p. 25.
19 Ibid. p. 153.
20 Cited in Devji (2005: 69).
21 Cited in Lawrence (2005: 121).
22 In 1924, Kemal Atatürk, leader of the recently formed Turkish Republic, constitutionally abolished the institution of the *Caliphate*.
23 Cited in Lawrence (2005: 202).
24 Cited in Faksh (1997: 10). Ironically, Qutb is most closely associated with the nation-state of Egypt.
25 Cited in Hamzeh (2004: 40).
26 Cited in al-Zayyat, (2004: 63).
27 Cited in Brisard (2005: 153).
28 Bin Laden has tried to embed the attention upon Saudi Arabia within the wider struggle, arguing 'this (Saudi) conflict is partly a local conflict but in other respects it is conflict between world heresy and with it today's apostates – under the leadership of America on the one hand, and on the other, the Islamic nation with brigades of the mujahideen in its vanguard' (quoted in Fradkin 2005: 6–7).
29 In some respects, this could be considered to be a further extension of the role that Egyptians have played within international Islamic movements. For example, in the 1950s, many members of the Muslim Brotherhood were denied opportunities in Egypt because of their religious beliefs and gained employment in other Muslim societies and communities, especially in the Gulf states.
30 Smith (2003: 217).

4 Social closure and *takfir*: the interrelationship between secular and militant 'switchmen'

1 Murphy also includes state ownership within the communist bloc that existed at the time of writing.
2 Islamic government controlled by Muhammed's successor (*caliph*).
3 For example, women were granted the rights to divorce, inheritance and to stand for election (Davison 1990; Vertigans 2003).

4 Further details can be found in Ayubi (1991), Burke (2003), Halliday (2002) and Jerichow (1997).

5 Ahmad (1994), Mortimer (1982) and Saikal (2003) discuss these issues in some detail.

6 Rashid (2002) also notes how Islam generally was targeted particularly under Stalin's reign, when mosques were closed down, worship and ceremonies were banned and the veil was prohibited. However, these tactics failed to eradicate Islam: institutions and religious leaders instead operated 'underground'.

7 Further details can be found in Gerges (2005, 2006), Hafez (2003), Rashid (2002) and Vertigans and Sutton (2006).

8 The research of Köse (1999) and Sültan (1999) discovered that Western female converts were attracted by the security and regulation that Islam could provide, contrary to their perceptions of an overly permissive, individualistic and materialistic West.

9 Other studies like Ahmed (1992) have argued that wearing the veil is not only often a personal choice but can also be politicized as 'a symbol of resistance.'

10 In this respect, the militants are in agreement with Weber's (1965) argument that the *Sufi* brotherhoods' mysticism prevents asceticism.

11 For example, al-Zawahiri (2001) has raised this matter in detail.

12 Bin Laden (2004) discusses these issues in his intervention in the 2004 American Presidential election (transcript is in Lawrence 2005).

13 Further details can be found in Ayubi (1991), Devji (2005), Hiro (2002), Kepel (2004b, 2005) and Milton-Edwards (2005). Again differences can be noticed within militancy. For example, Gerges (2005) describes how the Egyptian group al-Jama'a al-Islamiya has reversed the tendency to discredit the *ulema* by arguing that *jihad* is a collective duty determined by qualified and representative religious scholars.

14 Bin Laden has sought to exploit the distance of many *ulema* from the populace by openly criticizing their engagement with corrupt kingdoms and dictatorships and most notably their role in providing a judicial decree in support of the presence of American troops in Saudi Arabia.

15 Qutb died before fully developing the concepts of *jahiliyya* and *takfir* and a range of different approaches exists within contemporary militancy.

16 Steinberg (2006) points out that perceptions of the West vary across the country according to a range of variables like differing relations with the Saudi government, economic infrastructure, exposure to pilgrims and migrants, local histories and tribal loyalties.

17 For example, despite involvement within the sectarian Lebanese civil war, Hizbullah has since encouraged Muslim–Christian dialogue, the identification of common denominators and peaceful resolution of conflicts across Christian denominations (Qassem 2005).

18 Comments reported in Ulph (2006b).

19 Rahman was sentenced to life imprisonment in 1996 for his involvement in the 1993 attack on the World Trade Centre.

5 Challenging the risk society: contextualizing the impact of 'Islamic' terrorism

1 Beck appears to ignore the mundane reality that the vast majority of genetic variation occurs within ethnic groups, not between them.

6 Reacting to the militant risk: decivilizing in the name of civilization?

1 Consequently, it could be argued that the system of justice that sought to both punish and protect had been circumvented.
2 For example, in two days, Wall-Mart sold 450,000 flags compared with 26,000 during the same period in the previous year (CNN 2001).
3 Hedges (2003) discusses these issues in greater detail.
4 Reported in Milbank and Dean (2003).
5 Discussed in Croft (2006), Faath (2006), Furedi (2007b) and Halliday (2002).
6 Drury and Cocking's (2006) study of disasters identified that significant proportions of those involved felt a sense of togetherness and common identity and referred to examples of assistance and resilience during particular emergencies.
7 Cited in Croft (2006: 38).
8 Quoted in Lustick (2006: 104).
9 For example, Furedi (2007b) reviews studies of respondents in Western Europe, South America and the Middle East with the majority believing that 11 September was a turning point in history.
10 Rumsfeld and G. W. Bush are cited in Croft (2006: 107).
11 For example, in October 2001, George Bush (2001) declared that 'The object of terrorism is to try to force us to change our way of life, is to force us to retreat, is to force us to be what we're not'.
12 National Security Strategy of the USA, 2002.
13 Cited in Croft (2006: 52).
14 Data are available from the White House (2002).
15 'Torture taxis' refers to the planes that transported suspected terrorists to countries that practiced torture.
16 Discussed in CNN (2001).
17 Cited in Furedi (2007b: 153).
18 Luntz proposed 'No speech about homeland security or Iraq should begin without reference to 9/11' (cited in Lustick 2006: 104).
19 Cited in Furedi (2007b: 157).
20 Mueller (2005) examines the ways in which the 'terrorism industry' including politicians, the media, risk entrepreneurs and bureaucrats has overreacted to the threat and inflamed levels of fear.
21 For example, the then British Prime Minister, Tony Blair, declared in 2003 that 'it is only a matter of time before terrorists get hold of it [nuclear weapons]' (quoted in Furedi 2007b: 9).
22 Such opinions are exemplified by Vice President Dick Cheney's statement in October 2001 that the 'war' was different to any previous conflict 'in the sense that it may never end . . . at least not in our lifetime' (Washington Post, 7 October 2001).
23 Today people in the West tend to consider terrorism to be one of the biggest threats to them. For instance, in a survey carried out by the BBC (2006), respondents suggested that one of the reasons that Britain was considered to be a worse place to live than 20 years previously was due to the threat of terrorism.
24 Further details can be found in Drury and Cocking (2007), Fritz (1996), Robin (2004) and Sheppard *et al.* (2006).
25 Bauman (1994) details how symbolic communities are created through events and ceremonies associated with sporting occasions and issues of national importance, invariably reported by the media.

26 Furedi (2007b) refers to a YouGov survey in 2006 in which 35 per cent of those questioned believed that British politicians exaggerated the threat from terrorism.

27 'Martyrs' within the Palestinian territories are remembered on images, posters and pocket-sized cards distributed throughout neighbourhoods, within songs, poems and dramas, used to illustrate 'martyr of the month' calendars, their pre-attack announcements are visually recorded and frequently replayed and their actions celebrated within children's chanting and the giving of sweets and delicacies. The 9/11 paraphernalia includes the celebration of the role of firefighters in pictures and postage stamps, images of the Twin Towers, remembrance bears, candles, label badges and tattoos (Croft 2006) depicting different aspects of the nation's reaction and 'recovery'.

28 This point was developed in discussion with Philip W. Sutton.

29 Frum is quoted in Croft (2006: 104).

30 For example, in 2005, Amnesty International (2005) denounced the Guantanamo retention centre as 'the gulag of our times' cited in Kaplan (2006: 30).

31 These draw upon criteria Fletcher (1997) identified within decivilizing processes. However, characteristics within societies like growing acceptance of violence in public, individual and group standards of behaviour are eroded and increases in cruelty, aggressiveness and impulsiveness which would interact with the criteria are not at present noticeable.

32 Furedi (2007b) also reports upon the involvement of Hollywood directors and screenwriters in subsequent months as US officials sought to approach terrorism with greater imagination.

33 Santorum is quoted in Furedi (2007b: ix).

7 Conclusion

1 The 'dark side' includes treatment of women, gays, lesbians and different religious denominations.

2 Gerges (2006) reports on the angry responses of Muslims to attacks in Egypt, England, Indonesia, Jordan and Saudi Arabia. He and Burke (2006) discuss polls undertaken across the Middle East that indicate that support for al-Qa'ida has dropped considerably with the overwhelming majority now considering the 'group' to be a terrorist organization.

3 Further details can also be found in Abdallah (2003) and Pollack (2003).

4 Assurances by the United States administration about consumption that encouraged people to purchase were highlighted by Altheide (2006: 65) who discusses the role in 'Keep America Rolling' which emerged shortly after the 2001 attacks. He suggests that 'these messages made giving and buying commensurate with patriotism and national unity'.

Bibliography

Abdallah, A. (2003) 'Causes of Anti-Americanism in the Arab World: A Socio-Political Perspective', *Middle East Review of International Affairs*, 7(4): 62–73.

—— (2006) 'Egypt', in Faath, S. (ed.) *Anti-Americanism in the Islamic World*, London: C. Hurst & Co.

Abu-Amr, Z. (1994) *Islamic Fundamentalism in the West Bank and Gaza*, Bloomington, IN: Indiana University Press.

Abu-Rabi', I. (2004) 'Introduction', in al-Zayyat, M. (ed.) *The Road to al-Qaeda*, London: Pluto Press.

Abuza, Z. (2003) *Militant Islam in Southeast Asia: Crucible of Terror*, Boulder, CO: Lynne Riener.

—— (2005) 'Beyond Bali: A New Trend for Terrorism in Southeast Asia?', *Terrorism Monitor*, III(19): 1–3.

—— (2006) 'MILF's Stalled Peace Process and Its Impact on Terrorism in South-East Asia', *Terrorism Monitor*, IV(14): 8–10.

Acharya, A. (2006) 'The Bali Bombings: Impact on Indonesia and Southeast Asia', *Center for Eurasian Policy Occasional Research Paper, Series II (Islamism in Southeast Asia)* No. 2: 1–5.

Adams, J. (2003) 'Risk and Morality: Three Framing Devices', in Ericson, R. and Doyle, A. (eds) *Risk and Morality*, Toronto: University of Toronto Press.

Adey, P. (2004) 'Secured and Sorted Mobilities: Examples from the Airport', *Surveillance and Society*, 1(4): 500–19.

Admon, Y. (2007) 'Saudis criticize their School Curricula – Again', *Middle East Media Research Institute* (Inquiry and Analysis No. 325). Available at http://memri.org/bin/articles.cgi?Page = archives&Area = ia&ID = IA32507.

Ahmad, F. (1977) *The Turkish Experiment in Democracy 1950–1975*, London: C. Hurst & Co.

Ahmad, M. (1994) 'Islamic Fundamentalism in South Asia: The Jamaat-I-Islami and the Tablighi Jamaat of South Asia', in Marty, M. E. and Scott Appleby, R. (eds) *Fundamentalisms Observed*, Chicago: University of Chicago Press.

Ahmed, L. (1992) *Women and Gender in Islam: Historical Roots of a Modern Debate*, New Haven: Yale University Press.

Ahsan, M. (1977) *Islam: Faith and Practice*, Leicester: The Islamic Foundation.

Akhtar, S. (1999) 'The Psychodynamic Dimension of Terrorism', *Psychiatric Annals*, 29(6): 350–6.

Akşit, B. (1991) 'Islamic Education in Turkey: Medrese Reform in Late Ottoman Times and Imam-Hatip Schools in the Republic', in Tapper, R. (ed.) *Islam in Modern Turkey*, London: I. B. Tauris.

Al-Berry, K. (2005) 'Inside the Yearnings of a Potential Suicide Bomber', *The Observer*, 24 July.

Alexander, Y. (2002) 'September 11: US Reactions and Responses', paper presented at the *ESRC Conference of the St Andrews/Southampton Research Project on the Domestic Management of Terrorist Attacks*, 19–20 September.

Altheide, D. (2002) *Creating Fear: News and the Construction of Crisis*, New York: Aldine de Gruyter.

—— (2003) 'Mass Media, Crime, and the Discourse of Fear', *Hedgehog Review*, 5(3): 9–25.

—— (2006) 'Terrorism and the Politics of Fear', *Cultural Studies Critical Methodologies*, 6(4): 415–39.

al-Zawahiri, A. (2001) 'Fursan tahta rayat al-nabbi', *Al-Sharq al-Awsat*, 2–12 December.

al-Zayyat, M. (2004) *The Road to al-Qaeda*, translated by Fekry, A., London: Pluto Press.

Amoore, L. and de Goede, M. (2005) 'Governance, Risk and Dataveillance in the War on Terror', *Crime, Law and Social Change*, 43(2–3): 149–73.

Anderson, A. (2003) 'Risk, Terrorism, and the Internet', *Knowledge, Technology and Policy*, 16(2): 24–33.

Anderson, B. (1998) *The Spectre of Comparison – Nationalism, Southeast Asia, and the World*, London: Verso.

—— (2006) *Imagined Communities*, revised edition, London: Verso.

Aouragh, M. (2003) 'Cyber Intifada and Palestinian Identity', *International Institute for the Study of Islam in the Modern World*.

Appadurai, A. (1996) *Modernity at Large: Cultural Dimensions of Globalization*, Minneapolis: University of Minnesota Press.

Aradeau, C. and van Munster, R. (2005) 'Governing Terrorism and the (Non-)Politics of Risk', *Political Science Publications 11/2005*, Odense: University of Southern Denmark.

—— (2007) 'Governing Terrorism Through Risk: Taking Precautions, (Un)Knowing the Future', *European Journal of International Relations*, 13(1): 89–115.

Arendt, H. (1963) *On Revolution*, Harmondsworth: Penguin.

—— (1973) *The Origins of Totalitarianism*, New York: Harcourt.

Ariès, P. (1974) *Western Attitudes Towards Death: From the Middle Ages to the Present*, translated by Ranum, P., Baltimore, MD: The Johns Hopkins University Press.

Armstrong, K. (2000) *The Battle for God*, London: Harper Perennial.

—— (2002) *Islam: A Short History*, London: Phoenix Press.

Atran, S. (2004) 'Mishandling Suicide Terrorism', *The Washington Quarterly*, Summer: 67–90.

Ayubi, N. (1991) *Political Islam*, London: Routledge.

Bagguley, P. (1992) 'Social Change, the Middle Class and the Emergence of New Social Movements: A Critical Analysis', *The Sociological Review*, 40(1): 26–48.

Baker, T. (2002) 'Liability and Insurance after September 11: Embracing Risk Meets the Precautionary Principle', *Working Paper No. 4: University of Connecticut School of Law Articles and Workings Papers*.

Bandura, A. (1998) 'Mechanisms of Moral Disengagement', in Reich, W. (ed.) *Origins of Terrorism: Psychologies, Ideologues, Theologies, States of Mind*, Washington, DC: Woodrow Wilson Center Press.

Barbalet, J. (1982) 'Social Closure in Class Analysis: A Critique of Parkin', *Sociology*, 16(4): 484–97.

Barber, B. (2001) *Jihad vs. McWorld*, New York: Ballantine Books.

Barkun, M. (1997) *Religion and the Racist Right: The Origins of the Christian Identity Movement,* Chapel Hill, NC: The University of North Carolina Press.

Basch, L., Glick Schiller, N., and Szanton Blanc, C. (eds) (1994) *Nations Unbound,* Langhorne, PA: Gordon and Breach.

Bauman, Z. (1989) *Modernity and the Holocaust,* Cambridge: Polity Press.

—— (1992) *Mortality, Immortality and Other Life Strategies,* Stanford, CA: Stanford University Press.

—— (1993) *Postmodern Ethics,* Cambridge: Polity Press.

—— (1994) 'Desert Spectacular', in Tester, K. (ed.) *The Flâneur,* London: Routledge.

—— (1995) *Life in Fragments,* Cambridge: Polity Press.

—— (1997) *Postmodernity and Its Discontents,* Cambridge: Polity Press.

—— (1998) *Work, Consumerism and the New Poor,* Buckingham: Open University Press.

—— (2000) *Liquid Modernity,* Cambridge: Polity Press.

—— (2002) 'Foreword: Individually, Together', in Beck, U. and Beck-Gernsheim, E. (eds) *Individualization,* London: Sage.

—— (2004) *Europe: An Unfinished Adventure,* Cambridge: Polity Press.

—— (2006) *Liquid Fear,* Cambridge: Polity Press.

BBC (2005a) 'Suicide bombers' Ordinary Lives'. Available at http://news.bbc.co.uk/1/hi/uk/4678837.stm.

—— (2005b) 'London Bomber: Text in Full'. Available at http://news.bbc.co.uk/1/hi/uk/4206800.stm.

—— (2006) 'Britain "Worse Than 20 Years Ago"', 4 September. Available at http://news.bbc.co.uk/1/hi/uk/5310016.stm.

Beattie, L., Miller, D., Miller, E., Philo, G. (1999) 'The Media and Africa: Images of Disaster and Rebellion', in Philo, G. (ed.) *Message Received: Glasgow Media Group Research 1993–1998,* Harlow: Longman.

Beck, U. (1992) *Risk Society: Towards a New Modernity,* London: Sage.

—— (1995) *Ecological Politics in an Age of Risk,* Cambridge: Polity Press.

—— (1999) *World Risk Society,* Cambridge: Polity Press.

—— (2002a) 'The Cosmopolitan Society and Its Enemies', *Theory, Culture and Society,* 19(1–2): 17–44.

—— (2002b) 'The Terrorist Threat: World Risk Society Revisited', *Theory, Culture and Society,* 19(4): 39–55.

—— (2003) 'The Silence of Words: On Terror and War', *Security Dialogue,* 34(3): 255–67.

Beckford, J. (2003) *Social Theory and Religion,* Cambridge: Cambridge University Press.

Bennett, R. (2004) 'Inside the Mind of a Terrorist', *The Observer,* 22 August.

Ben-Yehuda, N. (2005) 'Terror, Media and Moral Boundaries', in Oliverio, A. and Lauderdale, P. (eds) *Terrorism: A New Testament,* Whitby, ON: de Sitter.

Bergen, P. (2001) *Holy War Inc.,* London: Weidenfeld and Nicolson.

Berger, P. (ed.) (1999) *The Desecularization of the World,* Washington and Grand Rapids, MI: Ethics and Public Policy Center and William B. Eerdmans Publishing Company.

Bergesen, A. and Han, Y. (2005) 'New Directions for Terrorism Research', in Oliverio, A. and Lauderdale, P. (eds) *Terrorism: A New Testament,* Whitby, ON: de Sitter.

Berkes, N. (ed.) (1959) *Turkish Nationalism and Western Civilization: Selected Essays of Ziya Gökalp,* London: Allen and Unwin.

—— (1964) *The Development of Secularism in Turkey,* Montreal: McGill University Press.

Bernton, H., Carter, M., Heath, D. and Neff, J. (2002) 'Terrorist Within: The Ahmed Ressam Story', canada.com. Available at http://www.canada.com/national/features/terrorist/story.html.

Berrebi, C. (2003) 'Evidence About the Link Between Education, Poverty and Terrorism Among Palestinians'. Available at http://www.cprs-alestine.org/il.articles/articledet.cfm? article3id = 508.

bin Laden, O. (1996) 'Declaration of War against the Americans Occupying the Land of the Two Holy Places'. Available at http://www.pbs.org/newshour/terrorism/international/ fatwa_1996.html.

—— (1998a). *World Islamic Front Statement*, 23 February. Available at http://www .fas.org/irp/world/para/docs/980223-fatwa.htm.

—— (1998b) *Interview Osama bin Laden*, May. Available at http://www.pbs.org/wgbh/ pages/frontline/shows/binladen/who/interview.html.

—— (2001a) Statements released by *al-Jazeera satellite TV*, aired 7 October.

—— (2001b) Statements released by *al-Jazeera satellite TV*, aired 3 November.

—— (2002a) *Bin Laden in His Own Words*, translated by BBC, last updated 15 April 2004. Available at http://newswww.bbc.net.uk/2/hi/south_asia/2827659.stm.

—— (2002b) *Letter to America*, issued November 2002. Available at http://observer .guardian.co.uk/worldview/story/0,11581,845725,00.html.

—— (2007) *The Solution*. Transcript 'Osama Bin Laden's Video Message to the American People', *Middle East Media Research Institute*. Available at http://www.memri.org/bin/ articles.cgi?Page=subjects&Area=jihad&ID=SP170907.

Bjørgo, T. (ed.) (2005) *Root Causes of Terrorism: Myths, Reality and Ways Forward*, Abingdon, UK: Routledge.

Blair, A. (2003) Address delivered to the Congress of the United States of America, Washington, DC, 17 July.

Blau, P. (1977) *Inequality and Heterogeneity: A Primitive Theory of Social Structure*, New York: Free Press.

Blom, A. (2007) 'Kashmiri Suicide Bombers: "Martyrs" of a Lost Cause', in Blom, A., Bucaille, L. and Martinez, L. (eds) *The Enigma of Islamist Violence*, London: C. Hurst & Co.

Blom, A., Bucaille, L. and Martinez, L. (eds) (2007) *The Enigma of Islamist Violence*, London: C. Hurst & Co.

Bloom, M. (2005) *Dying to Kill: The Global Phenomenon of Global Terror*, Columbia: Columbia University Press.

Bougen, P. (2003) 'Catastrophe Risk', *Economy and Society*, 32(2): 253–74.

Boukhars, A. (2005) 'The Challenge of Radical Islam in Mauritania', *Terrorism Monitor*, III(19).

Bourdieu, P. (1984) *Distinction: A Social Critique of the Judgement of Taste*, London: Routledge.

Bourdieu, P. and Passeron, J. (1977) *Reproduction in Education, Society and Culture*, London: Sage.

Bourke, J. (2005) *Fear: A Cultural History*, London: Virago.

Bourne, R. (1991 [1918]) *War is the Health of the Nation*, New York: Gordon Press.

Brady, B. and Phillips, J. (2005) '"Confession" Lifts Lid on London Bomb Plot', *Scotland on Sunday*. Available at http://news.scotsman.com/uk.cfm?id = 1707652005.

Brand, K.-W. (1990) 'Cyclical Aspects of New Social Movements', in Dalton, R. J. and Kuechler, M. (eds), *Challenging the Political Order: New Social and Political Movements in Western Democracies*, Cambridge: Polity Press.

Brisard, J.-C. (2005) *Zarqawi: The New face of al-Qaeda*, translated by Martinez, D., Cambridge: Polity Press.

Brown, C. S. (2001) 'The Shot Seen Around the World: The Middle East Reacts to September 11th', *Middle East Review of International Affairs*, 5(4): 69–89.

Brown, P. (2000) 'The Globalisation of Positional Competition', *Sociology*, 34(4): 633–53.

Buchta, W. (2006) 'Iran', in Faath, S. (ed.) *Anti-Americanism in the Islamic World*, London: C. Hurst & Co.

Bunt, G. (2003) *Islam in the Digital Age*, London: Pluto Press.

Burdman, D. (2003) 'Education, Indoctrination, and Incitement: Palestinian Children on Their Way to Martyrdom', *Terrorism and Political Violence*, 15(1): 96–123.

Burke, J. (2003) *Al-Qaeda*, London: I. B. Tauris.

—— (2004) 'What Exactly Does al-Qaeda Want?', *The Observer*, 21 March.

—— (2006) *On the Road to Kandahar: Travels though Conflict in the Islamic World*, London: Allen Lane.

Burke, J., Barnett, A., Bright, M., Townsend, M., Panja, T. and Thompson, T. (2005) 'Three Cities, Four Killers', *The Observer*, 17 July.

Birkitt, I. (1996) 'Civilization and Ambivalence', *British Journal of Sociology*, 47(1): 135–50.

—— (2005) 'Powerful Emotions: Power, Government and Opposition in the "War on Terror"', *Sociology*, 39(4): 679–95.

Bush, G. W. (2001) 'President Says Terrorists Won't Change American Way of Life', 23 October. Available at http://www.whitehouse.gov/news/releases/2001/10/20011023-33.html.

—— (2002a) 'President's Remarks at National Prayer Breakfast', 7 February. Available at http://www.whitehouse.gov/news/releases/2002/02/20020207-1.html. Accessed 23 December 2007.

—— (2002b) 'President Outlines Plan to Help World's Poor'. Available at http://www.whitehouse.gov/news/releases/2002/03/20020322-1.html.

—— (2005) 'President Discusses War on Terror at National Endowment for Democracy', 6 October. Available at http://www.whitehouse.gov/news/releases/2005/10/20051006-3.html.

Butko, T. (2004) 'Unity through Opposition: Islam as an Instrument of Radical Political Change', *Middle East Review of International Affairs*, 8(4).

Byman, D. L. and Green, J. D. (1999) 'The Enigma of Political Stability in the Persian Gulf Monarchies', *Middle East Review of International Affairs*, 3(3).

Byrne, E. (2004) 'Quranic Schools', *Middle East International*, No. 731.

Calhoun, C. (1995) '"New Social Movements" of the Early Nineteenth Century', in Traugott, M. (ed.) *Repertoires and Cycles of Collective Action*, Durham, NC: Duke University Press.

—— (1999) 'Symposium on Religion', *Sociological Theory*, 17(3): 237–39.

Calvert, J. (2004) 'Mythic Foundations of Radical Islamic Violence', paper presented at the *International Conference on Muslims and Islam in the 21st Century: Image and Reality*, Kuala Lumpur, Malaysia.

Campbell, C. (1987) *The Romantic Ethic and the Spirit of Modern Consumerism*, Oxford: Blackwell.

Castel, R. (1991) 'From Dangerousness to Risk', in Burchell, G., Gordon, C. and Miller, P. (eds) *The Foucault Effect: Studies in Governmentality*, Chicago: University of Chicago Press.

Cederroth, S. (1996) 'Islamism in Multi Religious Societies: The Experience of Malaysia and Indonesia', in Westerlund, D. (ed.) *Questioning the Secular State: The Worldwide Resurgence of Religion in Politics*, London: Hurst & Co.

Chalk, P. (2002a) 'Militant Islamic Separatism in Southern Thailand', in Isaacson and Rubenstein, C. (eds) *Islam in Asia: Changing Political Realities*, New Brunswick, NJ: Transaction.

—— (2002b) 'Militant Islamic Extremism in Southern Philippines', in Isaacson and Rubenstein, C. (eds) *Islam in Asia: Changing Political Realities*, New Brunswick, NJ: Transaction.

Chatterjee, P. (1993) *The Nation and its Fragments: Colonial and Post-Colonial Histories*, Princeton, NJ: Princeton University Press.

Chiozza, G. (2002) 'Is there a Clash of Civilizations? Evidence from Patterns of International Conflict Involvement, 1946–97', *Journal of Peace Research,* 39(6).

Clark, J. (2004) 'Social Movement Theory and Patron-Clientelism: Islamic Social Institutions in Egypt, Jordan, and Yemen', *Comparative Political Studies*, 37(8): 941–68.

CNN, (2001) 'President tours New York Devastation', CNN.com. Available at http://archives.cnn.com/2001/US/09/14/america.under.attack/.

Coaffee, J. (2003) *Terrorism, Risk and the City*, Aldershot: Ashgate.

—— (2006) 'From Counter-terrorism to Resilience: New Security Challenges and the Multidisciplinary Counter-Challenge in the "Age of Terror"', *European Legacy*, 11(4): 389–403.

Cohen, J. (1985) 'Strategy or Identity – New Theoretical Paradigms and Contemporary Social Movements', *Social Research*, 52(4): 663–716.

Cohen, R. and Rai, S. M. (eds) (2000) *Global Social Movements*, London: The Athlone Press.

Cohen, S. (2002) *Folk Devils and Moral Panic: The Making of Mods and Rockers*, 30th Anniversary Edition, London: Routledge.

Collins, R. (1979) *The Credential Society: An Historical Sociology of Education and Stratification*, New York: Academic Press.

Cooper, H. (1977) 'What is a Terrorist: A Psychological Perspective', *Legal Medical Quarterly*, 1: 16–32.

Cooper, M. (2006) 'Pre-empting Emergence: The Biological Turn in the War on Terror', *Theory, Culture and Society*, 23(4): 113–35.

Corrado, R. (1981) 'A Critique of the Mental Disorder Perspective of Political Terrorism', *International Journal of Law and Psychiatry*, 4(3): 293–310.

Crenshaw, M. (1992) 'Decisions to use Terrorism: Psychological Constraints on Instrumental Reasoning', *International Social Movement Research*, 4: 29–42.

—— (1998) 'The Logic of Terrorism: Terrorist Behaviour as a Product of Strategic Choice', in Reich, W. (ed.) *Origins of Terrorism: Psychologies, Ideologues, Theologies, States of Mind*, Washington, DC: Woodrow Wilson Center Press.

—— (2003a) 'The Causes of Terrorism', in Kegley, C. W. (ed.) *The New Global Terrorism: Characteristics, Causes & Controls*, New Jersey: Prentice Hall.

—— (2003b) 'Why is America the Primary Target? Terrorism as Globalized Civil War', in Kegley, C. W. (ed.) *The New Global Terrorism: Characteristics, Causes & Controls*, New Jersey: Prentice Hall.

Croft, S. (2006) *Culture, Crisis and America's War on Terror*, Cambridge: Cambridge University Press.

Cromer, L. (1913) 'The Government of Subject Races', in *Political and Literary Essays, 1908–1913*, London: Macmillan.

Crossley, N. (2002) *Making Sense of Social Movements*, Buckingham: Open University Press.

Curry, M. (2004) 'The Profiler's Question and the Treacherous Traveler: Narratives of Belonging in Commercial Aviation', *Surveillance and Society*, 1(4): 475–99.

Dake, K. (1992) 'Myths of Nature: Culture and the Social Construction of Risk', *Journal of Social Issues*, 48(4): 21–37.

Dalton, R. J. and Kuechler, M. (1990) 'New Social Movements and the Political Order: Inducing Change for Long-term Stability?', in Dalton, R. J. and Kuechler, M. (eds)

Challenging the Political Order: New Social and Political Movements in Western Democracies, Cambridge: Polity Press.

D'Anieri, P., Ernst, C. and Kier, E. (1990) 'New Social Movements in Historical Perspective', *Comparative Politics*, 22(4): 445–56.

Dankowitz, A. (2005) 'Saudi Prince Khaled Al-Faisal against the Islamist Ideology', *Middle East Media Research Institute*, 16 March, No. 212.

Das, V., Kleinman, A., Ramphele, M. and Reynolds, P. (eds) (2000) *Violence and Subjectivity*, Berkeley, CA: University of California Press.

Davis, J. M. (2003) *Martyrs: Innocence, Vengeance and Despair in the Middle East*, New York: Palgrave Macmillan.

Davison Hunter. J. (1990) 'Fundamentalism in Its Global Contours', in Cohen, N. (ed.) *The Fundamentalist Phenomenon: A View from Within: A Response from Without*, Grand Rapids, MI: William B. Eerdmans.

Davison, R. (1990) *Essays in Ottoman and Turkish History – The Impact of the West*, University of Texas: Saqi Books.

Dawkins, R. (2001) 'Religion's Guided Missiles', *Guardian Newspaper*. Available at http://www.guardian.co.uk/Archive/Article/0,4273,4257777,00.html.

Dean, M. (1999) *Governmentality: Power and Rule in Modern Society*, London: Sage.

Debray, R. (1994) 'God and the Political Planet', *New Perspectives Quarterly*, 11: 15.

Deleuze, G. (1992) 'Postscript on Societies of Control', *October*, 59(4): 3–7.

della Porta, D. and Diani, M. (1999) *Social Movements: An Introduction*, Oxford: Blackwell.

Devji, F. (2005) *Landscapes of the Jihad: Militancy, Morality, Modernity*, London: C. Hurst & Co.

de Waal, A. (ed.) (2004) *Islamism and Its Enemies in the Horn of Africa*, London: C. Hurst & Co.

de Waal, A. and Salam, A. (2004) 'Africa, Islamism and America's "War on Terror"', in de Waal, A. (ed.) *Islamism and Its Enemies in the Horn of Africa*, London: Hirst & Co.

Diani, M. (1992) 'The Concept of Social Movement', *The Sociological Review*, 40(1): 1–19.

Dieckhoff, A. (2005) 'Beyond Conventional Wisdom: Cultural and Political Nationalism Revisited', in Dieckhoff, A. and Jaffrelot, C. (eds) *Revisiting Nationalism: Theories and Processes*, London: C. Hurst & Co.

Dieckhoff, A. and Jaffrelot, C. (eds) (2005) *Revisiting Nationalism: Theories and Processes*, London: C. Hurst & Co.

Douglas, M. (1985) *Risk Acceptability According to the Social Sciences*. New York: Russell Sage.

—— (1990) 'Risk as a Forensic Resource', *Daedalus*, 119(4): 1–16.

Douglas, M. and Wildavsky, A. (1982) *Risk and Culture: An Essay on the Selection of Technological and Environmental Dangers*, Berkeley, CA: University of California Press.

Drury, J. and Cocking, C. (2006) *The Mass Psychology of Disasters and Emergency Evacuations: A Research Report and Implications for Practice*, Falmer, Brighton: University of Sussex. Available at http://www.sussex.ac.uk/affiliates/panic/.

Dunning, E., Murphy, P. and Williams, J. (1988) *The Roots of Football Hooliganism: A Historical and Sociological Study*, London: Routledge.

Du Pasquier, R. (1992) *Unveiling Islam*, Cambridge: Islamic Texts Society.

Durkheim, E. (1982 [1895]) *Rules of Sociological Method*, Basingstoke: Macmillan.

—— (1984 [1893]) *The Division of Labour in Society*, Basingstoke: Palgrave Macmillan.

—— (1996 [1912]) *The Elementary Forms of the Religious Life: A Study in Religious Sociology*, London: Simon & Schuster.

Durodié, B. (2004a) 'The Limitations of Risk Management: Dealing with Disasters and Building Social Resilience', *Årgang*, 8(1): 14–21.

—— (2004b) 'Facing the Possibility of Bioterrorism', *Current Opinion in Biotechnology*, 15(3): 264–8.

Duyvesteyn, I. (2004) 'How New is the New Terrorism', *Studies in Conflict and Terrorism*, 27(5): 439–54.

Dynes, R. (2003) 'Finding Order in Disorder: Continuities in the 9-11 Response', *International Journal of Mass Emergencies*, 21(3).

Elias, N. (1978) *What is Sociology?*, New York: Columbia University Press.

—— (1987) *Involvement and Detachment*, Oxford: Blackwell.

—— (1988) 'Violence and Civilization: On the State Monopoly of Physical Violence and Its Infringements', in Keane, J. (ed.) *Civil Society and the State: New European Perspectives*, London: Verso.

—— (1991) *The Society of Individuals*, Oxford: Blackwell.

—— (1996) *The Germans*, Cambridge: Polity Press.

—— (2000 [1939]) *The Civilizing Process: Sociogenetic and Psychogenetic Investigations*, Oxford: Blackwell.

Ellin, N. (2001) 'Thresholds of Fear: Embracing the Urban Shadow', *Urban Studies*, 38(5–6): 869–83.

Elsarraj, E. (1997) 'Palestinian Children and Violence', *Palestine-Israel Journal*, 4(1): 12–15.

Elshtain, J. B. (2003) *Just War Against Terror*, New York: Basic Books.

Enhali, A. and Adda, Q. (2003) 'State and Islamism in the Maghreb', *Middle East Review of International Affairs*, 7(1): 66–76.

Ericson, R. (2006) 'Ten Uncertainties of Risk-Management Approaches to Security', *Canadian Journal of Criminology and Criminal Justice*, 48(3): 135–73.

Ericson, R. and Doyle, A. (2004) 'Catastrophe Risk, Insurance and Terrorism', *Economy and Society*, 33(2): 135–73.

Esposito, J. L. (1999) *The Islamic Threat: Myth or Reality?*, New York: Oxford University Press.

—— (2002) *Unholy War: Terror in the Name of Islam*, New York: Oxford University Press.

Ewald, F. (1986) *L'Etat Providence*, Paris: Bernard Grasset.

—— (1990) 'Norms, Discipline and the Law', *Representations*, 30(1): 138–61.

—— (1991) 'Insurance and Risk', in Burchell, G., Gordon, C. and Miller, P. (eds) *The Foucault Effect: Studies in Governmentality*, Chicago: University of Chicago Press.

—— (1993) 'Two Infinities of Risk', in Massumi, B. (ed.) *The Politics of Everyday Fear*, Minneapolis: University of Minnesota Press.

—— (2002) 'The Return of Descartes's Malicious Demon: An Outline of a Philosophy of Precaution', in Baker, T. and Simon, J. (eds) *Embracing Risk: The Changing Culture of Insurance and Responsibility*, London: University of Chicago Press.

Faath, S. (ed.) (2006) *Anti-Americanism in the Islamic World*, London: C. Hurst & Co.

Faath, S. and Mattes, H. (2006) 'Conclusion and Outlook: Between Anti-Americanism, Criticism of America and Americanism', in Faath, S. (ed.) *Anti-Americanism in the Islamic World*, London: C. Hurst & Co.

Faksh, M. (1997) *Fundamentalism in Egypt, Algeria and Saudi Arabia*, London: Praeger.

Feely, M. and Simon, J. (1992) 'The New Penology: Notes on the Emerging Strategy of Corrections and Its Implications', *Criminology*, 30(4): 449–74.

Fielding, N. (2005) 'Battle for the Heart of Islam', *The Times*, 24 July.

Fitzpatrick, M. (2000) *The Tyranny of Health: Doctors and the Regulation of Lifestyle*, London: Routledge.

Fletcher, J. (1997) *Violence and Civilization: An Introduction to the work of Norbert Elias*, Cambridge: Polity.

Foucault, M. (1991) 'Governmentality', in Burchell, G., Gordon, C. and Miller, P. (eds) *The Foucault Effect: Studies in Governmentality*, Chicago: University of Chicago Press.

Fox, J. (2001) 'Two Civilizations and Ethnic Conflict: Islam and the West', *Journal of Peace Research*, 38(4): 459–72.

Fradkin, H. (2005) 'Recent Statements of Islamist Ideology: bin Laden and Zarqawi Speak', in Fradkin, H., Haqqani, H. and Brown, E. (eds) *Current Trends in Islamist Ideology Vol. 1*, Washington DC: Hudson Institute.

Fradkin, H., Haqqani, H. and Brown, E. (eds) (2005) *Current Trends in Islamist Ideology Vol. 1*, Washington, DC: Hudson Institute.

Freud, S. (1989 [1930]) *Civilisation and Its Discontents*, New York: W. W. Norton.

Friedland. N. (1992) 'Becoming a Terrorist: Social and Individual Antecedents', in Howard, L. (ed.) *Terrorism: Roots, Impact, Responses*, New York: Praeger.

Frisch, H. (2003) 'The Palestinian Media and Anti-Americanism: A Case Study', *Middle East Review of International Affairs*, 7(4): 74–82.

Fritz, C. (1996) 'Disasters and Mental Health: Therapeutic Principles Drawn from Disaster Studies', *DRC Historical and Comparative Series* No. 10, Wilmington, DE: DRC.

Furedi, F. (1992) *Mythical Past, Elusive Future: History and Society in an Anxious Age*, London: Pluto Press.

—— (2002a) *Culture of Fear: Risk-taking and the Morality of Low Expectation*, revised edition, London: Continuum.

—— (2002b) *Refusing to be Terrorised: Managing Risk after September 11th*, Global Futures. Available at http://www.terrorismresearch.net/docs/gobal_futures01.pdf.

—— (2004) *Therapy Culture: Cultivating Vulnerability in an Uncertain Age*, London: Routledge.

—— (2005a) *Politics of Fear: Beyond Left and Right*, London: Continuum.

—— (2005b) 'Terrorism and the Politics of Fear', in Hale, C., Hayward, K., Wahidin, A., and Wincup, E. (eds) *Criminology*, Oxford: Oxford University Press.

—— (2007a) 'From the Narrative of the Blitz to the Rhetoric of Vulnerability', *Cultural Sociology*, 1(2): 235–54.

—— (2007b) *Invitation to Terror: The Expanding Empire of the Unknown*, London: Continuum.

Gaddis, J. L. (2004) *Surprise, Security and the American Experience*, Cambridge, MA: Harvard University Press.

Gandy, O. (2003) 'Data Mining and Surveillance Post-9/11', in Ball, K. and Webster, F. (eds) *The Intensification of Surveillance: Crime, Terrorism and Warfare in the Information Age*, London: Pluto.

Garland, D. (2003) 'The Rise of Risk', in Ericson, R. and Doyle, A. (eds) *Risk and Morality*, Toronto: University of Toronto Press.

Geertz, C. (ed.) (1963) *Old Societies and New States*, London: The Free Press of Glencoe.

Gellner, E. (1978) 'Nationalism, or the New Confessions of a Justified Edinburgh Sinner', *Political Quarterly*, 49(1): 103–11.

—— (1983) *Nations and Nationalism*, Oxford: Blackwell.

—— (1997) *Nationalism*, London: Weidenfeld and Nicolson.

Gerges, F. (2005) *The Far Enemy: Why Jihad went Global*, Cambridge: Cambridge University Press.

—— (2006) *Journey of the Jihadist: Inside Muslim Militancy*, Orlando: Harcourt.

Gershoni, I. and Jankowski, J. (1987) *Egypt, Islam and the Arabs: The Search for Egyptian Nationhood, 1900–1930*, Oxford: Oxford University Press.

Giddens, A. (1990) *The Consequences of Modernity*, Cambridge: Polity Press.

—— (1991) *Modernity and Self-Identity: Self and Society in the Late Modern Age*, Cambridge: Polity Press.

Gilroy, P. (2002) *There Ain't No Black in the Union Jack: The Cultural Politics of Race and Nation*, 3rd edition, London: Routledge.

Glassner, B. (1999) *Culture of Fear: Why Americans are Afraid of the Wrong Things*, New York: Basic Books.

Goodwin, J. and Jasper, J. (eds) (2003) *The Social Movements Reader: Cases and Concepts*, Oxford: Blackwell.

Gordon, H. (2002) 'The Suicide Bomber: Is It a Psychiatric Phenomenon?', *Psychiatric Bulletin*, 26(8): 282–7.

Gould, P. (1988) *Early Green Politics: Back to Nature, Back to the Land and Socialism in Great Britain 1880–1900*, Brighton: Harvester Press.

Greenfeld, L. (1992) *Nationalism – Five Roads to Modernity*, Cambridge, MA: Harvard University Press.

Griset, P. and Mahan, S. (2003) *Terrorism in Perspective*, Thousand Oaks, CA: Sage.

Guibernau, M. (2004) 'Anthony D. Smith on Nations and National Identity: A Critical Assessment', *Nations and Nationalism*, 10(1–2): 125–41.

Guindy, A. (2006) 'The Islamization of Egypt', *Middle East Review of International Affairs*, 10(3): 92–102.

Gunaratna, R. (2004) 'The Post-Madrid Face of al Qaeda', *The Washington Quarterly*, 27(3): 91–100.

Gupta, D. (2005) 'Exploring Roots of Terrorism', in Bjørgo, T. (ed.) *Root Causes of Terrorism: Myths, Reality and Ways Forward*, Abingdon, UK: Routledge.

Gurr, T. (1970) *Why Men Rebel*, Princeton, NJ: Princeton University Press.

—— (2003) 'Terrorism in Democracies: When It Occurs, Why It Occurs, Why It Fails', in Kegley, C. W. (ed.) *The New Global Terrorism: Characteristics, Causes & Controls*, New Jersey: Prentice Hall.

Habeck, M. (2006) *Knowing the Enemy: Jihadist Ideology and the War on Terror*, New Haven, CT: Yale University Press.

Habermas, J. (1981) 'New Social Movements', *Telos*, 49 (Fall): 35–7.

Hacking, I. (1990) *The Taming of Chance*, Cambridge: Cambridge University Press.

—— (2003) 'Risk and Dirt', in Ericson, R. and Doyle, A. (eds) *Risk and Morality*, Toronto: University of Toronto Press.

Haddad, S. (2004) 'A Comparative Study of Lebanese and Palestinian Perceptions of Suicide Bombings: The Role of Militant Islam and Socio-Economic Status', *International Journal of Comparative Sociology*, 45(5): 337–63.

Hadden, J. and Shupe, A. (eds) (1989) *Secularization and Fundamentalism Reconsidered*, Vols I–III, New York: Paragon House.

Hafez, M. (2003) *Why Muslims Rebel: Repression and Resistance in the Islamic World*, Boulder, CO: Lynne Rienner.

Haggerty, K. (2003) 'From Risk to Precaution: The Rationalities of Crime Prevention', in Ericson, R. and Doyle, A. (eds) *Risk and Morality*, Toronto: University of Toronto Press.

Halliday, F. (2000) *Nation and Religion in the Middle East*, London: Saqi Books.

—— (2002) *Two Hours that Shook the World*, London: Saqi Books.

Hamas (1988) *The Charter of Hamas*. Available at http://www.hamasonline.com/indexx .php?page = Hamas/hamas_convenant.

Hamid, T. (2007) 'The Development of a Jihadist's Mind', *Center on Islam, Democracy and the Future of the Muslim World*, Washington, DC: Hudson Institute.

Hamzeh, A. (2004) *In the Path of Hizbullah*, Syracuse: Syracuse University Press.

Harries-Jones, P. (1995) *A Recursive Vision: Ecological Understanding and Gregory Bateson*, Toronto: University of Toronto Press.

Hass, A. (2003a) 'Confessions of a Suicide Bomber', *Middle East Resource Exchange Database*. Available at http://mered.org/article_read.asp?id = 75.

—— (2003b) *Reporting from Ramallah*, Los Angeles: Semiotext(e).

Hassan, N. (2001) 'An Arsenal of Believers: Talking to the "Human Bombs"', *Bint Jbeil*. Available at http://www.bintjbeil.com/articles/en/011119_hassan.html.

Hassan, R. (2002) *Faithlines: Muslim Conceptions of Islam and Society*, Pakistan: Oxford University Press.

Hassner, P. (2005) 'Nationalism and Violence in International Relations', in Dieckhoff, A. and Jaffrelot, C. (eds) *Revisiting Nationalism: Theories and Processes*, London: C. Hurst & Co.

Hatina, M. (2006) 'Restoring a Lost Identity: Models of Education in Modern Islamic Thought', *British Journal of Middle Eastern Studies*, 33(2): 179–97.

Havel, V. (1988) 'Anti-Political Politics', in Keane, J. (ed.) *Civil Society and the State: New European Perspectives*, London: Verso Press.

Heartfield, J. (2002) *The Death of the Subject Explained*, Sheffield: Sheffield-Hallam University Press.

Hedges, C. (2003) *War is a Force that Gives Us Meaning*, New York: Anchor Books.

Hegghammer, T. (2006) 'Terrorist Recruitment and Radicalization in Saudi Arabia', *Middle East Policy*, XIII(4): 39–60.

Heper, M. (1985) *The State Tradition in Turkey*, Beverley, CA: Eothen Press.

Hiro, D. (2002) *War Without End*, London: Routledge.

Hobsbawn, E. (1990) *Nations and Nationalism since 1870*, Cambridge: Cambridge University Press.

Hodgson, M. G. S. (1974) *The Venture of Islam: Conscience and History in a World Civilization*, Volumes 1–3, Chicago: The University of Chicago Press.

Hoffman, B. (1998) *Inside Terrorism*, London: Victor Gollancz.

—— (2003) 'The Logic of Suicide Terrorism', *The Atlantic Online*. Available at http://the-atlantic.com/issues/2003/06/hoffman.htm.

—— (2004) 'The Changing Face of Al Qaeda and the Global War on Terrorism', *Studies in Conflict and Terrorism*, 27(6): 549–60.

Hofheinz, A. (2006) 'Sudan', in Faath, S. (ed.) *Anti-Americanism in the Islamic World*, London: C. Hurst & Co.

Holloway, W. and Jefferson, T. (1997) 'The Risk Society in an Age of Anxiety: Situating Fear of Crime', *British Journal of Sociology*, 48(2): 255–66.

Horgan, J. (2005) *The Psychology of Terrorism*, London: Routledge.

Horsman, M. and Marshall, A. (1994) *After the Nation-State: Citizens, Tribalism and the New World Disorder*, London: Harper Collins.

Houben, V. (2003) 'South East Asia and Islam', *ANNALS, AAPSS*, 588: 149–70.

House of Commons (2006) *Report of the Official Account of the Bombings in London on 7 July 2005*, London: The Stationery Office.

Hudson, R. (1999) *The Sociology and Psychology of Terrorism: Who Becomes a Terrorist and Why?* Report prepared under an Interagency Agreement by the Federal Research Division, Library of Congress. Available at http:wwwloc.gov/rr/frd/pdf-files/Soc_Psych_of_Terrorism.pdf.

Hunt, A. (2003) 'Risk and Moralization in Everyday Life', in Ericson, R. and Doyle, A. (eds) *Risk and Morality*, Toronto: University of Toronto Press.

Huntington, S. P. (1998) *The Clash of Civilizations and the Remaking of World Order*, New York: Simon and Schuster.

Husain, E. (2007) *The Islamist*, London: Penguin Books.

Hutchinson, J. and Smith, A. (1994) *Nationalism*, Oxford: Oxford University Press.

Ibrahim, S. E. (1980) 'Anatomy of Egypt's Militant Islamic Groups: Methodological Note and Preliminary Findings', *International Journal of Middle East Affairs*, 12.

Ignatieff, M. (1998) *The Warrior's Honour: Ethnic War and the Modern Conscience*, London: Vintage.

Inglehart, R. (1977) *The Silent Revolution: Changing Values and Political Styles Among Western Publics*, Princeton, NJ: Princeton University Press.

—— (1990) 'Values, Ideology, and Cognitive Mobilization', in Dalton, R. J. and Kuechler, M. (eds) *Challenging the Political Order: New Social and Political Movements in Western Democracies*, Oxford: Blackwell.

Intelligence and Security Committee (2006) *Report into the London Terrorist Attacks on 7 July 2005*, Norwich, UK: HMSO.

International Crisis Group (ICG) (2002) 'Indonesia Backgrounder: How the *Jemaah Islamiyah* Terrorist Network Operates', *Asia Report* No. 43.

—— (2003) 'Islamic Social Welfare Activism in the Occupied Palestinian Territories: A Legitimate Target?', *ICG Middle East Report* No. 13, 2 April.

—— (2004a) 'Islamism in North Africa I: The Legacies of History', *Middle East and North Africa Briefing*, 1–15.

—— (2004b) 'Islamism, Violence and Reform in Algeria: Turning the Page', *ICG Middle East Report* No. 29.

—— (2004c) 'Saudi Arabia Backgrounder: Who Are the Islamists', *ICG Middle East Report* No. 31, 21 September.

—— (2005) 'Understanding Islamism', *ICG Middle East/North Africa Report*.

International Institute for Strategic Study (2003) *The Military Balance 2003–2004*, Arundel House: London, 15 October.

Ismail, N. (2006) 'The Role of Kinship in Indonesia's Jemaah Islamiya', *Terrorism Monitor*, IV(11): 6–9.

Israeli, R. (2004) 'Palestinian Women: The Quest for a Voice in the Public Square through "Islamikaze Martyrdom"', *Terrorism and Political Violence*, 16(1): 66–96.

Iveković, I. (2002) 'Nationalism and the Political Use and Abuse of Religion: The Politicization of Orthodoxy, Catholicism and Islam in Yugoslav Successor States', *Social Compass*, 49(4): 523–36.

Jaffrelot, C. (2002) *Pakistan: Nationalism Without a Nation*, London: Zed Books.

James, C. and Özdamar, Ö. (2005) 'Religion as a Factor in Ethnic Conflict: Kashmir and Indian Foreign Policy', *Terrorism and Political Violence*, 17(3): 447–67.

Jenkins, B. (1975) *International Terrorism*, Los Angeles: Crescent.

—— (2001) 'Terrorism and Beyond: A 21st Century Perspective', *Studies in Conflict and Terrorism*, 24(5): 321–7.

Jerichow, A. (1997) *Saudi Arabia: Outside Global Law and Order*, Richmond, Surrey: Curzon Press.

Johnston, D. and Sanger, D. (2004) 'New Generation of Leaders is Emerging for al Qaeda', *Middle East Information Center*, August 23. Available at http://middleeastinfo.org/article4666.html.

Jones, E., Woolven, R., Durodié, B. and Wessely, S. (2006) 'Public Panic and Morale: Second World War Civilian Responses Re-examined in the Light of the Current Anti-Terrorist Campaign', *Journal of Risk Research*, 9(1): 57–73.

Jordan, J. and Boix, L. (2004) 'Al-Qaeda and Western Islam', *Terrorism and Political Violence*, 16(1): 1–17.

Juergensmeyer, M. (1993) *The New Cold War: Religious Nationalism Confronts the Secular State*, Berkeley, CA: University of California Press.

—— (2003a) 'The Religious Roots of Contemporary Terrorism', in Kegley, C. W. (ed.) *The New Global Terrorism: Characteristics, Causes & Controls*, New Jersey: Prentice Hall.

—— (2003b) *Terror in the Mind of God*, London: University of California Press.

Kalpakian, J. (2005) 'Building the Human Bomb: The Case of the 16 May 2003 Attacks in Casablanca', *Studies in Conflict and Terrorism*, 28: 113–27.

Kaplan, J. (2006) 'Islamophobia in America? September 11 and Islamophobic Hate Crime', *Terrrorism and Political Violence*, 18(1): 1–33.

Karpat, K. (1959) *Turkey's Politics*, Princeton, NJ: Princeton University Press.

Kazamias, A. (1966) *Education and the Quest for Modernity in Turkey*, London: George Allen and Unwin.

Keddie, N. (1998) 'The New Religious Politics: Where, When, and Why Do "Fundamentalisms" Appear?', *Comparative Studies in Society and History*, 40(4): 696–723.

Kedourie, E. (1960) *Nationalism*, London: Hutchinson.

—— (ed.) (1971) *Nationalism in Asia and Africa*, London: Weidenfeld & Nicolson.

Kepel, G. (2004a) *Jihad: The Trail of Political Islam*, London: I. B.Tauris.

—— (2004b) *The War for Muslim Minds*, Cambridge, MA: Harvard University Press.

—— (2005) *The Roots of Radical Islam*, London: Saqi Books.

Khashoggi, J. (2001) 'Hijacker List Raises More Questions', *Jeddah Arab News*, 20 September.

Khatib, L. (2003) 'Communicating Islamic Fundamentalism as Global Citizenship', *Journal of Communication Inquiry*, 27(4): 389–409.

Khosrokhavar, F. (2005) *Suicide Bombers: Allah's New Martyrs*, London: Pluto Press.

Kimhi, S. and Even, S. (2004) 'Who are the Palestinian Suicide Bombers?', *Terrorism and Political Violence*, 16(4): 815–40.

Kinnvall, C. (2002) 'Nationalism, Religion and the Search for Chosen Traumas', *Ethnicities*, 2(1).

Kitschelt, H. P. (1990) 'New Social Movements and the Decline of Party Organization', in Dalton, R. J. and Kuechler, M. (eds) *Challenging the Political Order: New Social and Political Movements in Western Democracies*, Cambridge: Polity Press.

Kleinman, A. and Kleinman, J. (1997) 'The Appeal of Experience; The Dismay of Images: Cultural Appropriations of Suffering in our Times', in Kleinman, A., Das, V., and Lock, M. (eds) *Social Suffering*, Berkeley, CA: University of California Press.

Kleinman, A., Das, V. and Lock, M. (eds) (1997) *Social Suffering*, Berkeley, CA: University of California Press.

Knight, F. H. (1971) *Risk, Uncertainty and Profit*, Chicago: University of Chicago Press.

Kohn, H. (1944) *The Idea of Nationalism*, New York: Macmillan.

Köse, A. (1999) 'The Journey from the Secular to the Sacred: Experiences of Native British Converts to Islam', *Social Compass*, 46(3): 301–12.

Kramer, M. (1998) 'What You Should Know about Muslim Politics and Society', in Zelikow, P. and Zoellick, R. (eds) *American and the Muslim Middle East: Memos to a President*, Washington, DC: Aspen Institute.

—— (2001) *Ivory Towers on Sand: The Failure of Middle Eastern Studies in America*, Washington, DC: The Washington Institute of Near East Policy.

Kreckel, R. (1980) 'Unequal Opportunity Structure and Labour Market Segmentation', *Sociology*, 14(4): 525–50.

Krueger, A. and Malecková, J. (2003a), 'Seeking the Roots of Terrorism', *The Chronicle of Higher Education*. Available at http://chronicle.com/free/v49/i39/39b01001.htm.

—— (2003b) 'Education, Poverty and Terrorism: Is There a Causal Connection', *Journal of Economic Perspectives*, 17(4): 119–44.

Kurth, Cronin (2003) 'Terrorists and Suicide Attacks', *CRS Report for Congress*, The Library of Congress. Available at http://www.fas.org/irp/crs/RL32058.pdf.

Kurzman, C. (1994) 'A Dynamic View of Resources: Evidence from the Iranian Revolution', *Research in Social Movements, Conflict and Change*, 17: 53–84.

—— (1996) 'Structural Opportunities and Perceived Opportunities in Social Movement Theory: Evidence from the Iranian Revolution of 1979', *American Sociological Review*, 61: 153–70.

—— (2002) 'Bin Laden and Other Thoroughly Modern Muslims', *Contexts*, 4(1), Fall/Winter: 13–20.

—— (2004) 'Social Movement Theory and Islamic Studies', in Wiktorowicz, Q. (ed.) *Islamic Activism: A Social Movement Theory Approach*, Bloomington: Indiana University Press.

Lanceley, F. (1981) 'The Anti-Social Personality as a Hostage Taker', *Journal of Police Science and Adminstration*, 9(1): 28–34.

Lapidus, I. (2002) *A History of Islamic Societies*, 2nd edition, Cambridge: Cambridge University Press.

Laqueur, W. (2001a) *The New Terrorism: Fanaticism and the Arms of Mass Destruction*, London: Phoenix Press.

—— (2001b) 'Left, Right and Beyond: The Changing Face of Terror', in Hoge, J. and Rose, G. (eds) *How Did This Happen? Terrorism and the New War*, Oxford: Public Affairs.

—— (2003) 'Postmodern Terrorism', in Kegley, C. W. (ed.) *The New Global Terrorism: Characteristics, Causes & Controls*, New Jersey: Prentice Hall.

Larzillière, P. (2007) 'Chechnya: Moving Toward Islamic Nationalism?', in Blom, A., Bucaille, L. and Martinez, L. (eds) *The Enigma of Islamist Violence*, London: C. Hurst & Co.

Lawrence, B. (ed.) (2005) *Messages to the World: The Statements of Osama bin Laden*, London: Verso.

le Bon, G. (1968 [1895]) *The Crowd: A Study of the Popular Mind*, Dunwoody, GA: Norman S. Berg.

Lester, D., Yang, B. and Lindsay, M. (2004) 'Suicide Bombers: Are Psychological Profiles Possible?', *Studies in Conflict and Terrorism*, 27(4): 283–95.

Levi, M. and Wall, D. (2004) 'Technologies, Security, and Privacy in the Post-9/11 European Information Society', *Journal of Law and Society*, 31(2): 194–220.

Levitt, M. (2006) *Hamas: Politics, Charity and Terrorism in the Service of Jihad*, New Haven: Yale University Press.

Lewis, B. (1990) 'The Roots of Muslim Rage', *Atlantic Monthly*, September.

—— (2002) *What Went Wrong? The Clash between Islam and Modernity in the Middle East*, New York: Perennial.

Lewis, G. (1974) *Nations of the Modern World – Turkey*, London: Ernest Benn.

Li, Q. and Schaub, D. (2004) 'Economic Globalization and Transnational Terrorism', *Journal of Conflict Resolution*, 48(2): 230–58.

Lieven, A. (1998) *Chechnya: Tombstone of Russian Power*, New Haven, CT: Yale University Press.

Llobera, J. (1994) *The God of Modernity: The Development of Western Europe*, Oxford: Berg.

Lubeck, P. (2000) 'The Islamic Revival: Antinomies of Islamic Movements under Globalization', in Cohen, R. and Rai, S. M. (eds) *Global Social Movements*, New Brunswick, NJ: Athlone Press.

Luhmann, N. (1993) *Risk: A Sociological Theory*, New York: Walter de Gruyter.

Lupton, D. (1999) *Risk*, London: Routledge.

Lustick, I. (2006) *Trapped in the War on Terror*, Philadelphia, PA: University of Pennsylvania Press.

Lyon, D. (1994) The *Electronic Eye: The Rise of Surveillance Society*, Minneapolis: University of Minnesota Press.

—— (2001) *Surveillance and Society: Monitoring Everyday Life*, Buckingham: Open University Press.

—— (2003) 'Surveillance as Social Sorting: Computer Codes and Mobile Bodies', in Lyon, D. (ed.) *Surveillance as Social Sorting: Privacy, Risk and Digital Discrimination*, London: Routledge.

—— (2006) 'Airport Screen, Surveillance, and Social Sorting: Canadian Responses to 9/11 in Context', *Canadian Journal of Criminology and Criminal Justice*, 48(3): 397–411.

McAdam, D., McCarthy, J. D. and Zald, M. N. (eds) (1996) *Comparative Perspectives on Social Movements: Political Opportunities, Mobilizing Structures, and Cultural Framings*, Cambridge: Cambridge University Press.

McCauley, C. (ed.) (1991) *Terrorism and Public Policy*, London: Frank Cass.

—— (1998) 'The Readiness to Kill and Die: Suicidal Terrorism in the Middle East', in Reich, W. (ed) *Origins of Terrorism: Psychologies, Ideologues, Theologies, States of Mind*, Washington, DC: Woodrow Wilson Center Press.

—— (2002) 'Understanding the 9/11 Perpetrators: Crazy, Lost in Hate or Martyred?', in Matuszak, N. (ed) *History behind the Headlines*, Vol. 5, New York: Gale.

McCrone, D. (1998) *The Sociology of Nationalism*, London: Routledge.

McDermott, M. and Ahsan, M. (1980) *The Muslim Guide*, Leicester: The Islamic Foundation.

MacDonald, K. (1985) 'Social Closure and Occupational Registration', *Sociology*, 19(4): 541–56.

McGregor, A. (2006) 'Military Jama'ats in the North Caucasus: A Continuing Threat', *The Jamestown Foundation*. Available at http://www.jamestown.org/.

McKenna, T. (1998) *Muslim Rulers and Rebels: Everyday Politics and Armed Separatism in the Southern Philippines*, Berkeley, CA: University of California Press.

Maddy-Weitzman, B. and Litvak, M. (2003) 'Islamism and the State in North Africa', in Rubin, B. (ed.) *Revolutionaries and Reformers: Contemporary Islamist Movements in the Middle East*, Albany, NY: State University of New York Press.

Malecková, J. (2005) 'Impoverished Terrorists: Stereotype or Reality', in Bjørgo, T. (ed.), *Root Causes of Terrorism: Myths, Reality and Ways forward*, Abingdon, UK: Routledge.

Malik, J. (1996) *The Meaning of Race: Race, History and Culture in Western Society*, Basingstoke: Palgrave.

—— (2001) *Man, Beast and Zombie: What Science Can and Cannot Tell Us About Human Nature*, London: Phoenix.

—— (2002) 'Traditional Islamic Learning and Reform in Pakistan', *ISIM Newsletter*, 10 February.

Mannheim, K. (1956) *Essays on the Sociology of Culture*, London: Routledge and Kegan Paul.

Manning, P. (2006) 'Reflections on Risk Analysis, Screening, and Contested Rationalities', *Canadian Journal of Criminology and Criminal Justice*, 48(3): 453–69

Marranci, G. (2006) *Jihad beyond Islam*, Oxford: Berg.

Marron, D. (2007) 'Lending by Numbers: Credit Scoring and the Constitution of Risk within American Consumer Credit', *Economy and Society*, 37(1): 103–33.

Martin, G. (2003) *Understanding Terrorism*, Thousand Oaks, CA: Sage.

Martinez, L. (2007) 'The Distinctive Development of Islamist Violence in Algeria', in Blom, A., Bucaille, L. and Martinez, L. (eds) *The Enigma of Islamist Violence*, London: C. Hurst & Co.

Marty, M. E. and Scott Appleby, R. (eds) (1994) *Fundamentalisms Observed*, Chicago: University of Chicago Press.

Mattausch, J. (1989) *A Commitment to Campaign: A Sociological Study of CND*, Manchester: Manchester University Press.

Mawdudi, S. (1986) *The Islamic Way of Life*, Leicester: The Islamic Foundation.

Mehmet, O. (1990) *Islamic Identity and Development – Studies of the Islamic Periphery*, London: Routledge.

Melucci, A (1985) 'The Symbolic Challenge of Contemporary Movements', *Social Research*, 52: 789–816.

—— (1989) *Nomads of the Present: Social Movements and Individual Needs in Contemporary Society*, London: Hutchinson Radius.

Merari, A. (1991) 'Academic Research and Government Policy on Terrorism', in Reich, W. (ed.) *Origins of Terrorism: Psychologies, Ideologues, Theologies, States of Mind*, Washington, DC: Woodrow Wilson Center Press.

Merton, R. K. (1967) *Social Theory and Social Structure*, New York: The Free Press.

Mezran, K. (2001) 'Negotiating National Identity in North Africa', *International Negotiation*, 6(2): 141–73.

Middle East Media Research Institute (MEMRI) (2004) *Interview with Osama bin Laden's Former Bodyguard*, 20 August. Available at http://www.memri.org/bin/opener_latest.cgi?ID = SD76704.

—— (2007) 'al-Zawahiri Attacks Hamas for Signing Mecca Agreement', Islamist Web Sites Monitors # 75–76, *MEMRI Special Dispatch Series – No. 1507*. Available at http://memri.org/bin/articles.cgi?Page = archives&Area = sd&ID = SP150707.

Milbank, D. and Dean, C. (2003) 'Hussein Link to 9/11 Lingers in Many Minds', *Washington Post*, 6 September.

Mili, H. (2005) 'Xinjiang: An Emerging Narco-Islamist Corridor', *Terrorism Monitor*, III(8): 3–5.

Miller, S. (2002) 'The End of Unilateralism or Unilateralism Redux?', *Washington Quarterly*, 25(1): 15–29.

Mills, C. W. (1959) *The Sociological Imagination*, New York: Galaxy.

Milton-Edwards, B. (2005) *Islamic Fundamentalism since 1945*, London: Routledge.

Moaddel, M. (2001) *Jordanian Exceptionalism: The Alliance of the State and the Muslim Brothers*, Basingstoke: Palgrave Macmillan.

Moaddel, M. and Talattof, K. (eds) (2002) *Modernist and Fundamentalist Debates in Islam: A Reader*, Basingstoke: Palgrave Macmillan.

Morris, D. (1997) 'About Suffering: Voice, Genre, and Moral Community', in Kleinman, A., Das, V. and Lock, M. (eds) *Social Suffering*, Berkeley, CA: University of California Press.

Mortimer, E. (1982) *Faith and Power: The Politics of Islam*, New York: Random House.

Moughrabi, F. (n.d.) *A Nation at Risk: The Impact of Violence on Palestinian Children*. Available at http://www.gcmhp.net/File_files/NationAtrisk.html.

Mueller, J. (2005) 'Simplicity and Spook: Terrorism and the Dynamics of Threat Exaggeration', *International Studies Perspective*, 6(2): 208–34.

—— (2006) *Overblown: How Politicians and the Terrorism Industry Inflate National Security Threats and Why We Believe Them*, New York: Free Press.

Munson, H. (1995) 'Not all Crustaceans Are Crabs: Reflections on the Comparative Study of Fundamentalism and Politics,' *Contention*, 4(3): 151–66.

Murphy, C. and Ottaway, D. (2001) 'Some Light Shed on Saudi Suspects: Many Raised in Area of Religious Dissent', *Washington Post*, September 25.

Murphy, F. (1988) *Social Closure: The Theory and Monopolization and Exclusion*, Oxford: Clarendon.

Mythen, G. and Walklate, S. (2006a) 'Criminology and Terrorism: Which Thesis? Risk Society or Governmentality?', *British Journal of Criminology*, 46(3): 379–98.

—— (2006b) 'Communicating the Terrorist Risk: Harnessing a Culture of Fear', *Crime, Media, Culture*, 2(2): 123–42.

Nayyar, A. and Selim, A. (2002) *The Subtle Subversion: The State of Curricula and Textbooks in Pakistan: Urdu, English, Social Studies and Civics*, Islamabad: Sustainable Development Policy Institute.

Noorhaidi, H. (2002) 'Faith and Politics: The Rise of the Laskar Jihad in the Era of Transition in Indonesia', *Indonesia*, 73 (April): 145–69.

Norton-Taylor, R. (2006) 'Iraq War Motivated London Bombers', *The Guardian*. Available at http://politics.guardian.co.uk/iraq/story/0,1745696,00.html.

Oberschall, A. (2004) 'Explaining Terrorism: The Contribution of Collective Action Theory', *Sociological Theory*, 22(1): 26–37.

O'Driscoll, C. (2007) 'Jean Bethke Elshtain's Just War against Terror: A Tale of Two Cities', *International Relations*, 21(4): 485–92.

Offe, C. (1985) 'New Social Movements: Challenging the Boundaries of Institutional Politics', *Social Research*, 52, Winter: 817–68.

—— (1990) 'Reflections on the Institutional Self-Transformation of Movement Politics: A Tentative Stage Model', in Dalton, R. J. and Kuechler, M. (eds) *Challenging the Political Order: New Social and Political Movements in Western Democracies*, Cambridge: Polity Press.

Office of Homeland Security (2002) *The National Strategy for Homeland Security*, Washington, DC. Available at http://www.whitehouse.gov/homeland/book/.

Oliver, A.-M. and Steinberg, P. (2005) *The Road to Martyrs Square*, Oxford: Oxford University Press.

Oliverio, A.-M. (1998) *The State of Terror*, Albany, NY: State University of New York Press.

Oliverio, A.-M. and Lauderdale, P. (eds) (2005) *Terrorism: A New Testament*, Whitby, ON: de Sitter.

Olofsson, G. (1987) 'After the Working Class Movement? An Essay on What's "New" and What's "Social" in the New Social Movements', *Acta Sociologica*, 31(1): 15–34.

O'Malley, P. (1996) 'Risk and Responsibility', in Barry, A., Osbourne, T. and Rose, N. (eds) *Foucault and Political Reason: Liberalism, Neo-Liberalism and Rationalities of Government*, pp. 189–207, London: University College London Press.

—— (2003) 'Governable Catastrophe: A Comment on Bougen', *Economy and Society*, 32(2): 275–9.

—— (2004) *Risk, Uncertainty and Government*, London: Glasshouse.

—— (2006) 'Risk, Ethics, and Airport Security', *Canadian Journal of Criminology and Criminal Justice*, 48(3): 413–21.

O'Neill, B. (2006) '7/7: A Very British Bombing', *Rising East Online*, 5. Available at http://www.uel.ac.uk/risingeast/archive05/feedback/oneill.htm.

Orbach, B. (2001) 'Usama bin Ladin and al-Qa'ida: Origins and Doctrines', *Middle East Review of International Affairs*, 5(4): 54–68.

Papadakis, E. (1988) 'Social Movements, Self-Limiting Radicalism and the Green Party in West Germany', *Sociology*, 22(3): 433–54.

Pape, R. (2003) 'The Strategic Logic of Suicide Terrorism', *American Political Science Review*, 97(3): 343–61.

Pappé, I. (2005) *The Modern Middle East*, Abingdon, UK: Routledge.

Pargeter, A. (2006) 'Libyan Fighters Join the Iraqi Jihad', *Terrorism Monitor*, IV(23): 7–10.

Parkin, F. (ed.) (1974) *The Social Analysis of Class Structure*, London: Tavistock.

—— (1979) *Marxism and Class Theory: A Bourgeois Critique*, London: Tavistock.

—— (1982) *Max Weber*, London: Routledge.

Parsa, M. (2000) *States, Ideologies, and Social Revolutions: A Comparative Analysis of Iran, Nicaragua, and the Philippines*, Cambridge: Cambridge University Press.

Paz, R. (2001) *Radical Islamist Terrorism*. Available at http://www.ict.org.il/articles/arti cledet.cfm?articleid+367.

—— (2002) *Qa'idat al-Jihad*. Available at http://www.ict.org.il/articles/articledet.cfm? articleid = 436.

—— (2003) 'Islamists and Anti-Americanism', *Middle East Review of International Affairs*, 7(4): 53–61.

Pedahzur, A. and Perliger, A. (2003) 'Altruism and Fatalism: The Characteristics of Palestinian Suicide Terrorists', *Deviant Behaviour: An Interdisciplinary Journal*, 24: 405–23.

Pels, T. (2000) 'Muslim Families from Morocco in the Netherlands: Gender Dynamics and Father's Roles in a Context of Change', *Current Sociology*, 48(4): 75–93.

Philo, G., Hilsum, L., Beattie, L. and Holliman, R. (1999) 'The Media and the Rwanda Crisis: Effects on Audiences and Public Policy', in Philo, G. (ed.) *Message Received: Glasgow Media Group Research 1993–1998*, Harlow: Longman.

Pipes, D. (1989) 'Fundamentalist Muslims in World Politics', in Hadden, J. and Shupe, A. (eds) *Secularization and Fundamentalism Reconsidered*, New York: Paragon House.

Pollack, J. (2003) 'Anti-Americanism in Contemporary Saudi Arabia', *Middle East Review of International Affairs*, 7(4): 30–43.

Post, J. (1984) 'Notes on a Psychodynamic Theory of Terrorist Behaviour', *Terrorism*, 7(3): 241–56.

—— (1998) 'Terrorist Psycho-logic: Terrorist Behaviour as a Product of Psychological Forces', in Reich, W. (ed) *Origins of Terrorism: Psychologies, Ideologues, Theologies, States of Mind*, Washington, DC: Woodrow Wilson Center Press.

—— (2005) 'The Socio-cultural Underpinnings of Terrorist Psychology: When Hatred is Bred in the Bone', in Bjørgo, T. (ed.) *Root Causes of Terrorism: Myths, Reality and Ways Forward*, Abingdon, UK: Routledge.

Post, J., Sprinzak, E. and Denny, L. (2003) 'The Terrorists in Their Own Words: Interviews with 35 Incarcerated Middle Eastern Terrorists', *Terrorism and Political Violence*, 15(1): 171–84.

Power, M. (1999) *The Audit Society: Rituals of Verification*, Oxford: Oxford University Press.

—— (2004) *The Risk Management of Everything: Rethinking the Politics of Uncertainty*, London: Demos.

Prior, L. (1989) *The Social Organisation of Death: Medical Discourse and Social Practices in Belfast*, London: Macmillan.

Putnam, R. (2001) *Bowling Alone: The Collapse and Revival of American Community*, New York: Touchstone.

Qassem, N. (2005) *Hizbullah: The Story from Within*, London: Saqi.

Qutb, S. (1991) *The Islamic Concept and Its Characteristics*, Plainfield: American Trust Publications.

—— (2001 [1996]) *Milestones*, New Delhi: Islamic Book Service.

Rahman, T. (1998) 'Language, Religion and Identity in Pakistan: Language-Teaching in Pakistan', *Medressas: Ethnic Studies Report*, XVI(2): 197–214.

Ramphele, M. (1997) 'Political Widowhood in South Africa: The Embodiment of Ambiguity', in Kleinman, A., Das, V. and Lock, M. (eds) *Social Suffering*, Berkeley, CA: University of California Press.

Rapoport, D. (ed.) (1988) *Inside Terrorist Organizations*, London: Frank Cass.

—— (2003) 'The Four Waves of Rebel Terror and September 11', in Kegley, C. W. (ed.) *The New Global Terrorism: Characteristics, Causes & Controls*, New Jersey: Prentice Hall.

Rao, A. (1999) 'The Many Sources of Identity: An Example of Changing Affiliations in Rural Jammu and Kashmir', *Ethnic and Racial Studies*, 22(1): 56–91.

Rashid, A. (1999) 'The Taliban: Exporting Extremism', *Foreign Affairs*, 78(6): 22–35.

—— (2000) *Taliban: Islam, Oil and the New Great Game in Central Asia*, London: I. B.Tauris.

—— (2002) *Jihad: The Rise of Militant Islam in Central Asia*, New Haven, CT: Yale University Press.

—— (2005) 'The Reason for Arab Muslim Youth Involvement in Terrorism is Religious Brainwashing', in *Arab Columnists: Terrorists are Motivated by Cultural and Religious Factors, Not Poverty*, MEMRI No. 853.

Reddy, S. (1996) 'Claims to Expert Knowledge and the Subversion of Democracy: The Triumph of Risk over Uncertainty', *Economy and Society*, 25(2): 222–54.

Reetz, D. (2006) 'Pakistan', in Faath, S. (ed.) *Anti-Americanism in the Islamic World*, London: C. Hurst & Co.

Reeve, S. (1999) *The New Jackals*, London: Andre Deutsch.

Reith, G. (2004) 'Uncertain Times: The Notion of "Risk" and the Development of Modernity', *Time and Society*, 13(2): 383–402.

Reuter, C. (2004) *My Life is a Weapon*, Princeton, NJ: Princeton University Press.

Rieffer, B. (2003) 'Religion and Nationalism: Understanding the Consequences of a Complex Relationship', *Ethnicities*, 3(2): 215–42.

Robertson, R. (1992) *Globalization: Social Theory and Global Culture*, London: Sage.

Robin, C. (2004) *Fear: The History of a Political Idea*, Oxford: Oxford University Press.

Rodinson, M. (1973) *Mohammed*, Harmondsworth: Pelican.

Roschin, M. (2006) 'Islam in the Northern Caucasus: Dagestan', *The Jamestown Foundation*.

Roscigno, V., Garcia, L. and Bobbitt-Zeher, D. (2007) 'Social Closure and Processes of Race/Sex Employment Discrimination', *The ANNALS of the American Academy of Political and Social Science*, 609(1): 16–48.

Rose, N. (1999) *Powers of Freedom: Reframing Political Thought*, Cambridge: Cambridge University Press.

Rothstein, H., Huber, M. and Gaskell, G. (2006) 'A Theory of Risk Colonization: The Spiralling Regulatory Logics of Societal and Institutional Risk', *Economy and Society*, 35(1): 91–112.

Rowland, R. (2001) 'Experts: Trauma, Fear, Natural Reactions', *CNN*. Available at http://archives.cnn.com/2001/HEALTH/09/14/traumatic.stress/index.html.

Roy, O. (1994) *The Failure of Political Islam*, London: I. B.Tauris.

—— (2004) *Globalised Islam: The Search for a New Ummah*, London: C. Hurst & Co.

Roy, S. (2000) 'The Transformation of Islamic NGOs in Palestine', *Middle East Report*, 214.

Rubenstein, J. (2002) 'Introduction', in Isaacson and Rubenstein, C. (eds) *Islam in Asia: Changing Political Realities*, New Brunswick: Transaction.

Rumsfeld, D. (2001) 'DoD News Briefing – Secretary Rumsfeld and Gen. Myers', 4 December. Available at http://www.defenselink.mil/Transcripts/Transcript.aspx?Transcript ID = 2598.

Russell, C. and Miller, B. (1977) 'Profile of a Terrorist', *Terrorism: An International Journal*, 1(1): 17–34.

Russett, B. M., Oneal, J. R. and Cox, M. (2000) 'Clash of Civilizations or Realism and Liberalism Déjà Vu? Some Evidence', *Journal of Peace Research,* 37(5).

Saarnivaara, M. (2004) 'Internationalisation of Local Conflict? The Case of Palestine', paper presented at the *International Conference of Muslims and Islam in the 21st Century*, Kuala Lumpur, Malaysia, 4–6 August.

Sageman, M. (2004) *Understanding Terror Networks*, Philadelphia, PA: University of Pennsylvania Press.

Saghieh, H. (2002) 'On Suicide, Martyrdom and the Quest for Individuality', *ISIM Newsletter*, 10 February.

Saïd, E. (1995) *Orientalism: Western Conceptions of the Orient*, London: Penguin.

Saikal, A. (2003) *Islam and the West*, Basingstoke: Palgrave Macmillan.

Sakr, N. (2001) *Satellite Realms*, London: I. B.Tauris.

Saleh, B. A. (2004) 'Economic Conditions and Resistance to Occupation in the West Bank and Gaza Strip'. Available at http://www.mafhoum.com/press7/197E14.htm.

Salem, A. and de Waal, A. (2004) 'On the Failure and Persistence of *Jihad*', in de Waal, A. (ed.) *Islamism and Its Enemies in the Horn of Africa*, London: Hurst & Co.

Salib, E. (2003) 'Suicide Terrorism: a case of folie à plusieurs', *British Journal of Psychiatry*, 182(6): 475–6.

Sarraj, E. (2001) 'Why We Have Become Suicide Bombers'. Available at www.missionis lam.com/islam/conissue/palestine.htm.

Sassen, S. (2002) 'Governance Hotspots: Challenges We Must Confront in the Post-September 11 World', *Theory, Culture and Society*, 19(4): 233–44.

Schmid, A. (1993) 'Defining Terrorism: The Response Problem as a Definitional Problem', in Schmid, A. and Crelinsten, R. (eds) *Western Responses to Terrorism*, London: Frank Cass.

Schwartz, S. (2005) 'Islamic Extremism on the Rise in Nigeria', *Terrorism Monitor,* III(20).

Sedgwick, M. (2004) 'Al-Qaeda and the Nature of Religious Terrorism', *Terrorism and Political Violence*, 16(4): 795–814.

Seeseman, R. (2006) 'Sub-Saharan Africa', in Faath, S. (ed.) *Anti-Americanism in the Islamic World*, London: C. Hurst & Co.

Seitz, C. (2004) 'A New Kind of Killing', *Middle East Report and Information Project*. Available at http://www.merip.org/mero/mero03304.html.

Sennott, C. (2002) 'Driving a Wedge: Why bin Laden Plot Relied on Saudi Hijackers', *Boston Globe*, 3 March.

Shaw, E. (1986) 'Political Terrorists: Dangers of Diagnosis and an Alternative to the Psychopathology Model', *International Journal of Law and Psychiatry*, 8(3): 359–68.

Sheppard, B., Rubin, J., Wardman, J. and Wessley, S. (2006) 'Terrorism and Dispelling the Myth of a Panic Prone Public', *Journal of Public Health Policy*, 27(3): 219–45.

Shils, E. (1957) 'Primordial, Personal, Sacred and Civil Ties', *British Journal of Sociology*, 8(2): 130–45.

Shiqaqi, K. (2001) 'The Views of Palestinian Society on Suicide Terrorism', in The International Policy Institute for Counter-Terrorism (ed.) *Countering Suicide Terrorism*, Herzliya, Israel: The International Policy Institute for Counter-Terrorism.

Shuja, S. (2005) 'Gauging Jemaah Islamiyah's Threat to Southeast Asia', *Terrorism Monitor*, III(8): 1–3.

Silke, A. (2003) (ed.) *Terrorists, Victims and Society: Psychological Perspectives on Terrorism and Its Consequences*, Chichester, UK: John Wiley & Sons.

Sivan, E. (1997) *Radical Islam: Medieval Methodology and Modern Politics*, New Haven, CT: Yale University Press.

Smith, A. (1986) *The Ethnic Origins of Nations*, Oxford: Blackwell.

—— (1991) *National Identity*, Harmondsworth: Penguin Books.

—— (1999) *Myths and Memories of the Nation*, Oxford: Oxford University Press.

—— (2003) *Chosen Peoples*, Oxford: Oxford University Press.

Sofsky, W. (2002). *Zeiten des Schreckens. Amok, Terror, Krieg*, Frankfurt: Fischer.

Solomon, J. (2006) 'Saudi Arabia's Shiites and Their Effect on the Kingdom's Stability', *Terrorism Monitor*, IV(15): 5–8.

Sparks, R. (2001) 'Degrees of Estrangement: The Cultural Theory of Risk and Comparative Penology', *Theoretical Criminology*, 5(2): 159–76.

Sparks, R., Girling, E. and Loader, I. (2001) 'Fear and Everyday Urban Lives', *Urban Studies*, 38(5–6): 885–98.

Steger, M. A. E., Pierce, J. C., Steel, B. S and Lovrich, N. P. (1989) 'Political Culture, Postmaterial Values, and the New Environmental Paradigm: A Comparative Analysis of Canada and the United States', *Political Behavior*, 11(3): 233–54.

Steinberg, G. (2005) 'The Amman Suicide Bombings', *Stiftung Wissenschaft und Politik Comments*, German Institute for International and Security Affairs, 51: 1–4.

—— (2006) 'Saudi Arabia', in Faath, S. (ed.) *Anti-Americanism in the Islamic World*, London: C. Hurst & Co.

Stemmann, J. (2006) 'Middle East Salafism's Influence and the Radicalization of Muslim Communities in Europe', *MERIA*, 10(3): 1–14.

Stern, J. (2003a) *Terror in the Name of God*, New York: Ecco.

—— (2003b) 'Fearing Evil', *Social Research*, 71(4): 1111–17.

Sültan, M. (1999) 'Choosing Islam: A Study of Swedish Converts', *Social Compass*, 46(3): 325–35.

Sunstein, C. (2005) *The Laws of Fear: Beyond the Precautionary Principle*, Cambridge: Cambridge University Press.

Sutton, P. W. (2000) *Explaining Environmentalism: In Search of a New Social Movement*, Aldershot: Ashgate.

Sutton, P. and Vertigans, S (2005) *Resurgent Islam: A Sociological Approach*, Cambridge: Polity Press.

—— (2006) 'Islamic "New Social Movements?" al-Qa'ida, Radical Islam and Social Movement Theory', *Mobilization: An International Journal of Social Movement Research*, 11(1): 101–16.

Taheri, A. (1987) *Holy Terror: The Inside Story of Islamic Terrorism*, London: Hutchinson.

Tamimi, A. (2007) *Hamas: Unwritten Chapters*, London: C. Hurst & Co.

Tarrow, S. (1998) *Power in Movement: Social Movements, Collective Action and Politics*, Cambridge: Cambridge University Press.

Taylor, M. and Quayle, E. (1994) *Terrorist Lives*, London: Brassey's Defence Publishers.

Terdman, M. (2005) 'The Libyan Islamic Fighting Group', *The Project for the Research of Islamist Movements Occasional Papers*, 3(2): 1–9.

—— (2006) 'Muslims Persecution of Christians: The Unknown Side of Radical Islam in Somalia', *Islam in Africa Newsletter*, The Project for the Research of Islamist Movements, 1(2): 1–4.

Tessler, M. (2003) 'Do Islamic Orientations Influence Attitudes toward Democracy in the Arab World: Evidence from the World Values Survey in Egypt, Jordan, Morocco and Algeria', *International Journal of Comparative Sociology*, Spring: 3–5.

Thompson, T., Townsend, M., Bright, M. and McMahon, B. (2005) 'Terror Suspects Gives First Account of London Attack', *The Observer*, 31 July 2005.

Thornton, W. (2005) *New World Empire: Civil Islam, Terrorism and the Making of Neoglobalism*, Oxford: Rowman and Littlefield.

Tilly, C. (2003) *The Politics of Collective Violence*, Cambridge: Cambridge University Press.

—— (2004) 'Terror as Strategy and Relational Process', paper presented at the American Sociological Association Conference, 14–17 August 2004.

—— (2005) 'Terror as Strategy and Relational Process', in Oliverio, A.-M. and Lauderdale, P. (eds) (2005) *Terrorism: A New Testament*, Whitby, ON: de Sitter.

Tönnies, F. (1965 [1887]) *Community and Society (Gemeinschaft und Gesellschaft)*, London: Harper Torchbooks.

Toprak, B. (1981) *Islam and Political Development in Turkey*, Leiden, The Netherlands: E. J. Brill.

Touraine, A. (1971) *The Post-Industrial Society: Tomorrow's Social History: Classes, Conflict and Culture in the Programmed Society*, New York: Random House.

—— (1981) *The Voice and the Eye: An Analysis of Social Movements*, Cambridge: Cambridge University Press.

Tsfati, Y. and Weimann, G. (2002) 'www.terrorism.com: Terror on the Internet', *Studies in Conflict and Terrorism*, 25(5): 317–32.

Tudor, A. (2003) 'A (Macro) Sociology of Fear?', *Sociological Review*, 51(2): 238–56.

Tumelty, P. (2005) 'An In-depth Look at the London Bombers', *Terrorism Monitor*, III(15): 1–4.

—— (2006) 'The Rise and Fall of Foreign Fighters in Chechnya', *Terrorism Monitor,* IV(2).

Turner, B. (1974) *Weber and Islam*, London: Routledge and Kegan Paul.

—— (1978) *Marx and the End of Orientalism*, London: George Allen and Unwin.

—— (1993) *Max Weber: From History to Modernity*, London: Routledge.

—— (1994) *Orientalism, Postmodernism and Globalism*, London: Routledge.

—— (2001) 'Cosmopolitan Virtue: On Religion in a Global Age', *European Journal of Social Theory*, 4(2): 131–52.

—— (2002) 'Sovereignty and Emergency: Political Theory, Islam and American Conservatism', *Theory, Culture and Society*, 19(4): 103–19.

—— (2003) 'Class, Generation and Islamism: Towards a Global Sociology of Political Islam', *British Journal of Sociology*, 54(1): 139–47.

Turner, B. S. (2004) 'Weber and Elias on Religion and Violence: Warrior Charisma and the Civilizing Process', in Loyal, S. and Quilley, S. (eds) *The Sociology of Norbert Elias*, Cambridge: Cambridge University Press.

Ufen, A. (2006) 'Southeast Asia (Indonesia and Malaysia)', in Faath, S. (ed.) *Anti-Americanism in the Islamic World*, London: C. Hurst & Co.

Ulph, S. (2006a) 'Islamists Criticize Muslims Who Abstain from Jihad', *Terrorism Focus*, III(7): 3–6.

—— (2006b) 'al-Zawahiri's New Video Calls on Muslims to Support the Mujahideen', *Terrorism Focus*, III(15).

Ungar, S. (2001) 'Moral Panic Versus the Risk Society: the Implications of the Changing Sites of Social Anxiety', *British Journal of Sociology*, 52(2): 271–92.

United Nations Development Programme (UNDP) (2002) *Human Development Report*, New York.

US Department of State (2003) *American National Strategy for Combating Terrorism.* Available at http://www.state.gov/documents/organization/60172.pdf.

Urry, J. (2002) 'The Global Complexities of September 11th', *Theory, Culture and Society*, 19(4): 57–69.

Valiyev, A. (2005) 'Azerbaijan: Islam in a Post-Soviet Republic', *The Middle East Review*, 9(4): 12–13

—— (2006) 'Al-Qaeda in Azerbaijan: Myths and Realities', *Terrorism Monitor*, IV(10): 9–11.

van der Veer, P. (1994) *Religious Nationalism: Hindus and Muslims in India*, London: University of California Press.

van Krieken, R. (1999) 'The Barbarism of Civilization: Cultural Genocide and the "Stolen Generations"', *British Journal of Sociology*, 50(2): 297–315.

Vertigans, S. (2003) *Islamic Roots and Resurgence in Turkey*, Westport, CT: Praeger.

—— (2004) 'Social Barriers to Peace', *Sociological Research Online*, 9(3). Available at http://www.socresonline.org.uk/9/3/vertigans.html.

—— (2007a) 'Beyond the Fringe? Radicalisation within the American Far-Right', *Totalitarian Movements and Political Religions*, 8(3–4): 41–59.

—— (2007b) 'Routes into "Islamic" Terrorism: Dead Ends and Spaghetti Junctions', *Policy: A Journal of Policy and Practice*, 1(2): 447–59.

—— (2007c) 'Militant Islam and Weber's Social Closure', *Contemporary Islam*, 1(4): 303–21.

—— (2008) *Terrorism and Societies*, Aldershot: Ashgate.

Vertigans, S. and Sutton, P. W. (2001) 'Back to the Future: "Islamic Terrorism" and Interpretations of Past and Present', *Sociological Research Online*, 6(3). Available at http://www.socresonline.org.uk/6/3/vertigans.html.

—— (2006) 'The Role of Anti-terror Measures in the Development of "Islamic" Terrorism', *International Journal of the Humanities*, 4(4): 87–94.

Victor, B. (2004) *Army of Roses*, London: Constable & Robinson.

Voll, J. O. (2001) 'Bin Laden and the New Age of Global Terrorism', *Middle East Policy*, 8(4): 1–5.

Volpi, F. (2003) *Islam and Democracy: The Failure of Dialogue in Algeria*, London: Pluto Press.

Wallerstein, I. (1980) *The Modern World – System II: Mercantilism and the Consolidation of the European World-Economy, 1600-1750*, New York: Academic Press.

—— (1983) *Historical Capitalism*, London: Verso.

—— (1984) *The Politics of the World Economy*, London: Cambridge University Press.

Walzer, M. (2007) 'On Fighting Terrorism Justly', *International Relations*, 21(4): 480–4.

Wang, J. (2003) 'Eastern Turkistan Islamic Movement: A Case Study of a New Terrorist Organisation in China', *International Journal of Offender Therapy and Comparative Criminology*, 47(5): 568–84.

Waters, M. (1998) *Globalization*, London: Routledge.

Watt, W. M. (1968) *Islamic Political Thought*, Edinburgh: Edinburgh University Press.

Weber, M. (1958) *From Max Weber*, translated and edited by Gerth, H. H. and Wright Mills, C., New York: Galaxy.

—— (1965) *The Sociology of Religion*, London: Methuen.

—— (1978) *Economy and Society, Vols I & II*, edited by Roth, G. and Wittich C., Berkeley, CA: University of California Press.

Weinberg, L. and Pedahzur, A. (2004) 'The Challenges of Conceptualizing Terrorism', *Terrorism and Political Violence*, 16(4): 777–94.

West, C. and Zimmerman, D. (1987) 'Doing Gender', *Gender and Society*, 1(2): 125–51.

White House, The (2002) 'Securing the homeland, strengthening the nation'. Available at http://www.whitehouse.gov/homeland/homeland_security_book.html.

Wickham, C. R. (2002) *Mobilizing Islam: Religion, Activism and Political Change in Egypt*, New York: Columbia University Press.

Wiktorowicz, Q. (2001) *The Management of Islamic Activism: Salafis, the Muslim Brotherhood, and State Power in Jordan*, Albany, NY: State University of New York Press.

—— (ed.) (2004) *Islamic Activism: A Social Movement Theory Approach*, Bloomington, IN: Indiana University Press.

Wiktorowicz, Q. and Kaltner, J. (2003) 'Killing in the Name of Islam: Al-Qaeda's Justification for September 11', *Middle East Policy*, X(2): 76–92.

Wildavsky, A. and Dake, K. (1990) 'Theories of Risk Perception: Who Fears What and Why?', *Daedalus*, 119(4): 41–60.

Wilkinson, I. (2005) *Suffering: A Sociological Introduction*, Cambridge: Polity Press.

Wilkinson, P. (2003) 'Why Modern Terrorism? Differentiating Types and Distinguishing Ideological Motivations', in Kegley, C. W. (ed.) *The New Global Terrorism: Characteristics, Causes & Controls*, New Jersey: Prentice Hall.

Williamson, B. (1987) *Education and Social Change in Egypt and Turkey*, Basingstoke: MacMillan Press.

Yehoshua, Y. (2005) 'Are Saudi Summer Camps Encouraging Terrorism?', *Middle East Media Research Institute*. Available at http://memri.org/bin/articles.cgi?Page = archives& Area = ia&ID = IA24105.

Young, J. (1999) *The Exclusive Society: Social Exclusion, Crime and Difference in Late Modernity*, London: Sage.

—— (2007) *The Vertigo of Late Modernity*, London: Sage.

Zawadzki, P. (2005) 'Nationalism, Democracy and Religion', in Dieckhoff, A. and Jaffrelot, C. (eds) *Revisiting Nationalism: Theories and Processes*, London: C. Hurst & Co.

Zedner, L. (2006) 'Neither Safe Nor Sound? The Perils and Possibilities of Risk', *Canadian Journal of Criminology and Criminal Justice*, 48(3): 423–34.

Zimmerman, J. (2004) 'Sayyid Qutb's Influence on the 11 September Attacks', *Terrorism and Political Violence*, 16(2): 222–52.

Zisser, E. (2003) 'Hizbollah: Between Armed Struggle and Domestic Politics', in Rubin, B. (ed.) *Revolutionaries and Reformers: Contemporary Islamist Movements in the Middle East*, Albany, NY: State University of New York Press.

Zubaida, S. (1989) 'Nations: Old and New. Comments on Anthony D. Smith's "The Myth of the 'Modern Nation' and the Myth of Nation"', *Ethnic and Racial Studies*, 12(3): 329–39.

Index

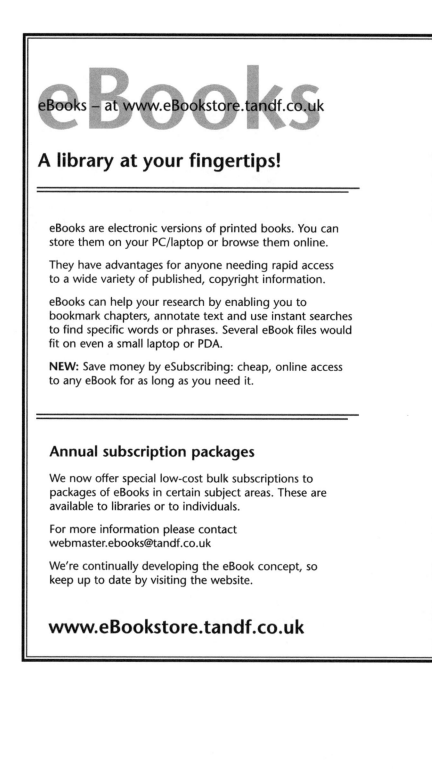